SUZANNE METHOT

LEGACY

TRAUMA, STORY, AND INDIGENOUS HEALING

Published by ECW Press
665 Gerrard Street East
Toronto, Ontario, Canada M4M 1Y2
416-694-3348 / info@ecwpress.com

Editor for the Press: Susan Renouf
Cover design: Tania Craan, based on *Pictograph*, mixed
media on page, by Patricia June Vickers
Author photo: © Nadya Kwandibens, Red Works

LIBRARY AND ARCHIVES CANADA CATALOGUING IN PUBLICATION

Methot, Suzanne, author
    Legacy : trauma, story, and Indigenous healing /
Suzanne Methot.

Issued in print and electronic formats.
ISBN 978-1-77041-425-9 (softcover)
ISBN 978-1-77305-297-7 (PDF)
ISBN 978-1-77305-296-0 (HTML)

    1. Native peoples—Canada—Social conditions.
2. Native peoples—Health and hygiene—Canada. 3.
Colonization—Social aspects—Canada. 4. Colonization—
Psychological aspects. 5. Psychic trauma—Canada. I. Title.

E78.C2M486 2019   971.004'97
C2018-905335-6   C2018-905336-4

PRINTED AND BOUND IN CANADA
PRINTING: MARQUIS   5   4

The publication of *Legacy* has been generously supported by the Canada Council for the Arts which last year invested
$153 million to bring the arts to Canadians throughout the country and is funded in part by the Government of Canada.
*Nous remercions le Conseil des arts du Canada de son soutien. L'an dernier, le Conseil a investi 153 millions de dollars pour mettre
de l'art dans la vie des Canadiennes et des Canadiens de tout le pays. Ce livre est financé en partie par le gouvernement du Canada.*
We acknowledge the support of the Ontario Arts Council (OAC), an agency of the Government of Ontario, which last
year funded 1,737 individual artists and 1,095 organizations in 223 communities across Ontario for a total of $52.1 million.
We also acknowledge the contribution of the Government of Ontario through the Ontario Book Publishing Tax Credit,
and through Ontario Creates for the marketing of this book.

Produced with the support of the City of Toronto through the Toronto Arts Council. The author also gratefully
acknowledges financial assistance from the people of Ontario through the Writers' Reserve and Writers' Works-in-
Progress programs of the Ontario Arts Council.

PERMISSIONS
Chapter 4: Photograph of the Duplessis Orphans courtesy of the collections of Bibliothèque et Archives nationales du
        Québec.
Chapter 5: The author received permission from her mother in 1995 to quote the contents of her mother's diary.
Chapter 6: Image capture from the film *Hollow Water*, directed by Bonnie Dickie, courtesy National Film Board of
        Canada.
Chapter 7: Image of *Shaking Tent*, by Carl Ray, courtesy Thunder Bay Art Gallery. Efforts made to contact the estate of
        Carl Ray were unsuccessful.
Chapter 7: Photograph of the Niisitapiikwan Siksika kidney dress courtesy Ethnology Department, McCord Museum,
        Montreal, QC.

We may be through with the past,
but is the past through with us?

REG CROWSHOE (AWAKAASEENA),
PIIKANI ELDER AND CEREMONIALIST

To create health, you need a new kind of knowledge,
based on a deeper concept of life.

DEEPAK CHOPRA, MD

We work in the direction of ending the trauma,
and letting our children be children.

SHELLEY NIRO, KANIENKEHAKA ARTIST

CONTENTS

CHAPTER 1:   How Things Work, and Why Stories Matter   1

CHAPTER 2:   What It Means to Be Colonized   31

CHAPTER 3:   Becoming Human   62

CHAPTER 4:   The Angry Indian and a Culture of Blame   88

CHAPTER 5:   Invisible Roots   124

CHAPTER 6:   Fractured Narratives   149

CHAPTER 7:   What the Body Remembers   177

CHAPTER 8:   Sacred Being   215

CHAPTER 9:   Recreating the Structures of Belonging   240

CHAPTER 10: Killing the Wittigo   266

AUTHOR'S NOTE   323

ACKNOWLEDGEMENTS   324

SOURCES   326

INDEX   342

CHAPTER 1

HOW THINGS WORK, AND WHY STORIES MATTER

Indigenous people do funerals really, really well.

When a young man I know is stabbed and killed in a street fight in Toronto in 2016, there are no fewer than three memorial services: one at the local friendship centre, one at his workplace, and one on his mother's reserve. A vigil is also held at the site of his death. News of his passing filters through the Indigenous community on Tuesday and Wednesday, and by Thursday, the first memorial is in progress. The events come together beautifully: drummers, elders, a photo slideshow, room rentals, social media invitations, a written program, a speakers' list, gifts for the family, a basket of tobacco ties (cobbled together from at least three different urban organizations), platters of food, his favourite music piped into the auditorium, a guestbook, and people gathered to support the family and discuss This Thing That Has Happened.

I have lived in and worked for Indigenous communities in Ontario since 1992, and I can tell you: this kind of co-operation, positive energy, and amenability does not exist on an everyday basis.

If you don't believe me, then believe the Aboriginal Healing Foundation (AHF). Between 1998 and 2014, the AHF — a non-profit organization managed by Indigenous peoples — conducted research and supported community-based healing initiatives across the country. These projects were meant to address the legacy of residential schools in Canada, including intergenerational impacts. According to the AHF, as a result of the physical, sexual, and psychological abuse suffered by those who attended residential schools, the capacity of Indigenous peoples to build and sustain healthy families and communities has been compromised and, in some places, completely erased.

The AHF says psychological and emotional abuse in Indigenous communities is common. Rage and anger are widespread at all levels — individual, family, and community. Indigenous peoples carry multiple layers of unresolved grief and loss, and they suffer chronic physical illness related to their emotional and spiritual states. Families, communities, and workplaces suffer from toxic communication patterns. According to the AHF, there is disunity and conflict among individuals, families, and factions within Indigenous communities. Indigenous people in positions of authority often misuse their power to control others. The social structures that hold families and communities together — trust, common ground, shared purpose and direction, a vibrant ceremonial and civic life, co-operative networks and associations — have broken down, and in many families and communities, there are only a few people working for the common good. Many Indigenous people fear personal growth, transformation, and healing.

In addition to those listed above, the AHF has documented 22 other impacts of intergenerational trauma that it says are contributing to dysfunction and negative outcomes in Indigenous communities. These findings have been corroborated by other organizations, including the National Collaborating Centre for Aboriginal Health, which released a 2015 report on the increased prevalence and root causes of depression among Indigenous peoples in Canada.

The AHF makes a direct connection between residential schools and the challenges we see in Indigenous communities today. In so doing, it delegitimizes the notion that colonization — or "civilization," as some people like to call it — has benefitted Indigenous peoples. It also delegitimizes the notion that current challenges within Indigenous communities are the result of inherent deficiencies in Indigenous peoples and cultures. The AHF list of intergenerational impacts makes it very clear: where Indigenous peoples and communities are dysfunctional and/or in crisis, it is because of colonialism, not because they are Indigenous.

The way in which the Indigenous community in Toronto came together in 2016 to mourn the death and celebrate the life of the murdered young man shows that age-old philosophies — of respect, responsibility, reciprocity, and relationships — continue to underpin our communities despite the negative effect of colonization and settler colonialism. These philosophies also support the transformative healing work underway in many Indigenous communities across the country. However, I have seen the dysfunction and negative outcomes described by the AHF at every level of Indigenous society, from my own life and the life of my family, to the people I know, the communities I have worked with, and the Indigenous organizations I have worked for.

Indigenous peoples are more than victims, and they are not defined only by the traumatic events of colonization. As Nehiyaw poet Billy-Ray Belcourt wrote in a blog post after being named a Rhodes Scholar in 2015 (an achievement that was inevitably framed around Belcourt's experiences with racism and the trauma of residential school), "Dear Media: I am more than just violence." Despite the Indigenous desire to leave the past behind, however, the past doesn't seem quite done with us.

This past-as-present reality is reflected in the lives of many Indigenous people in Canada, including the life of Robert Arthur Alexie. Alexie was chief of the Tetlit Gwich'in band council in Fort McPherson, Northwest Territories, and chief negotiator for the Gwich'in regional land claim in 1992. After serving his people in multiple roles, he was elected president of the Gwich'in Tribal Council in 2012. Alexie was also a musician, a photographer, and the author of two novels including the groundbreaking *Porcupines and China Dolls*, which deals with the impacts of the residential school system on Indigenous peoples. Alexie was knowledgeable, principled, and funny, and he made enduring contributions to his nation and to the country. And in 2014, at the age of 58, he was found at the side of the Dempster Highway in the Northwest Territories, dead from a self-inflicted gunshot wound. In a 2015 piece about Alexie's contribution to Indigenous and Canadian literature, journalist Noah Richler surmised that Alexie's "terrifying private demons" had finally caught up with him.

These demons are a persistent reality in the lives of all the Indigenous people I know and have known, affecting those on the fringes of society and those in positions of influence and authority. They exist in people who seem to be functioning just fine, thank you — the kind of people who are profiled in good-news media stories that seek to overturn common myths and stereotypes about Indigenous peoples and communities.

The young man whose death brought the Toronto community together in an all-too-familiar ritual of mourning was certainly a success story. He worked at a major cultural institution. He had graduated from high school, studied a trade at the college level, and was registered in another college program when he died. He had pursued his goals, even completing a course to overcome his fear of public speaking. He bicycled to and from work and was trying to quit smoking. He had a girlfriend and he was saving up so they could move out of her father's house. He was well liked and he wanted to work for his community. He did everything the student support workers at his high school and college said he should do. And he still died at age 20, stabbed in the neck and chest, after taking a bar fight outside.

Behind all our goals, our successes, and our attempts at success, there is a story. It is a story of terror, anger, grief, and loss. It is a story that still, after hundreds of years, determines Indigenous lives in Canada. The young man in Toronto carried this story, as all Indigenous peoples do. It is not the only story we tell — there are stories of happiness and achievement, too — but it is the one that sometimes seems to have the most influence. The time has come to understand this story and the mechanisms of its transmission.

European stories usually follow a linear conflict-crisis-resolution format. They are discrete and almost always aim to communicate a central moral or lesson. For Indigenous peoples, however, stories are spirals: they exist in time and space as they happen, and they also exist in each subsequent telling, spiralling off from a common root to become part of the lives of successive generations. There is no separation between "fact" and "fiction" in Indigenous stories, only a distinction between everyday stories and sacred stories, which means that all stories are true. These stories belong to people, families, and communities — and they are as important today as they were 50 years ago, 100 years ago, and 500 years ago.

For Indigenous peoples, stories are about movement, transition, and change. Instead of being centred on events, Indigenous stories tend to reveal an emotional narrative. The purpose behind Indigenous storytelling is to evoke the same emotions in listeners, so that they can make connections to their own lives — sparking the learning and the transformation that Indigenous peoples consider sacred.

The AHF correctly identifies residential schools as a major part of the story of terror, anger, grief, and loss. But this story actually begins long before the first residential school opened.

So. This story starts here.

In his book *The Conquest of Paradise*, Kirkpatrick Sale quotes Christopher Columbus's initial impression of the Taíno he encountered in the Bahamas in 1492. Columbus describes them as noble and kind, and says, "They are very gentle and without knowledge of what is evil; nor do they murder or steal . . . Your Highness may believe that in all the world there can be no better people . . . They love their neighbours as themselves . . . and are gentle and always laughing."

Columbus's thoughts are echoed by the Spanish historian and missionary Bartolomé de Las Casas. Before his ordination as a Catholic priest in 1513, Las Casas took part in the 1502 conquest of Hispaniola and the 1513 conquest of Cuba. In 1542, he wrote a chapbook entitled "A Short Account of the Destruction of the Indies," in which he writes that the Taíno of Hispaniola "are devoid of wickedness and duplicity . . . by nature the most humble, patient, and peaceable, holding no grudges, free from embroilments, neither excitable nor quarrelsome . . . devoid of rancors, hatreds, or desire for vengeance of any people in the world. . . . [T]hey are not arrogant, embittered, or greedy . . . They are very clean in their persons, with alert, intelligent minds."

Las Casas mentions "the very few Indians who are hardhearted and impetuous" and, as if to assure readers that he is not speaking from a religious bias, also takes care to point out that "[s]ome of the secular Spaniards who have been here for many years say that the goodness of the Indians is undeniable."

The events of the 15th to 20th centuries — the height of European colonial endeavour — have changed Indigenous peoples and communities in political, economic, cultural, and social terms. These events, which Las Casas described as a holocaust, were an attempt to destroy Indigenous systems and societies.

As Las Casas wrote about Hispaniola (today's Dominican Republic and Haiti), "[T]he Christians, with their horses and swords and pikes, began to carry out massacres and strange cruelties against [the Indigenous people]. They attacked the towns and spared neither the children nor the aged nor pregnant women nor women in childbed, not only stabbing them and dismembering them but cutting them to pieces as if dealing with sheep in the slaughterhouse. They laid bets as to who, with one stroke of the sword, could split a man in two or could cut off his head or spill out his entrails with a single stroke of the pike. They took infants from their mothers' breasts, snatching them by the legs and pitching them headfirst against the crags, or snatched them by the arms and threw them into the rivers . . . Other infants they put to the sword . . . They made some low, wide gallows on which the hanged victim's feet almost touched the ground . . . then set burning wood at their feet and thus burned them alive. To others they attached straw or wrapped their whole bodies in straw and set them afire. . . . And because all the people who could do so fled to the mountains, the Spanish captains . . . pursued them with the fierce dogs they kept, which attacked the Indians, tearing them to pieces and devouring them."

Writing about Nicaragua, Las Casas said, "Who could exaggerate the felicity, the good health, the amenities of that prosperous and numerous population? Verily it was a joy to behold that admirable province with its big towns . . . full of gardens and orchards and prosperous people. . . . And since these Indians were by nature very gentle and peace-loving, the tyrants and his comrades (all of whom had aided him in destroying other kingdoms) inflicted such damage, carried out such slaughters, took so many captives, perpetrated so many unjust acts that no human tongue could describe them."

When English colonists entered into what is today known as the United States, the terror continued. During the Pequot Massacre of 1637, the governor of the Plymouth Colony, William Bradford, celebrated the Pilgrim victory in his *History of the Plymouth Plantation*: "Those [Indigenous people] that escaped the fire were slain with the sword; some hewed to pieces, others run through with their rapiers, so as they were quickly dispatched and very few escaped. It was conceived [the Pilgrims] thus destroyed about 400 at this time. It was a fearful sight to see them thus frying in the fire, and the streams of blood quenching the same, and horrible was the stink and scent thereof, but the victory seemed a sweet sacrifice, and [the Pilgrims] gave the prayers thereof to God, who had wrought so wonderfully for them."

But it wasn't just the English. In New Netherland in 1643, at a site in New York City that is now the home of the National Museum of the American Indian, Governor Willem Kieft ordered his soldiers to destroy two refugee camps filled with displaced Lenape: "Infants were torn from their mother's breast and hacked to death in the presence of their parents, and the pieces thrown into the fire and in the water," wrote David Pietersz de Vries, a Dutch witness. "Other sucklings, being bound to small boards, were cut, stuck, and pierced, and miserably massacred in a manner to move a heart of stone. Some were thrown into the river, and when the fathers and mothers endeavoured to save them, the soldiers would not let them come on land but made both parents and children drown."

Most Canadians think that genocide did not occur in Canada.

In fact, Sir John A. Macdonald, Canada's first prime minister, deliberately starved Indigenous peoples on the Canadian prairies in order to open the west to settlers and clear the way for the Canadian Pacific Railroad (CPR). After the CPR was built and the bison were hunted to extirpation by settlers — as a result of industrial-scale hunting and the colonial government's plan to destroy the food source of Indigenous peoples on the Plains — Indigenous peoples were left hungry and desperate. When they asked the federal government to honour the treaties, which guaranteed food in times of famine, Macdonald denied their request and ordered the Department of Indian Affairs to withhold food until they moved to designated reserves far from the CPR line.

Once on the reserve, Indigenous peoples were trapped and could leave only with the permission of the Indian Agent. Hunters could not hunt and subsistence farming was impossible on substandard reserve land — especially when the government failed to provide tools as specified in the treaties. If Indigenous peoples complained, their rations were cut. Food was withheld for so long that much of it rotted, while Indigenous peoples fell sick from malnutrition and disease. Thousands died. As James Daschuk, an associate professor at the University of Regina and the author of *Clearing the Plains: Disease, Politics of Starvation, and the Loss of Aboriginal Life*, wrote in the *Globe and Mail*, "The uncomfortable truth is that modern Canada is founded upon ethnic cleansing and genocide . . . Canadian officials used food, or rather denied food, as a means to ethnically cleanse a vast region from Regina to the Alberta border as the Canadian Pacific Railway took shape."

The genocide continued under the national system of Indian Residential Schools. From the 1870s to 1996, the Truth and Reconciliation Commission (TRC) states that at least 150,000

Indigenous children were removed from their families and communities and sent to residential schools funded by the federal
government and operated by the Anglican, Catholic, United,
Methodist, and Presbyterian churches, where Indigenous children were forced to adhere to European societal and cultural
norms, forbidden to speak their own languages, and alienated
from their cultures, families, and communities. Parents were
threatened with imprisonment or denied treaty rations if they
failed to surrender their children. The RCMP were employed to
forcibly remove children from their homes. Many students were
physically, psychologically, emotionally, and sexually abused in
the schools. According to the TRC, more than 3,000 children died
in residential schools across the country, but the actual number is
believed to be much higher, as the federal government stopped
collecting annual death reports after 1917. In fact, former TRC
chairman (now senator) Murray Sinclair believes the number
could be as much as 10 times higher — which would mean that
30,000 children died in residential schools.

When Europeans arrived in the Americas, the Indigenous population is estimated to have been approximately 100 million. Up to
90 per cent of the population — or 90 million people — died in the
first 250 years after contact due to epidemics, slavery, war, and mass
extermination. By the late 1700s, when explorer George Vancouver
landed in what is today British Columbia, entire Indigenous villages were littered with corpses and emptied of people due to
epidemic outbreaks of smallpox, tuberculosis, and influenza that
spread through migration and Indigenous trade (before first-hand
contact with European peoples). The trauma inflicted on survivors
is almost unimaginable; the genocide unprecedented. According
to Las Casas, the Spaniards "spread terror throughout those kingdoms and filled the people with bitterness, anguish, and revolt.
That calamity . . . meant, for them, the end of their world, and

they have never ceased lamenting and recounting the story in their songs and dances . . . They have never recovered from that loss."
Contemporary statistics tell us the same thing.

Research conducted by Statistics Canada in the 1996 and 2006 censuses, the Environics Institute in the 2010 Urban Aboriginal Peoples Study, Indian and Northern Affairs Canada, the *Toronto Star*, the Office of the Correctional Investigator of Canada, and the World Health Organization has identified a wide range of issues within Indigenous communities, both on- and off-reserve. Tuberculosis rates are 17 times higher in Indigenous communities in Canada. Nearly half the on-reserve population has type 2 diabetes, putting diabetes rates at nearly six times higher than the national average. Suicide is two times higher for Indigenous peoples, six times higher for Indigenous youth, and Inuit have the highest suicide rate in the world. The overall death rate for Indigenous peoples is three to four times higher than for non-Indigenous Canadians and life expectancy is six to ten years lower. Unemployment is three times higher than for non-Indigenous peoples. Forty-eight per cent of Indigenous youth have no high school diploma, 54 per cent of Indigenous adults lack a diploma, and 44 per cent of adults between the ages of 50 and 64 living off-reserve have less than grade 9. Indigenous males make up 25 per cent of the inmate population in federal men's prisons and 50 per cent of all inmates in the Prairie provinces, while Indigenous women make up over 40 per cent of all inmates in federal women's prisons. Nationally, Indigenous peoples make up just over 4 per cent of the population, but 17 per cent of homicide victims and 23 per cent of those accused of that crime. Nearly 50 per cent of youth inmates in Canada are Indigenous, although that figure rises to 80 per cent in the province of Manitoba.

These socio-economic challenges are not the result of an innate deficiency in Indigenous peoples, communities, or societies. They are not the result of so-called primitive societies unable to adapt to "civilization," or of what is often described as a "culture clash." They are responses to prolonged, repeated trauma. They are manifestations of unresolved terror, anger, grief, and loss.

In Indigenous philosophy and science, the only thing that is constant is change. For Indigenous peoples, the only fixed static "law" is that the world and everything in it is in a constant process of movement, transition, and transformation. Human beings are dependent upon creation, and we learn from creation. This means that we, too, must adapt and change over time. One of the tools Indigenous peoples use to understand and accomplish movement and transformation is the medicine circle (or medicine wheel).

In its simplest form, the medicine wheel is shown as a circle divided into four quadrants. The quadrants and lines are often drawn at different angles, but each is correct, because there are two parts to the whole:

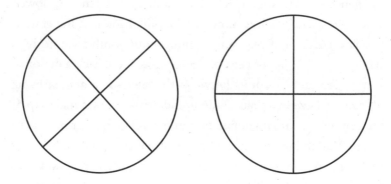

According to Nehiyaw grandfather/elder Michael Thrasher, the two versions of the medicine circle represent the sun and the moon, or fire and water. Both ground our ways of knowing and being in the world. Both measure time and distance — through the equinoxes, solstices, and cardinal directions — and both illustrate the balance of active and receptive energy in the universe (fire is active, water is receptive). The 13 moons that are seen during one cycle of the sun are each named by, and for, the seasons. This grounds us in our geographic location. In essence, the medicine wheel is about where we live over time. The purpose of the medicine circle is to help human beings learn how to live in a particular place — our body, mind, and spirit, as well as our families, communities, or places on the land — at any particular moment.

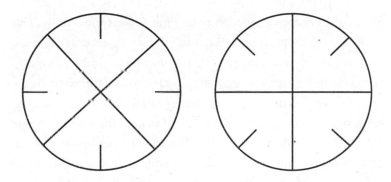

The medicine wheel represents a vast store of knowledge. Multiply it by the many people who adapt the wheel for their own purposes — in counselling, addictions treatment, or as a model for sustainability — and it becomes a wide-ranging tool for understanding interconnectedness, human development, balance, and change.

According to grandfather/elder Thrasher, the east quadrant of the medicine wheel represents vision: the ability to engage in the hopeful thinking necessary for change. When a guiding vision is created or received, we see what needs to be done, and we begin to envision strategies that will enact that change. For this reason, the east is matched with the spiritual — the stories, ceremonies, and teachings that must be respected because they bring us awareness and vision. The south quadrant of the wheel represents time: the time it takes to relate to an idea or vision and to understand it. For this reason, the south is matched with the physical — the land around us and the body we inhabit, which change over time and teach us about relationship. The west quadrant represents feeling and reason: the ability to gain knowledge and figure things out. This is why the west is matched with the emotional — because the head and the heart are both involved in making sense of life and the world around us. Knowledge can only be gained through this balance. The north quadrant of the medicine wheel represents movement: the ability to do things, and the transition from knowledge to the wisdom that accomplishes movement and change. This is why the north quadrant is matched with the intellectual: because each individual must engage in behaviours that embrace change in a conscious way. We begin each cycle around the circle in the east and we end in the north, gaining awareness, understanding, knowledge, and wisdom with each turn around the wheel. Change is only possible when each stage in the wheel is acknowledged and undertaken — when we embody the wholeness that exists in the universe and when we maintain balance while embracing change.

The centre of the wheel represents humanity and the energy of human agency, because it represents the planet's core. We live inside that power and are connected to it. If we are in tune with it, we can access it to create movement and change. In that way, the centre of the wheel is an axis: a place of individual movement around the various aspects of the circle, where all the aspects

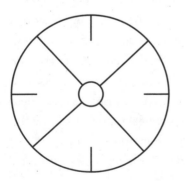 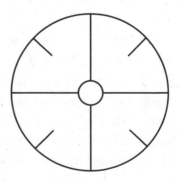

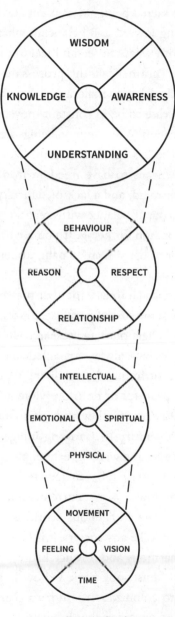

Medicine Wheel

converge to create sacred being. Movement and change is accomplished by reflecting inward and balancing what we see and feel inside ourselves with what we see and feel in the external world. Grandfather/elder Thrasher calls this process the "right inner measure" of the individual, key to maintaining health and wellness.

When people cease to be in constant movement, they are out of balance with creation. When human beings are out of balance, it results in dis-ease. The "dis-" prefix is from the Latin, meaning "apart" or "away." "Ease" means to have freedom from pain or trouble, comfort of body or mind, and a lack of difficulty. If you are away from the world and out of balance with creation, you are away from yourself and your reason for being. If you are away from yourself and your reason for being, you are in pain, troubled, in discomfort, and having difficulty.

It would be a mistake to assume that pre-contact Indigenous communities were some sort of paradise. In fact, as Val Napoleon, the director of the Indigenous Law Research Unit at the University of Victoria, says, "We have always struggled, as every other society has, with problems of human beings living together. Our societies were no more peaceful or no more violent than any others." Virginia colonist William Strachey also commented on this reality, writing in the 17th century that among Indigenous peoples, "as amongst Christians," some were "great people . . . some very little . . . some speaking likewise more articulate and plaine, and some more inward and hollow . . . some curteous and more civill, others cruel and bloody." The Indigenous world is (and was) neither idyllic nor depraved. Like any society, it is (and was) a mixture of hardship and joy, harmony and conflict, brutality and compassion.

The reason we must look back at how Indigenous societies functioned prior to colonization is not to claim that they were idyllic but to remind ourselves that Indigenous peoples once lived in a world of movement and balance that fostered connection and relationship. The writings of Las Casas and Columbus tell us how relationships were destroyed, joy extinguished, harmony disrupted, and compassion annihilated in the face of seven generations of genocide and colonial rule. Indigenous peoples are no longer in constant movement; instead, we are stuck in an event-centred story that has an undue influence on contemporary Indigenous emotional narratives. Indigenous peoples are no longer in relationship with one another or the world; instead, we are stuck in the disruption and disharmony created by colonialism. This has resulted in dis-ease that will continue to affect contemporary Indigenous peoples until it is addressed.

As Senator Murray Sinclair said in a speech to the Aboriginal Justice Learning Network, "As a result of the dysfunction within some of our communities, people believe this is the way all Aboriginal people would tend to be if it were not for the grand civilizing process we have come through with the help of the churches and Canadian society. When we look around us at our communities . . . we see great discordance, we see great pain. Our young people are killing themselves at incredibly high rates, six to eight times the national average rate of suicide among young people. We have among our women incredibly high rates of domestic violence, of sexual abuse. Some of our communities are bordering on social chaos and anarchy, where people have no respect, not only for their brothers and their sisters, but they have no respect for their parents, they have no respect for their elders, they have no respect for their leaders — if there are any — and they have no respect for their society, however they see it, which is not to say that we all live that way."

"We have not always been this way," Sinclair said. "Our people did not appear to be acting out and committing crimes at such excessive rates. Our people did not appear to be abusing themselves and others in the the same way we see today. A part of it,

for me, is because of the way the government has treated our leadership, the way the government has treated our families, the way
the government has treated our cultures. There has been and there
still is great disruption among our people today as a direct result
of some of the laws that have been passed in this country. . . .
The government set out on a deliberate attempt to undermine the
very existence of Aboriginal communities, to undermine the very
nature of Aboriginal families within society. . . . The government
had a deliberate policy that it did not want the Aboriginal communities of this country to flourish economically. They did not want
Aboriginal communities to become self-sufficient and stable."

The ability of Indigenous peoples to maintain any form of culture or community in the face of genocide and colonialism speaks
to a resiliency created and sustained by spirituality, humour, and
a unique form of Indigenous adaptability characterized by the
interplay between accommodation and resistance. However, the
unresolved terror, anger, grief, and loss created by the holocaust
in the Americas has had deleterious effects on Indigenous identity, as well as on the interpersonal skills, parenting skills, and
emotional and physical well-being of most, if not all, Indigenous
peoples, leading to challenges in every aspect of contemporary life, from health and education to crime and victimization.
Pre-contact mores and values have been replaced with attitudes
and beliefs that negatively affect future generations, such as poor
self-concept (negative beliefs about self), internalized shame and
hatred, passive compliance, and learned helplessness. These negative inheritances are part of a process that results in a circular
reliving of the trauma of genocide and colonialism generation
after generation.

Intergenerational trauma was first identified in the children
of Holocaust survivors and the descendants of Japanese people
interned during the Second World War. It has also been identified

in the children of American veterans of conflicts including Korea, Vietnam, and the Gulf Wars. In one study, researchers reported that 45 per cent of American veterans' children exhibited "significant" signs of PTSD, with 83 per cent reporting "elevated hostility" scores and more dysfunctional social and emotional behaviours. Like contemporary Indigenous peoples, these children weren't there at the time of their parents' traumatic episode — yet they exhibit the same symptoms as their traumatized parents.

In one case in the research literature, a Jewish man tells his therapist about his dreams: he is hiding in the cellar from soldiers who want to kill him, standing in line for selection, the smell of burning flesh is in the air, shots are fired, and starving people in striped uniforms are marching to the crematoria. He is trapped in a pit full of skeletal dead bodies, and he attempts to bury them, but limbs keep sticking up from the mud, and he feels guilty for what has happened. He then awakes in a sweat "with a prevailing sense of numb grief for all those anonymously gone." According to Natan Kellermann, executive director of the National Israeli Center for Psychosocial Support of the Holocaust and Second Generation, this man was not interned in a concentration camp — he was born after the war, in another country, far away in both time and place from the horrors of the Second World War. However, his mother had survived the Auschwitz-Birkenau concentration camp. Kellermann asks, "Why was he dreaming such dreams half a century after the war? Why are children of Holocaust survivors still experiencing the effects of the Holocaust as if they themselves had actually been there? How do we explain that the so-called second generation seems to share the grief and terror of their traumatized parents?"

According to Kellermann, trauma can be transmitted across generations by four distinct but sometimes overlapping means: psychodynamic processes, sociocultural processes, the family system, and biological processes. When trauma is transmitted through psychodynamic processes, the anger, fear, and repressed grief of parents is externalized and projected onto their children, leading subsequent generations to engage in behaviours without insight or awareness as to the unconscious processes behind those behaviours. When intergenerational trauma is transmitted through sociocultural processes, the younger generation is socialized through behaviours modelled by the older generation and come to believe things about themselves and the world around them via their parents' parenting style. When the family system is the vehicle of transmission, children become enmeshed in the emotional issues of their parents; this lack of boundaries encourages children to ignore their own emotional needs in favour of meeting the parent's needs, resulting in problems with the child's development as an individual. Biological processes describe the physiological and genetic means by which trauma is transmitted across generations.

Many people believe that an individual's DNA is set at birth and remains unchangeable, but this is untrue. The science of epigenetics has shown that human genes respond to their social context, and traumatic experiences such as neglect during childhood and severe stress in adulthood actually change the expression of a person's DNA. These traumatic experiences leave molecular scars that also appear in a traumatized person's descendants.

In Indigenous science and philosophy, epigenetics is a part of "blood memory." For Indigenous peoples, blood memory is carried from generation to generation through psycho-spiritual-biological processes that encompass culture (for example, the belief that dreams are important sources of knowledge), the energy of the universe (known as *manitow* in the language of the Nehiyawak), and the systems of the body (life essence stored in the kidneys, for example, or grief stored in the lungs). Blood memory expresses both presence and what the late Anishinabe scholar Gail Guthrie Valaskakis calls "goneness," representing a connection to the past built through shared relationships and collective experience. These connections can be positive or negative. More than simply memories, blood memory is an inheritance. As Kiowa writer N. Scott Momaday, winner of the 1969 Pulitzer Prize for his novel *House Made of Dawn*, writes in his memoir, *The Names*, "Some of my mother's memories have become my own. That is the real burden of the blood."

The late Judith Kestenberg, a psychiatrist and professor emeritus at New York University Medical School, refers to the transmission of intergenerational trauma as "transposition." Kestenberg describes the process as an unconscious one, where the parent does not explicitly speak about their traumatic experiences, but the child picks up the parent's trauma through comments and actions that reveal the parent's worldview and approach to relationship-making. The parent never says outright that "the world is a dangerous place" or "people are not to be trusted," but these ideas are key to how these parents function in the world — and this style of engagement is transposed onto their children, in effect transplanting the trauma.

Kestenberg theorized that transposition might serve as a mechanism to resurrect the murdered and missing people whom the parent — the trauma survivor — cannot adequately mourn. Maria Yellow Horse Brave Heart, a Hunkpapa Lakota research associate professor at the University of New Mexico Department of Psychiatry, also recognizes this pattern. Yellow Horse Brave Heart says that Indigenous peoples have a loyalty to ancestral suffering that causes them to create suffering in their own lives. Yellow Horse Brave Heart says this is not a conscious process but a result of Indigenous peoples having internalized the suffering of their ancestors to the point where vitality in one's own life is seen as a betrayal of those ancestors. In order to remain loyal to their suffering community, individuals become fixated on the trauma, recreating the murdered and missing people in their minds and hearts at the cost of extinguishing their own spiritual and emotional centres. As Yellow Horse Brave Heart says, "It's hard for [Indigenous peoples] to be joyful in our own lives and really free and happy."

Indigenous knowledge is based upon thousands of years of observation, experience, and data. It is no less empirical than European knowledge. It does, however, illustrate a different way of seeing.

The European Enlightenment view of the universe is a mechanistic one, as described in the work of English physicist and mathematician Isaac Newton and his laws of motion and universal gravitation. In this view, the human body is composed of mechanical parts that work together like a machine. Although there is now some debate as to whether Enlightenment ideas are responsible for creating the health and prosperity that are often ascribed to them, the fact is, the philosophical underpinnings of these ideas still resonate in much of Western thought. In the Indigenous world, however, the physical body is connected to the mind, the spirit, and the emotion, and to the external forces of the universe — the particles and waves, the manitow, that form and act upon all living things. Human beings are created from this energy, acted upon by this energy, and in turn affect the energy of the universe. By observing the world, Indigenous peoples have seen that human beings do not exist in isolation. The human body-mind is a manifestation of the forces that surround it and a powerful force in determining how the universe unfolds. Intergenerational trauma, by definition, proves that humans do not exist in isolation from the forces that surround them.

Although many other ethnic groups have had adverse experiences, survived traumatic episodes, and been the victims of genocide, the ongoing cycle of trauma in Indigenous communities is perpetuated by the loss of land and the consequent loss of the stories and ceremonies that once connected Indigenous peoples to the land. These stories and ceremonies construct identity, ground us in our geographic locations, help us make meaning, and play a vital role in maintaining health and well-being; without them, Indigenous peoples have found it difficult to recover from the traumatic experiences of colonialism and colonization.

An interruption or disruption in the present that connects to the past is often referred to as a ghost, or a haunting. When this ghost/haunting becomes a collective experience — transferred from the realm of individual traumatic memory to collective traumatic memory — it creates what sociologists refer to as "post catastrophic memory." In the Indigenous world, the encounter with the ghost is often described as a form of possession.

In Nehiyawak and other Algonquian cultures, possession takes the form of the *wihtikiw* (or *wittigo*), a cannibal spirit-creature. According to oral tradition, the wittigo's heart, and sometimes its entire body, is made of ice. Its eyes roll in blood, its voice bellows and whistles, its hands and feet are clawed, and its lips are blackened by decay. The wittigo is strong, and it can travel as fast as the wind. It is greedy and has a ravenous appetite for human flesh. A wittigo can take possession of a person's soul, and it can also haunt a community — and once a wittigo appears, it is extremely difficult to get rid of. Once a person is overtaken by a wittigo, they lose their humanity, destroying their family members and those they love the most. No one can outrun a wittigo, and no one can outsmart it. Once possessed, an individual has to fight the wittigo and destroy the evil in order to be free again.

The wittigo often appears when peoples and communities are in crisis or transition. In the fur-trade era, for example, when Indigenous societies were under stress from outside social and economic forces, the wittigo appeared in oral tradition as a personification of greed and selfishness, serving as a cautionary tale against those who would turn away from the Indigenous belief in reciprocity and relationships and toward the European belief in individualism. In his 1978 book, *Columbus and Other Cannibals*, Powhatan-Renape/Delaware-Lenape writer Jack D. Forbes uses the wittigo to personify the forces of capitalism and colonialism, which separate human beings and human societies from their relationships with the earth and with each other. Nehiyaw poet Louise Halfe and Anishinabe novelist Louise Erdrich have both used the wittigo figure in their recent writing to describe the emotional and spiritual famine that has been created within Indigenous peoples and societies by the trauma of colonization, and the lateral violence that results when traumatized people try to regain a sense of power or control by becoming predators over others.

Some Indigenous peoples are not comfortable discussing inter-generational trauma. They believe that focusing on trauma-related issues within Indigenous communities — especially when those issues take the form of lateral violence — undermines the deliberate nature of genocide and colonization or recasts Indigenous peoples as somehow complicit in their own oppression. Neither is true. Acknowledging the damage that colonization has wrought on Indigenous communities is a crucial first step in healing and in reconciliation. Acknowledging the need for individual and collective change is also part of the process.

Wab Kinew, leader of the Manitoba NDP, has spoken openly about his family's struggle with intergenerational trauma. Kinew's father, Tobasonakwut Kinew, was a residential school survivor who self-medicated with alcohol and was abusive to his son. Kinew responded by acting out his own pain and anger, getting into conflict with the law. As Kinew told the CBC, "My father was put into a situation where he was powerless. It unleashed anger and rage inside of him . . . My experience growing up wasn't as severe as his was by any means, but it was similar in that I was made to feel powerless. Instead of a priest and a nun, it was my father." Kinew now says that he is mindful of his responsibility to create a healthy relationship with his wife and children. "Now, as an adult, I look at how I parent and I recognize that . . . I'm creating the same situations for my own sons to grow up with. I'm a hockey-coaching, homework-helping, bedtime-reading superdad. Yet I can also be too quick to raise my voice or make a cutting remark that can damage my sons' self-esteem. In these moments, I recognize my father in myself. I am still on the journey to dealing with my own anger . . . That's the thing that we're still carrying in our families and our communities today. If we understand the trajectory and the path by which it is transmitted, we might be able to work toward doing the hard internal work in our own hearts, in our own spirits, in our own minds, to be able to make ourselves better parents, to be able to make ourselves the generation where that is going to stop."

Indigenous prophecies tell us that human societies are in a time of change. According to the Anishinabek, we are in the time of the Eighth Fire; according to the Hopi, we are in the Fifth World; according to the Inca, the condor has met the eagle; and according to the Maya, the 13th *baktun* has ended and a new world has begun. The terror, anger, grief, and loss that has possessed Indigenous communities for the past 500 years is coming to an end. With Canada taking its first tentative steps toward reconciliation, this is an era of change in Canadian society. This is our collective opportunity to rewrite the narrative of genocide and oppression and envision another better way of living — not just within Indigenous communities but between Indigenous peoples and the settler population.

According to visual artist and photographer Jeff Thomas, a self-described "urban Iroquois" who curated *Where Are the*

Children?, the Aboriginal Healing Foundation's online photographic exhibition on residential schools, "To heal is to visualize what has happened to you. What are you fighting back against? In the residential schools, there were children who fought back. They could see their enemy. . . . In today's world, we have generations of people who cannot fight back because they cannot see the enemy their parents and grandparents saw."

At the young man's memorial in Toronto, many of those in attendance say he died because he was in the wrong place at the wrong time. Many others see him only as a victim, the helpless recipient of someone else's choice of action. Only his sister tells the real truth. When she gets to the stage and takes the microphone, she is angry and she doesn't always choose her words wisely — but she is brave enough to name the issue. After listening to everyone else speak, she gets up and says, "Our father abused us." This might seem like a non sequitur, but in fact her comment speaks to a developing awareness and understanding. This is the story she and her family must begin to tell. This is the story that will lead them toward healing. If the young man had understood this story, he would have understood the anger and grief that he carried, and he might not have decided to take that fight outside.

For Indigenous peoples, the work of the next seven generations will be to make meaning of present issues in light of past events and return to the habits and routines that ensure movement, balance, connection, and relationship. This will reframe how Indigenous youth understand themselves and their world, allowing them to carry the story of colonization in a way that does not define them or limit their opportunities.

Healing from intergenerational trauma isn't just work for Indigenous peoples, though. Non-Indigenous Canadians must recognize the wisdom contained within Indigenous science and philosophy and must accept this wisdom — this way of seeing

— as a legitimate body of knowledge within Canadian systems and institutions. This means going beyond "inclusion" and actually making room for another culture's worldview. Then, and only then, will Canada be a post-colonial country.

In a 2015 workshop, Rose LeMay, the director of Northern and Indigenous Health at the Canadian Foundation for Healthcare Improvement, told a story about learning to drive a really fast car. She couldn't make the course's hairpin turn until the instructor told her, "Don't look at the corner! You'll drive off the road! Look *ahead*. You go where you look." After that, LeMay made the turn. She now applies the lesson to her own healing and to her work with Indigenous communities. LeMay says Indigenous peoples must acknowledge where they came from, where they are now, and where they want to be in the future. To LeMay, "that is what balance is about."

Colonization has changed Indigenous communities. The only way to regain sovereignty — true independence, as opposed to the reductive political meaning — is to unlearn the worst of what Indigenous peoples have learned from colonial society and go back to the respect, responsibility, reciprocity, and relationship-building that we used to know and enact. That starts with a return to Indigenous ways of knowing and being, beyond mere ritual and toward the heart of what it means to be an Indigenous person on this land in the 21st century.

INTERGENERATIONAL IMPACTS OF TRAUMA

The unresolved trauma of Indigenous peoples who have experienced, witnessed, or inherited the memory of horrific events creates an ongoing cycle of patterns and behaviours that are passed down from generation to generation. These intergenerational impacts are felt on a day-to-day basis by survivors and their families. Different communities experience different impacts and to differing degrees.

PROCESSES OF COLONIZATION = TRAUMA

- Genocide
- Decimation by disease
- Sexual and physical abuse, primarily of women and children
- Banned ceremonies
- Residential schools (re-education, separation from family, banning of Indigenous languages)
- Imprisonment and murder of spiritual/political leaders
- Imposition of colonial/patriarchal governance systems
- Land appropriation and large-scale development (hydroelectric dams)
- Removal from land and relocation to unknown and/or non-viable territory
- Confinement to reserves
- Social welfare policies
- Racism
- Psychological and emotional abuse

= LOSS OF PERSONAL & COLLECTIVE AGENCY
= NEGATIVE EFFECT ON FEELINGS OF SAFETY
= SOCIO-ECONOMIC & POLITICAL DEPENDENCY
= INTERNALIZED HATRED
= LEARNED BEHAVIOURS
= LACK OF RESOURCES TO SUPPORT HEALTHY LIVING

↓

EVERYDAY IMPACTS OF TRAUMA (HISTORICAL & CONTEMPORARY)

- Cultural identity issues: Christianization and the loss of language and cultural foundations, resulting in assimilation, cultural confusion, and cultural dislocation
- Destruction of social support networks that individuals and families could once rely on
- Disconnection from the natural world as an important dimension of daily life, leading to spiritual dislocation
- Spiritual confusion: alienation from one's own spiritual life and growth process, as well as conflicts over religion
- Dysfunctional families and interpersonal relationships
- Parenting issues such as emotional coldness, rigidity, neglect, poor communication, and abandonment
- Chronic widespread depression
- Layer upon layer of unresolved grief and loss
- Deep-seated sense of shame and shame-based family dynamics
- Unconscious internalization of residential school behaviours including false politeness, not speaking out, passive compliance, excessive neatness, obedience without thought
- Breakdown of social glue that holds families and communities together, such as trust, common ground, shared purpose and direction, a vibrant ceremonial and civic life, and co-operative networks and associations working for the common good
- Flashbacks and associative trauma: certain smells, foods, sounds, sights, and people trigger flashback memories, anxiety attacks, and physiological symptoms of fear (e.g., the sight of a police vehicle)
- Becoming an oppressor and abuser of others after suffering abuse to oneself

↓

INTERGENERATIONAL IMPACTS MOST COMMON IN, BUT NOT EXCLUSIVE TO, CONTEMPORARY TIME PERIOD

- Chronic widespread anger and rage
- Disunity and conflict between individuals, families, and factions in the community
- Alcohol and drug abuse

- Fetal alcohol spectrum disorder (FASD)
- Low self-esteem
- Eating disorders
- Sleeping disorders
- Sexual abuse
- Physical abuse, especially but not exclusively of women and children
- Psychological/emotional abuse
- Chronic physical illness related to spiritual and emotional states
- Internalized sense of inferiority or aversion to white people, especially white people in positions of power
- Toxic communication patterns, including backbiting, gossip, criticism, putdowns, personal attacks, sarcasm, and secrets
- Suicide and the threat of suicide
- Teen pregnancy
- Accidental deaths
- Dysfunctional community environment, including patterns of paternalistic authority linked to passive dependency; patterns of misuse of power to control others; and community social patterns that foster whispering and malicious gossip but a refusal to support or stand with those who speak out or challenge the status quo
- Educational blocks: an aversion to formal learning programs that seem "too much like school," fear of failure, self-sabotage, and psychologically based learning disabilities
- Dysfunctional/co-dependent family behaviours replicated in the workplace
- Fear of personal growth, transformation, and healing
- Voicelessness: feeling that one cannot influence or shape the world one lives in; passive acceptance of powerlessness within community life; passively accepting whatever comes and feeling powerless to change it

Text for "Everyday Impacts" and "Intergenerational Impacts" sections adapted from the Aboriginal Healing Foundation Program Handbook, *Second Edition (Ottawa, 1999)*

CHAPTER 2

WHAT IT MEANS TO BE COLONIZED

As a child, my identity isn't my own. It's something that is decided for me and assigned to me based upon categories and rules that other people have drafted. I am never sure how or what to be, but I know that to keep other people happy I have to be what they want me to be.

I am entertainer-storyteller for my mother on her good days and parent-caregiver on her bad days. I am a dutiful daughter for one member of my family (who doesn't like it when I tell the truth about how I'm feeling) and the patient listener to another (who, when in crisis, tells me everything).

To the white boys in my northern Alberta hometown, I am a squaw. I know this because I am 12 years old and riding a bike up High School Hill and they toss a beer bottle at me, out the window of their pickup truck, as one of them yells, "Suck this, squaw!" To most of my teachers, I am a walking stereotype, or a convenient target for public shaming, or an anomaly because I do well in school and I talk a lot — it depends on the day. But I only figure this out later, as an adult. As a child, I'm just confused when Mr. Graeme subs in music class and he asks me why I'm a bass player, and shouldn't I be the drummer, since my ancestors played drums? On another day, when the student teacher says I can't know all the right answers and accuses me of cheating in front of the class, I just accept the fact that people will always have the wrong idea about me. When one teacher takes more than a professional interest in me, the other teachers tease him, but no one reports it. I don't realize this is a bad thing until I am in my 30s. Instead, at 14, I write "Sexy Suzi" on my binders over and over, glad to finally be someone. One teacher, a female friend of his, gives me a bad second-term mark, and I wonder what I've done wrong.

Indians are squaws. Indians are stupid. Squaws are sluts. These ideas are part of the fabric of everyday life in northern Alberta in the 1970s and 1980s; I know them as surely as I know my own name. I don't want to be a squaw, because squaws are bad. I don't want to be stupid. I don't want to be a slut. So I definitely don't want to be an Indian. But everyone tells me I am these things, so they must be true.

To Mr. Donnelly, who runs the general store and buys pelts from the local Nehiyawak, I am a dirty Indian. I know this because when I fart, he turns to his youngest daughter and says, "Did you do that?" and she says, "It was her!" and he turns to me and snorts and says, "Figures." To the Nehiyawak men in Mr. Donnelly's store, I am out of place. I run around the stuffed owls and used washing machines with my friend Moira, the second youngest daughter in her blond-haired family of 10, and when the trappers

The author, 1975

see me, they always look at me, and I know they're looking at me, but I don't know why. They make eye contact with me but never with Mr. Donnelly. I start hanging around the counter while Mr. Donnelly examines the pelts, until Moira tells me to stay away. Even though she doesn't come right out and say it, I understand what she means: Indians are dangerous.

To Mabel Osborne, a pioneer and the town historian, I am a potential friend to her granddaughter, Sandra, whose mother is gone. Like Lloyd Kozlow's mother, who is also gone. I am a stand-in for all the missing Indigenous women whose children are being raised by white fathers and, sometimes, white stepmothers. A little bit of cultural connection, or so Mabel assumes. Too bad, though: Lloyd and Sandra want nothing to do with Sexy Suzi. They are Good Ones, because they're quiet and don't act like Indians. I am not a Good One, because I call up the disc jockeys at the local radio station and talk dirty to them. I'm trying to be what other people want me to be, because I want to be good. But how can I be good when I am a dirty, slutty Indian? I am pulled back and forth; I am disjointed. When the DJs invite me to the studio and one of them says something about Indian chicks being easy, I tell him I'm French, and he says, "Yeah, that's what they all say." I have learned many things in my 14 years on the planet. One thing I've learned: when white people say "they," it means Indians. I begin to understand that there are sides in this town, like two opposing teams. I don't choose a side; my position is chosen by those around me.

When a family member puts an ad in the paper in 1980 to sell an old bike, an Indian guy shows up to buy the red 10-speed. When he gets out of the car, he looks around nervously. Then he sees me, smiles, and tells me he lives across the river in West Peace. He asks me where I'm from, and I don't know what to say — I mean, this is my house. Well, a family member's house, but I live here. Then he says, "Good price for what they're selling, eh?" Another thing I've learned: when Indians say "they," it means white people. He claims me, just like the trappers do. "They" do not.

I am Entertainer-Storyteller, Parent-Caregiver, Dutiful Daughter, Patient Listener, Squaw, Descendant of Drummers, Stupid, Anomaly (White Teacher Version), Sexy Suzi, Anomaly (Cree Trapper Version), Dirty Indian, Potential Friend Failure, Not a Good One, They (White Version), and Easy. These assigned identities become my guides as I negotiate the task of growing up in a family that doesn't teach me how to be, in a town that doesn't want me to be. If there is a Suzanne inside here, I have yet to meet her. I don't know who or what I am.

Every individual has two kinds of self: the subject and the object, or the knower and the known. The subject is the self that an individual knows inside themselves. This is how we know the world. The object is the self that is known by others. This is how we are seen by the world.

For most Indigenous peoples, the division between subject and object is blurred. Myths and stereotypes about Indigenous peoples persist within the dominant society, and they continue to shape Indigenous identity. Because Indigenous peoples are marginalized within the dominant society — they have little to no power to influence that society's systems and institutions of education, policing, justice, and media, for example — what Indigenous peoples know or believe about themselves is inevitably affected, if not entirely shaped, by the assumptions of others. This is a form of control.

Control is a central factor in intergenerational trauma, because it is central to the development of complex post-traumatic stress disorder (CPTSD). While post-traumatic stress disorder (PTSD) has become a well-known issue in the wake of retired senator Roméo Dallaire's 2000 hospitalization — he was found intoxicated and unconscious under a bench in a park in Gatineau, Quebec, after retiring from the Canadian Armed Forces, where he served during the genocide in Rwanda — CPTSD is less well known.

When an individual survives a single traumatic event (such as sexual assault or a car accident) or traumatic events that occurred within a limited timeframe or context (such as war), the experience can result in a set of responses and behaviours referred to as PTSD. These cognitive and physiological adaptations — including but not limited to hypervigilance, irritability, dissociation, problems with memory, negative beliefs about oneself and about the world, feelings of detachment or estrangement from others, and a persistent negative emotional state (fear, anger, shame) — are useful during the traumatic event, as they may contribute to the individual's ability to survive the incident in physical, emotional, and spiritual terms. However, when the individual returns to daily life, these adaptations become counterproductive, creating a disorder. Individuals with PTSD are essentially stuck in time, reacting to situations in daily life as they did at the moment of their trauma, unable to move past that traumatic event.

The rate of PTSD among the general population in the United States is 8 per cent, according to the National Center for PTSD at the U.S. Department of Veterans Affairs. Maria Yellow Horse Brave Heart says that the rate of PTSD for Indigenous communities in the U.S. is 28 per cent, or nearly four times higher. No national studies about the prevalence of PTSD in Indigenous peoples in Canada have been conducted, but in a 2003 sample of residential school survivors in the province of British Columbia, 64 per cent were diagnosed with PTSD. Studies of women in prison show that up to 50 per cent of incarcerated women have PTSD — important to the Indigenous context because although Indigenous women make up only 4 per cent of the total female population in Canada, they represent almost half of the population in federal women's prisons.

Clearly, the rates of PTSD in Indigenous populations in the Americas point to the fact that Indigenous peoples have experienced traumatic events as a result of colonization. The rate of PTSD in Indigenous populations also points to the underlying issue behind the ongoing cycle of intergenerational trauma: that Indigenous peoples are living those traumatic events as unfinished business in the present day.

Mae Katt, an Indigenous nurse at Dennis Franklin Cromarty First Nations High School in Thunder Bay, Ontario, has been working with remote First Nations communities for 30 years. Katt, who testified at a 2016 inquest into the deaths of seven First Nations students who died in Thunder Bay between 2000 and 2011, says that many students who leave their reserves to come to Thunder Bay for high school exhibit classic symptoms of PTSD, including recurrent distressing memories of traumatic events, sleeplessness, problems with concentration, and reckless and self-destructive behaviour. Katt believes the high rate of PTSD in the student population is related to the fact that children are being raised by parents who are themselves coping with unresolved terror, anger, grief, and loss. The resulting dysfunction creates a highly stressful environment for children and youth, resulting in post-traumatic stress.

When former Ontario Health Minister and War Child Canada co-founder Eric Hoskins visited the Mushkegowuk community of Attawapiskat, in northern Ontario, in 2016 after dozens of young people tried to kill themselves, he told media that what he saw reminded him of the years he spent as a medical doctor working in war zones around the world. This is an accurate comparison, and it's how most people conceptualize post-traumatic stress: as traumatic experiences happening within a limited timeframe or context.

The work of the late Nehiyaw author Larry Loyie, Sto:lo chief Ernie Crey, Nlaka'pamux educator Shirley Sterling, former Sagkeeng First Nation chief Theodore Fontaine, and Mi'kmaw writer Isabelle Knockwood, who have all written about their residential school experiences, points to the ways in which the residential school experience can be understood through the lens of PTSD: these individuals were taken from childhoods spent on the land or in their communities with extended family — where they felt safe and experienced normal personality development through their connection to family and community — and put into institutions where they experienced traumatic events that continued to have an impact on their lives after they left the schools.

An individual with PTSD experiences heavy stress during a limited period of time during which they are exposed to threats or demands that are at or near the limits of their internal capacity to cope. The traumatic incident is a shock to the individual's assumed path in life, and the unfinished business of PTSD is created partly by the individual's unanswered questions about why the traumatic incident happened. Constantly asking the question "Why?" and never receiving an answer creates an endless repetitive loop within the individual's mind, body, and spirit that constantly triggers the traumatic incident.

Generations of Indigenous peoples, however, have never had an assumed path in life or any belief that the world around them is safe. Their development has been marked by repeated traumatic episodes and instances of prolonged abuse, from genocide to residential schools to the ongoing racism and discrimination of the dominant society — and now to the lateral violence present in post-contact Indigenous communities. Contemporary Indigenous peoples are not shocked by their traumatic experiences, because these experiences are commonplace and, for some, even routine. For contemporary Indigenous peoples, the unfinished business of the past is related to a "Why?" that encompasses the past 200 to 500 years, depending on the time of contact. This reflects their own experiences as well as the traumatic experiences of their ancestors. Although PTSD is an issue for many Indigenous peoples — as evidenced by the BC study and the students in Thunder Bay — intergenerational trauma is different from PTSD and cannot be explained using the same framework.

The everyday impacts of intergenerational trauma catalogued by the Aboriginal Healing Foundation refer to a broad range of feelings, thoughts, and behaviours that describe the physical, mental, emotional, and spiritual suffering of a population that has experienced prolonged or repeated trauma within the context of colonial control. Although the signs, symptoms, and behaviours that result from this chronic trauma are related to PTSD, they are different in emphasis and origin, earning them the distinct title of *complex* post-traumatic stress disorder, or CPTSD.

The CPTSD classification was first proposed by pioneering American psychiatrists Judith Lewis Herman and Bessel van der Kolk in 1985 when they were working at a Harvard teaching hospital with people who had been diagnosed with borderline personality disorder. They discovered that more than 80 per cent of their patients had histories of severe childhood abuse and neglect, so they formulated a set of criteria that would describe the psychological impact of traumatic events that occur when an individual is subordinate and under control. Herman went on to study women who had survived domestic abuse and eventually expanded CPTSD to include any situation where an individual is in a state of captivity, unable to flee, and under the control of the perpetrator: hostages, prisoners of war, concentration camp survivors, survivors of some religious cults, women who had survived organized sexual exploitation, and survivors of childhood physical or sexual abuse. Other researchers have since suggested that the CPTSD category could be widened to include refugees fleeing violence or war, victims of human trafficking, and individuals who experience acute or chronic illness that requires intensive medical intervention.

Residential schools can certainly be understood as a contributing factor to CPTSD: the experience was prolonged in nature and was characterized by repeated acts of cruelty and terror within an environment of captivity, subordination, and control. For contemporary Indigenous peoples, however, the trauma of residential school is only one experience in a long list of colonial oppression that includes state-sanctioned policies (both historical and contemporary), the events of colonization, and contemporary racism and discrimination.

In 2013, a Human Rights Watch report stated that Royal Canadian Mounted Police (RCMP) officers in northern British Columbia "abuse" Indigenous women and girls — using racist comments, excessive force, rape, and sexual assault, among other tactics — leading to widespread fear of police and a general feeling of unsafety. The report says there is a longstanding "dysfunctional relationship between the Canadian police and Indigenous com-munities" and makes 20 recommendations urging the federal government, the provincial government, and the RCMP to address the systemic roots of the violence and create accountability in Canada's federal policing system. In 2015, Indigenous women near Val-d'Or, Quebec, tell Radio-Canada that officers with the Sûreté du Québec — the province's provincial police force — have phys-ically and sexually assaulted them on a routine basis over the past 20 years. According to the women, officers give them beer from the trunk of their police vehicles and take them to remote areas where they demand oral sex, paying them in cash or cocaine to stay silent. One woman told Radio-Canada she was assaulted in a police car on the road between Val-d'Or and the Eeyou commu-nity of Waswanipi: "He wanted a blow job. I said no. He threw me out and grabbed my hair. He left me alone on the highway."

When traumatic experiences occur repeatedly, over a pro-longed period of time, they become chronic. Complex trauma refers to chronic trauma experienced within a specific context of control. As Indigenous peoples living in a settler state — where a dominant and dominating society controls every aspect of Indigenous peoples' lives, from the child welfare and education systems to the medical-pharmaceutical industry to policing to the justice system to the Indian Act — Indigenous peoples are under the control of the very systems and institutions that conspired to take their land, re-educate their children, and disempower them through the denial of human rights and a distorted interpretation of the treaty relationship. These traumatic events are not confined to a past single incident or catastrophic period: they began cen-turies ago and continue today, and they occur within a context of control. As such, I argue that CPTSD is the most accurate framework for understanding the challenges faced by Indigenous peoples and communities in a settler colonial state.

For Indigenous peoples, the trauma of colonization is chronic because it happens across time as a result of a continual, persistent, and progressive process of loss. This traumatic history includes single incidents, such as the hanging of Louis Riel in Regina in 1885 and the effect that incident had on the Métis people and their dream of a homeland, and ongoing systemic and institutionalized processes of colonization, such as the residential school system (which affected seven generations and destroyed the Indigenous family) and the prison system (a contemporary tool of control). It also includes historical incidents and processes, such as the destruction of Indigenous economies and the consequent inability of Indigenous peoples to provide for themselves and their families; the replacement of pre-colonial governments with the colonial band council system and the consequent disempowerment of women; the banning of ceremonies and spiritual practices, which were made illegal under an 1884 amendment to the Indian Act; the confinement of Indigenous peoples to reserves; and the Sixties Scoop, where, beginning in the 1960s, children were removed from their communities and placed for adoption with non-Indigenous families, sometimes in other countries.

In some cases, the chronic trauma experienced by Indigenous peoples is a result not only of the original experience but also of the prolonged and repeated outcomes of that experience — including inherited outcomes.

Clifford Cardinal, a professor at the University of Alberta's Department of Family Medicine, attended a special "day school" at the Goodfish Lake First Nation near Edmonton, Alberta, when he was a child. Although it was called a school, the Goodfish Lake facility was actually the site of a polio vaccine experiment. From

1959 to 1962, 38 Nehiyawak children were isolated, denied learning (survivors recall watching television all day for three years), and given excessive doses of a polio vaccine known to be contaminated with a human carcinogen — the SV40 virus, which originated in the kidneys of the rhesus monkeys used to grow the vaccine. The SV40 virus induces replication of viral and cellular DNA and inactivates tumour suppressor genes. Of the 38 children who attended the Goodfish Lake facility, only seven were alive in 2000, when Cardinal did a research project on the participants. The others had died of cancer, during surgery or treatment for cancer, or by suicide due to chronic pain. The average age of death was 36 years, with the youngest subject dying at 30 and the oldest dying at 49. By 2000, the seven survivors were struggling with multiple occurrences and multiple forms of cancer. The trauma of the vaccine experiment — the children's captivity and dehumanization — did not end with the participants' release from the facility after three years: it continues throughout their lives, as they deal with multiple incidents of sickness and invasive treatment, lifelong pain, and feelings of guilt about the health of their children. They worry about their children because the suppressor gene inactivated by the SV40 virus is inheritable, which means that subsequent generations at Goodfish Lake will also have to deal with multiple forms and occurrences of cancer as a result of the vaccine experiment.

This ongoing multi-generational pain and worry is common to many Indigenous communities. In the Anishinabek community of Grassy Narrows (Asubpeeschoseewagong) in northern Ontario, children and youth of the contemporary generation are dealing with the legacy of the Reed Paper mill in Dryden, Ontario, which dumped at least 9,000 kilograms of mercury waste into the English-Wabigoon River in the 1960s and 1970s. Not only does the mercury continue to contaminate the water — poisoning the fish and the Indigenous people who eat the fish (and drink the water) — it also bio-accumulates, passing from one generation to the next through the placenta and into the developing fetus. Today, children and youth in Grassy Narrows exhibit a range of symptoms associated with mercury poisoning, including numbness in fingers and toes, seizures, and cognitive delays. They also suffer from the chronic trauma of seeing friends and family sickened and killed by mercury poisoning. In 2017, Chayna Loon, a teenage resident of Grassy Narrows, told the CBC, "We could all be dying. We probably are, already."

People who have experienced chronic trauma within the context of control are left with an altered sense of identity and self-perception, a lack of personal agency, and a lack of faith in the value and meaning of their own lives. When an individual is under someone's control, all of the structures of self — the individual's ideas about their body, internalized beliefs about others, and the values and ideals that give a person a sense of coherence and purpose — are invaded and systematically broken down. In some totalitarian systems, the process of breaking the structures and sense of self extends to the point where the survivor's name is taken away. This occurred in concentration camps during the Second World War and in Canada under the systems and institutions of colonization.

Prior to the imposition of the colonial state, Inuit did not use surnames. Instead, children were named after animals, animal parts, astronomical objects (the sun, moon, various stars), a body part, or after a relative or other person whom the parents respected. According to Inuk elder Peter Irniq, the purpose of naming Inuit children after people who have died "is to make sure that person lives on in life." Irniq's brother Isaia, for example, is named after his grandfather, so Isaia's aunts and uncles call him "my father," and his cousins call him "my grandfather." When Irniq's son Adam was born, Irniq gave him the Inuit name Katak, after

Irniq's mother. As a result, Irniq refers to his son as "my dear little mother." Rather than see the beauty of this system, however — and how it provides a sense of connection, history, and belonging — the Canadian government instituted a numbering system in the Arctic between 1941 and 1978. Every Inuk was assigned a number and a wearable disc that resembled a dog tag. The tags were stamped with "Eskimo Identification Canada" around the edge and had a crown in the middle. Just above the crown was the person's ID code: "E" if they lived in the eastern Arctic and "W" if they lived in the western Arctic, followed by a one- or two-digit number indicating the area the person was from, followed by a set of numbers that identified the individual. Inuk singer Lucie Idlout recorded a song in 2004 called "E5-770: My Mother's Name," after her mother's disc number.

When she was in residential school in northern Ontario, Anishinabe elder Mary Wemigwans was assigned the number 54, which replaced her name. Wemigwans remembers being told, "Number 54, close the window. Number 54, erase the blackboard. Number 54, stand in the corner."

As psychiatrist Judith Lewis Herman puts it, "While the [survivor] of a single acute trauma may say she is 'not herself' since the event, the [survivor] of chronic trauma may lose the sense that she has a sense of self." This erasure of identity and sense of self is at the root of colonial control and is the primary force behind many of the everyday impacts of intergenerational trauma as identified by the Aboriginal Healing Foundation: low self-esteem, chronic depression, chronic anger, chronic physical illness related to spiritual and emotional states, unresolved grief and loss, and voicelessness. The feeling that any independent action will amount to insubordination and result in punishment also contributes to what the AHF calls "fear of personal growth and healing" in Indigenous peoples and communities.

According to Herman, "captivity, which brings the victim into prolonged contact with the perpetrator, creates a special type of relationship, one of coercive control." Rendered confined by physical force (residential schools, prisons) and a combination of economic, social, and psychological means (government policy that denies on-reserve communities clean water, access to education, and suitable housing, for example), it is clear that Indigenous peoples are captives of a colonial system, which has negative effects on personal autonomy. For most Indigenous peoples, these experiences begin early in life, dramatically affecting how they develop their identity and self-concept.

Culture helps us understand and manage our life experiences, especially those that are terrifying or that cause us to feel grief and loss. When colonial governments outlawed Indigenous cultural and spiritual practices — including dancing, the sweat lodge, the sundance, and the potlatch — they removed the processes Indigenous peoples used to understand or manage the terrifying experiences of colonization. For those who attended residential school, cultural genocide was only one part of the equation. When children were separated from their families and forced to attend the schools, the separation from a support system meant that they struggled alone with their traumatic experiences, which made recovery difficult or impossible. This disruption in social structure is one of the main reasons why trauma has become intergenerational within Indigenous communities.

Because Indigenous peoples have been unable to process and recover from the chronic trauma of colonialism, these recurring memories and unresolved emotions have morphed into social narratives. Instead of stories that connect people to Indigenous belief systems or to the land, oral tradition after contact began to focus on stories of terror, pain, and degradation. Instead of hearing stories that make them feel safe and protected, Indigenous children today hear stories about the pain and suffering of their ancestors — if they hear anything at all. Sometimes, adults are incapable of communicating with their children, as they struggle with unresolved terror, anger, grief, and loss. Well-being has been replaced with hypervigilance (being constantly tense and on guard for possible danger) and the assumption that individuals — and Indigenous societies as a whole — will have a foreshortened future.

Once, when I am visiting my hometown in northern Alberta, I go to lunch with a friend and her brother. At the time, they are living in the Nehiyawak community of Little Buffalo, just outside town. As we talk, I ask my friend what is going on with the land claims process and the oil companies. How is her daughter doing? Would she ever consider moving into town? My friend's reply is not filled with hopes and dreams for the future. She doesn't have a plan. What she says is: "I know I won't get old."

As the trauma of colonization has become entrenched in the fabric of Indigenous societies, substance abuse and suicide have become common as individuals attempt to escape their unbearable situation.

The central issue behind trauma and complex post-traumatic stress is helplessness. Whether it is literal or cultural genocide committed by the state, racist violence committed by a member of the dominant society against an Indigenous person, interpersonal violence committed by one Indigenous individual toward another, or emotional abuse committed by a traumatized Indigenous parent toward a child, the defining issue is that survivors experience a loss of control. One minute, everything is fine, then the next, the individual is in serious danger, experiencing a threat toward their physical, emotional, or spiritual sense of self. The impact of this terrifying experience usually results in the survivor losing control over their conscious thought, as they attempt to bury the memory of the incident and deny the painful feelings associated with it.

However, just because the terror, anger, and grief is buried doesn't mean it has no effect on the survivor. Over time, these unconscious and unresolved memories and emotions can negatively affect an individual's personality and their ability to connect with others.

As Indigenous peoples internalized and mimicked the soul-destroying tactics of colonialism — the emotional and sexual abuse they experienced or witnessed in residential schools, for example — they began to engage in toxic communication patterns and lateral violence within their own communities. These behaviours have changed pre-colonial social dynamics, processes, and structures of Indigenous societies, resulting in an erosion of trust, changes to Indigenous norms and values, poor leadership, and a general lack of social cohesion. Passed down across generations, the dysfunction has now become normalized — accepted as the way things are — and part of the expectations of successive generations.

Thirteen-year-old Indigenous girls don't choose to turn tricks in townhouses rented by their Internet-savvy pimps in Edmonton. Indigenous people in Vancouver's Downtown Eastside don't choose to shoot up cocaine 15 or 20 times a day. Young Indigenous men in North Central Regina don't choose to join gangs. Missing and murdered Indigenous women don't choose to put themselves in dangerous situations in hotel rooms and cars. They've been forced into these situations because they think their lives don't matter, because they're looking for meaning, because they feel like they're not part of the real world, because they are shut down and not feeling anything, because they're self-medicating their pain, because they crave a sense of belonging and validation, because they're looking for love, and because they are unconsciously re-enacting the trauma they have witnessed or experienced in their own lives. Changing these behaviours isn't about making better choices: it's about healing from the trauma that impedes a person's ability to make choices. Someone who is angry, incapacitated by grief and fear, paralyzed by internalized shame, or who lacks a sense of identity and a corresponding sense of personal agency isn't able to make choices. For many Indigenous people, choosing to heal is the first choice they have ever made.

According to the AHF, unresolved trauma leads to chronic anger and chronic depression — and although the two emotions are on opposite ends of a spectrum, they are actually related. Anger helps people regain control (or feel as if they are in control). However, fear of retribution means that Indigenous people who experience chronic trauma cannot express their anger toward the abuser. As a result, they internalize their anger. Eventually, it becomes what Judith Lewis Herman calls a "malignant self-hatred" that morphs into chronic depression, self-destructive behaviour, and suicidal ideation.

When an individual or a community is under external control, it destroys their sense of autonomy. Although they may approach daily tasks with remarkable creativity and strength — typical of the resiliency it takes to survive — being under control and experiencing prolonged repeated trauma destroys the survivor's sense that they can act for themselves or change the situation. Herman calls this a "paralysis of initiative." The AHF calls it a lack of agency.

A Moravian minister who lived among the Cherokee in the early 19th century described their society: "Age confers rank, wisdom gives power, and moral goodness secures title to universal respect." A few decades later, after their lands were taken and the colonial government forcibly removed the Choctaw, Seminole, Creek, Chickasaw, and Cherokee nations from their traditional territories — sending 46,000 Indigenous peoples on a forced march west to Oklahoma between 1831 and 1837, during which thousands died — a U.S. colonel wrote, "You cannot have an idea of the deterioration which these Indians have undergone during these last two or three years, from a general state of comparative plenty to that of unqualified wretchedness and want. Encroaches upon their lands, even upon their cultivated fields; abuses of their person; hosts of traders who, like locusts, have devoured their substance and inundated their homes with whiskey. They are brow beat, and cowed, and imposed upon, and depressed with the feeling that they have no adequate protection and no capacity for self-protection in themselves." This feeling is common in survivors of trauma, and it is a major force behind the dysfunction and negative outcomes described by the AHF.

Trauma experienced in the context of control changes the way an individual interacts with the external world. First, as Holocaust research has shown, and as Herman discovered while working with survivors of domestic abuse, the perpetrator of the trauma — the controlling figure — becomes the most powerful entity in the life of the survivor. This means that the survivor will often attempt to please the control figure by internalizing the control figure's beliefs and acting in ways that they think will please or placate them. Second, as the process of internalization changes the personality of the survivor, the survivor comes to believe that any individual initiative amounts to insubordination, which carries the risk of punishment. This, along with the fact that they cannot control the traumatic events they experience, leaves survivors without a sense of agency. The world then becomes a very unsafe, unpredictable place. Survivors begin to expect that something bad will happen in the future, which prevents them from taking action in the present. When they do act, their internalized self-hatred — manifested through the cognitive and emotional processes by which the survivor attempts to make sense of their situation (*they must be treating me this way because I deserve it*) — means they attribute any failures to personal causes, which results in self-blame (*see, I did deserve it*).

When cancer began to surface at Goodfish Lake after the 1959–1962 vaccine experiment, very few of the test subjects chose to use traditional Nehiyawak medicine to combat their illnesses. According to Clifford Cardinal, 95 per cent of the community was Christianized and using Western medicine at the time of his study. Cardinal also says that those who used pre-colonial medicine or practised any Nehiyawak traditions were ostracized. At one point, Cardinal says, a band council resolution was introduced to remove Cardinal from his position on the council "due to the possibility of the return to the pagan ways of the traditional people." Cardinal says the intent was to please local nuns and priests and the federal Department of Indian Affairs and to "support all programs . . . initiated by white outsiders."

When the cancers began, people in the community blamed the test subjects for their illnesses, because they were considered to have received "special privileges" by attending the facility — where everyone knew that they watched television all day, did not study or learn, and did not pray — thereby avoiding residential school. Those who blamed the test subjects have clearly internalized what they learned from the colonizer: that Nehiyawak science, medicine, and cultural practices are wrong; that Indigenous peoples are bad; that they deserve to be punished; and that the test subjects therefore got what they deserved. These ideas would have been inculcated in the residents of the community through their attendance at residential schools and Christian churches, which taught generations of Indigenous people that their cultures were pagan and evil, and that they were dirty, backward savages who had to be taught how to be human.

Nehiyawak culture, like all Indigenous cultures, emphasizes respect, responsibility, reciprocity, and relationships. Everything an individual does has an effect on their internal world and on the external world, and individual and collective balance is maintained through right relationships that hinge upon awareness and self-control. Some things are assumed to be predestined

— especially when it comes to a person's talents and gifts, and the purpose they will serve within the community in this lifetime — but the medicine wheel also teaches that human beings have the power of volition. Although there are forces in the universe that can influence a person's life — such as bad medicine (negative energy sent from one person to another), visitors from the spirit world, and the energy of cosmological and astronomical forces — an individual can also change the energy around them and within them through spiritual practice. In so doing, an individual can influence the forces acting upon them.

When we look at the effect of chronic trauma on Indigenous peoples, the phenomenon of CPTSD, and the everyday impacts of intergenerational trauma, we see what it means to be colonized. Colonization is disconnection.

There are many ways in which Indigenous people and communities honour and reclaim pre-colonial social structures in order to resist colonialism and recover from colonization. We (re-) start women's circles in communities impacted by the oil and gas industry, as the Muskotew Sakahikan Enowuk did. We (re-)create warrior societies in communities resisting land appropriation, as the people of Kanehsatake did. We use Indigenous law and governance structures to assert title over unceded lands, as the Nisga'a did. We create safety patrols in urban communities. We start movements such as Idle No More. But the straightforward and insidious work of colonization has achieved its aim: many Indigenous people are disconnected from their bodies and spirits, disconnected from family and community, disconnected from pre-colonial social support networks, disconnected from personal and cultural identity, and disconnected from the dominant society. This disconnection has created the situations that the Aboriginal Healing Foundation documents on its list of everyday impacts of trauma: social issues from substance abuse to suicide; chronic physical illness; spiritual confusion and disconnection from the natural world; dysfunctional families and relationships; disunity and conflict at the community level; patterns of sexual abuse and child neglect; and a passive acceptance of powerlessness.

According to Nehiyaw grandfather/elder Michael Thrasher, there are knowable conditions for creating change in an individual and within a community: kindness and willingness, honesty and introspection, change and forgiveness, balance and creativity. Thrasher says that every individual is born with four gifts — vision, feeling, movement, and time — but that fear keeps most people from using these gifts to grow and transform. To stop the cycle of intergenerational trauma, Indigenous peoples must choose to see, to feel, and to move.

CPTSD is about being stuck: stuck in time at the moment of trauma, stuck in negative self-perception created by the internalization of the perpetrators' beliefs, stuck in a space where people feel they cannot create change, and stuck in patterns that communicate the trauma across generations. Instead of occupying the centre of the medicine wheel — the axis that represents the energy of human agency — Indigenous peoples are stuck in an old story, one of genocide and control, unable to enact the constant renewal and transformation once considered sacred. Returning to a state of constant movement and renewal as described by the medicine wheel will require Indigenous peoples to tell a new story: a story of hope and change.

In 2017, as part of a Resistance 150 project — an Indigenous response to the Canada 150 sesquicentennial celebrations — Mary Wemigwans cut up her Indian Status card. As she did so, she stated, "I am not a number. I am Mary Elizabeth Wemigwans, Anishinabe-kwe."

Healing is not just an individual process: it is also a social one. To heal from CPTSD, Indigenous peoples must regain identity, repair their self-concept, and reconnect their minds, bodies, spirits, and emotions so that they can recognize beauty within themselves and then extend that thinking to others. Indigenous peoples must also regain their sense of agency. This will require the systems and institutions of the dominant society to act as allies instead of instruments of colonial control.

Longtime Alberta youth court judge Steve Lipton is one of those allies. In 2017, he contacted the media about the case of a 14-year-old Indigenous boy who had been diagnosed with paranoia and hallucinations and who also required treatment for addictions to crystal meth and alcohol. Lipton told the CBC he was "frustrated" and "very, very angry" about the lack of services and supports available for the boy, who was charged with assault, failure to appear, mischief, and theft. According to Lipton, the boy — who fears that people are going to kill him or inject him with drugs while he is sleeping — needed to be in a secure treatment facility or a secure safe house for children and youth requiring treatment for substance abuse. However, because no beds were available in southern Alberta, Lipton was forced to keep him in jail, where treatment was not available. "He's mentally ill," Lipton said, "and I'm keeping him in jail, and he's a kid. What's wrong with this picture?"

There is a strong correlation between socio-economic disadvantage and involvement with the criminal justice system. Poverty, lack of educational opportunities, unemployment, and poor living conditions are part of the life stories of every Indigenous person now serving time in a Canadian prison. The everyday impacts of intergenerational trauma also play a role, as many offenders struggle with alcohol abuse and the effects of fetal alcohol spectrum disorder, and as the physical and sexual abuse many offenders experience in childhood become their own learned patterns of behaviour. The anger, disunity, conflict, breakdown of social glue, and disconnection from the natural world identified by the Aboriginal Healing Foundation also play a factor in the high rates of violent crime and property crime in Indigenous communities. However, Indigenous peoples are also overrepresented in Canadian prisons because the colonial state is increasingly using prison as a form of captivity and control. According to the Office of the Correctional Investigator, the Indigenous prison population increased by 39 per cent between 2007 and 2016.

Although a 1999 Supreme Court decision (*R. v. Gladue*) requires judges to consider an Indigenous person's history of trauma, abuse, addictions, displacement, family dysfunction, and other disadvantages during sentencing, many judges ignore the law. This means that Indigenous offenders (especially repeat offenders) are incarcerated for crimes that would net a non-Indigenous offender a discharge or a fine. In addition, Indigenous people are sent to prison for breaching the conditions of bail or parole at twice the rate of non-Indigenous people. As a result, they serve longer sentences. Indigenous people are also more likely to be placed in maximum security institutions and more likely to be placed in segregation. Once in segregation, Indigenous people spend a longer time there than non-Indigenous offenders do. These incarceration rates are becoming part of the chronic trauma experienced by Indigenous peoples at the hands of the colonial control figure. Such treatment also contributes to CPTSD, as it confirms what survivors of complex trauma have already come to believe: that the world is an unsafe place, no one will help them, and they have no control over what happens to them.

By creating conditions that ensure the overrepresentation of Indigenous peoples in the justice system, the colonial state also creates and sustains a distorted conception of Indigenous identity. According to a 2016 feature investigation in *Maclean's*, the number of Indigenous people labelled as "dangerous offenders"

— a categorization that allows the state to apply an indeterminate sentence, with no parole hearing for at least seven years — doubled between 2006 and 2016. And in some provinces, the dangerous offender category is populated almost exclusively by Indigenous people. In Saskatchewan, for example, Indigenous peoples make up only 11 per cent of the province's population, but 80 per cent of all dangerous offenders. Since only 4 per cent of dangerous offenders ever actually get out of prison, this means that Indigenous peoples are being sentenced to life in prison for crimes that one *Maclean's* source calls "really ludicrous offences," such as bar fights, which would put a non-Indigenous person in jail for only a short period of time. The overuse of the dangerous offender label denies Indigenous peoples control over their own lives and identities, perpetuating the control relationship that characterizes CPTSD.

Prior to colonization, Indigenous identities were self-determined and in constant flux, as people and communities defined and redefined themselves in response to individual and cultural change. After centuries of being trivialized, marginalized, dehumanized, and institutionalized, however, Indigenous identities have now become fixed within various systems of colonial control, from "at-risk student" to "dangerous offender" and everything in between.

For most contemporary Indigenous peoples, the need for identity grows out of confusion: the need to know and understand the components of Indigenous identity in the face of literal genocide, cultural genocide, disconnection from land, family breakdown, and the myths and stereotypes created and assigned by the control figure (the colonial state). When an Indigenous person selects an identity apart from those created for them by the control figure, they are expressing their agency and taking an early step on the path to healing and reconnection.

After I am born and my mother takes me home from the hospital, she brings me to the Catholic school that some of my family members attend, run by the nuns at Our Lady of Perpetual Help parish in Vancouver. The nuns know that my mother lost the child she carried before me, and they have been steadfast in their joy throughout this pregnancy. When my mother arrives at the parish, I am only a few days old. The nuns take me to the residence, place me on their personal altar, and say a special prayer. Although the sisters don't know it, their ceremony mirrors the tradition of some Indigenous nations, where a child is held up in the eastern door of the lodge and introduced to creation. Nearly 30 years later, I receive my Indigenous spirit name from a medicine person in Toronto.

In Nehiyawak tradition, a spirit name is not just invented and assigned — it exists in the universe and is *found*. A person's spirit name is a reconnection to the spirit world they inhabited before birth. Today, when I think about the sisters and their ceremony, and when I think about what it means to embody my name — what it means to have this particular relationship with creation and this particular responsibility to my community — I realize that my ancestors have always known me. I just needed to know myself.

POST-TRAUMATIC STRESS DISORDER (PTSD)

1. Exposure to actual or threatened death, serious injury, or sexual violence in one (or more) of the following ways:

   - directly experiencing the traumatic event(s)
   - witnessing, in person, the event(s) as it occurred to others
   - learning that a traumatic event(s) occurred to a close family member or close friend (in cases of actual or threatened death of a family member or friend, the events must have been violent or accidental)
   - experiencing repeated or extreme exposure to aversive details of the traumatic event(s) (e.g., first responders collecting human remains; police officers repeatedly exposed to details of child abuse, including work-related exposure through electronic media, television, movies, or pictures)

2. Presence of one (or more) of the following intrusion symptoms associated with the traumatic event(s), beginning after the traumatic event(s) occurred:

   - recurrent, involuntary, and intrusive distressing memories of the traumatic event(s) (in children younger than six, repetitive play may occur in which themes or aspects of the traumatic event(s) are expressed)
   - recurrent distressing dreams in which the content and/or affect of the dream are related to the traumatic event(s) (in children, there may be frightening dreams without recognizable content)
   - dissociative reactions (e.g., flashbacks) in which the individual feels or acts as if the traumatic event(s) were recurring (in children, trauma-specific re-enactment may occur in play)
   - intense or prolonged psychological distress at exposure to internal or external cues that symbolize or resemble an aspect of the traumatic event(s)

3. Persistent avoidance of stimuli associated with the traumatic event(s), beginning after the traumatic event(s) occurred, as evidenced by one or both of the following:

- avoidance of or efforts to avoid distressing memories, thoughts, or feelings about or closely associated with the traumatic event(s)
- avoidance of or efforts to avoid external reminders (people, places, conversations, activities, objects, situations) that arouse distressing memories, thoughts, or feelings about or closely associated with the traumatic event(s)

4. Negative alterations in cognitions and mood associated with the traumatic event(s), beginning or worsening after the traumatic event(s) occurred, as evidenced by two (or more) of the following:

- inability to remember an important aspect of the traumatic event(s) (typically due to dissociative amnesia and not to other factors such as head injury, alcohol, or drugs)
- persistent and exaggerated negative beliefs or expectations about oneself, others, or the world (e.g., "I am bad," "No one can be trusted," "The world is completely dangerous")
- persistent, distorted cognitions about the cause of consequences or the traumatic event(s) that lead the individual to blame themself or others
- persistent negative emotional state (e.g., fear, horror, anger, guilt, or shame)
- markedly diminished interest or participation in significant activities
- feelings of detachment or estrangement from others
- persistent inability to experience positive emotions (e.g., inability to experience happiness, satisfaction, or loving feelings)
- in children six years and younger, substantially increased frequency of negative emotional states (e.g., fear, guilt, sadness, shame, confusion), including constriction of play and socially withdrawn behaviour

5. Marked alterations in arousal and reactivity associated with the traumatic event(s), beginning or worsening after the traumatic event(s) occurred, as evidenced by two (or more) of the following:

- irritable behaviour and angry outbursts (with little or no provocation) typically expressed as verbal or physical aggression toward people or objects
- reckless or self-destructive behaviour
- hypervigilance
- exaggerated startle response
- problems with concentration
- sleep disturbance (e.g., difficulty falling or staying asleep or restless sleep)

In order to be considered PTSD, the above issues must be present for more than one month; cause significant distress or impairment in social, occupational, or other important areas of functioning; and, in children six years and younger, cause significant distress or impairment in relationships with parents, siblings, peers, or other caregivers or with school behaviour.

Adapted from the Diagnostic and Statistical Manual of Mental Disorders, *Fifth Edition (American Psychiatric Association, Washington, DC, 2013)*

COMPLEX POST-TRAUMATIC STRESS DISORDER (CPTSD)

1. A history of subjection to totalitarian control over a prolonged period (months to years). Examples include hostages, prisoners of war, concentration-camp survivors, survivors of some religious cults, survivors of genocide, and populations who have experienced colonization. Examples also include those subjected to totalitarian systems in sexual and domestic life, including survivors of domestic violence, childhood physical or sexual abuse, and organized sexual exploitation.

2. Alterations in affect regulation, including:

   - persistent mental unease or discomfort
   - chronic suicidal preoccupation
   - self-injury
   - explosive or extremely inhibited anger (may go back and forth)
   - compulsive or extremely inhibited sexuality (may go back and forth)

3. Alterations in consciousness, including:

   - amnesia or hyperamnesia of traumatic events
   - transient dissociative episodes
   - loss of one's sense of identity
   - the feeling that things are strange, unreal, or somehow altered
   - reliving experiences, either in the form of intrusive post-traumatic stress disorder symptoms or preoccupation with thoughts about past occurrences, that cause feelings of anxiety, sadness, shame, or guilt

4. Alterations in self-perception, including:

   - sense of helplessness or paralysis of initiative
   - shame, guilt, and self-blame

- sense of impurity or stigma
- sense of complete difference from others (may include utter aloneness or belief that no other person can understand)

5. Alterations in perception of perpetrator, including:

- preoccupation with relationship with perpetrator (includes preoccupation with revenge)
- unrealistic attribution of total power to perpetrator
- idealization of perpetrator or paradoxical gratitude
- acceptance of belief system or rationalizations of perpetrator

6. Alterations in relations with others, including:

- isolation and withdrawal
- disruption in intimate relationships
- repeated search for rescuer (may alternate with isolation and withdrawal)
- persistent distrust
- repeated failures of self-protection

7. Alterations in systems of meaning, including:

- loss of sustaining faith
- sense of hopelessness and despair

Excerpted and adapted from Judith Herman, Trauma and Recovery: The Aftermath of Violence from Domestic Abuse to Political Terror *(New York, Basic Books, 1997)*

CHAPTER 3

BECOMING HUMAN

My father never talks about his past, but my mother tells me three things. One: he grew up in an orphanage in Montreal. Two: the nuns at the orphanage would pull on the little boys' penises, laugh, and make disparaging remarks. The nuns also laughed and pointed at the boys when they were naked in the shower. Three: my father remembers the day he arrives at the orphanage with his older brother. They are holding hands, and he sees light coming through a window. He hasn't started school yet, so he's about four years old.

My father is born in 1938 to a single mother. In the 1940s and 1950s, under *Le Grande Noirceur* (The Great Darkness) of Quebec premier Maurice Duplessis's rule, thousands of children born to young unmarried women are rounded up and sent to orphanages run by the Catholic Church. These "children of sin," as they are called — many living in poverty and some, like my father, who are not *pure laine* (of purely French-Canadian ancestry) — are improperly diagnosed as mentally incompetent or psychotic so that the priests and nuns running the orphanages receive bigger subsidies from the federal government. Many of the Duplessis orphans have their names changed and identities erased, so that their mothers cannot search for them and families can never reunite.

The Duplessis orphans endure forced lobotomies, electroshock, straitjackets, experimental psychiatric drugs, and physical, sexual, psychological, and emotional abuse. Some children are sent out to work with farmers, while other children do the maintenance and janitorial work that enable the orphanages to function. They are treated as slave labour and receive harsh discipline if they refuse orders. As Hervé Bertrand, a Duplessis orphan, tells the *Toronto Star* in 1992, "I was beaten, I was tied up, I was made to work."

The Duplessis orphans are also victims of medical experiments performed at the St. Jean de Dieu insane asylum, which is now known as the Institut universitaire en santé mentale de Montréal. Albert Sylvio, a Duplessis orphan who lived at St. Jean de Dieu in the 1950s, tells the *National Post* in 2004 that he transported more than 60 bodies of fellow orphans from the operating rooms to the basement morgue: "I undressed them and washed them and prepared them for burial. We put them in cardboard boxes. Some of them were children." He says the bodies were taken to the cemetery and buried in unmarked graves. One government registry indicates that there are about 2,000 bodies buried at the St. Jean de Dieu cemetery; at least 42 are children.

In an interview in the *Montreal Gazette* in 1992, social worker Daniel Simard, who worked in the Duplessis orphanages in the 1950s, recalls the atmosphere: "What struck me the most when I visited the orphanages was the lack of love. The nuns showed no kindness or affection to the children. It was as though they were making the children expiate the sin of being born illegitimate."

After an abusive childhood during which they are not educated — because "hospitals," unlike orphanages, are not required to provide any schooling — the Duplessis orphans leave the orphanages completely unprepared to cope in the outside world. They cannot hold down jobs, do not know how to create successful friendships or marriages, and are unable to form relationships with or be parents to their own children. Some Duplessis orphans leave the orphanages as young as 10 years old, to live on the streets of Montreal.

My father meets my mother in Vancouver. She is in a laundromat, he asks for her telephone number, and then he barrages her with calls until she relents. They are married in August 1965. My brother Paul is stillborn in 1966, and I arrive in 1968, when my two

Duplessis Orphans in Huberdeau, Quebec

3762669 Orphelinat d'Huberdeau, P.Q. [image fixe]; Montreal : Published by International Post Card Cote : BAnQ, CP 023662 CON

half-siblings from my mother's first marriage are nine and seven. The verbal abuse begins when she is pregnant with me, when my father starts to say things like, "Be careful you don't kill this one like you killed the last one." The physical abuse will come later.

By 1971, my mother has embarked on a campaign to fix the man she has married. She convinces my father to open a business based on his skills repairing televisions, radios, and other electronic devices. She also asks her friends — including a pastor and a police officer — to write letters of support and secures him a federal pardon, which means my father's criminal record is wiped clean.

My father is 17 or 18 years old in 1956 when he is convicted of the offence of theft. In 1957, he is convicted of escaping lawful custody and theft, and in 1958 he is convicted of breaking and entering with intent. He is in and out of jail in a cycle of short sentences and even shorter periods of freedom stretching over several years, returning to crime soon after being released (or escaping custody), then being convicted and sentenced again. He would have left the Duplessis orphanage only a few years before, without any formal education, no family to rely on, and with a history of abuse that has negatively affected his development, his sense of self-worth and his interpersonal skills. By 1958, his career as a petty criminal comes to an end, when he commits an indictable offence and is sentenced to the big house: Oakalla Prison Farm in Burnaby, BC.

Oakalla has been described as "decrepit" by Dr. Guy Richmond, who was senior medical officer of the BC Corrections Branch in the 1950s and 1960s. The prison — which executed 44 prisoners between 1919 and 1959, when the death penalty was abolished – was originally designed to house a maximum of 500 prisoners but holds almost triple that number by 1963. Steam pipes make living conditions in some cells intolerable. There are fire hazards, and the prison is infested with rats. Prisoners lack adequate supervision, which results in frequent riots and no fewer than 890 prisoner escapes over 40 years. There are also dozens of suicides and thousands of suicide attempts. Despite these issues, Oakalla is the first institution in BC to offer a range of work programs, which are meant to rehabilitate offenders and ease their reintegration into society. So my father stays put this time and learns a trade: repairing small electronics.

My father writes captions on the bottom of every photograph for the family album. He always shows me what he writes, and I assume he writes in English because my mother and I do not understand French. Two decades later, as I uncover bits and pieces of the little-known and relatively undocumented history of the Duplessis orphans, I make a sudden realization: never educated as a Duplessis orphan, my father can't read or write in his native French. He reads and writes in English only, because he learned while he was in prison. It is these a-ha moments that give me a way to make sense of the situations in which I am enveloped as a child. Now I understand why he wouldn't help his stepchildren with their French homework. Now I understand the ongoing tension and the arguments over a grade 10 textbook. My mother and other family members think my father is an asshole. In truth, he is covering up the fact that he cannot read or write in French, ashamed to admit that he is the ignorant savage the nuns told him he was.

According to Bessel van der Kolk, a psychiatrist and expert on post-traumatic stress in children, traumatic experiences have a more pervasive impact when they are experienced during the first decade of life.

When an adult in otherwise normal circumstances experiences a single traumatic event — such as the death of a close relative or a violent or life-threatening situation — they have skills and abilities that enable them to manage the experience. They have the ability to maintain positive emotions and the capacity to learn from the experience. They have a sense of autonomy, which can help them take steps toward processing and recovery. They have a sense of identity that anchors them in a place they understand as "normal life," which helps them create a roadmap toward healing. As functioning adults, they have a sense that they are capable of creating change in their lives. As adults, they have developed the ability to manage their emotions, including the intense feelings created by a traumatic experience. And they have the skills to engage in basic forms of self-care — eating, sleeping, seeking support from others — even when they are managing those intense feelings. The adult survivor of a traumatic event may experience a stress reaction during that episode, and sometimes after, but these reactions are usually mild or moderate, short term, and do not interfere with their ability to continue functioning.

When a child experiences a traumatic incident or lives with chronic trauma, the trauma disrupts their development, preventing them from achieving many of the competencies of adulthood. Without these adult skills — planning, organizing, paying attention to (and remembering) detail, regulating emotion, and managing everyday stressors — they are likely to adopt behaviours that help them manage the traumatic memories but which are otherwise destructive to themselves and others. These behaviours and coping mechanisms will set the stage for ongoing difficulties in adulthood, as survivors of trauma deal with feelings of fear; an inability to trust other people or ask for help; feelings of isolation, anxiety, anger, and helplessness; and a sense of inferiority and shame.

There is currently no diagnostic label to describe the pervasive impact of trauma on childhood development, so children who have experienced trauma are usually given what is called "co-morbid diagnoses" — a laundry list of multiple labels including oppositional defiant disorder (ODD) and attention deficit hyper-activity disorder (ADHD). These labels concentrate on a child's problematic behaviours, helping teachers and others who work with children answer the standard question: *What's wrong with you?* Unfortunately, this is the wrong question to ask a child who is angry, oppositional, disengaged, or unable to focus. The real question we should be asking is: *What happened to you?*

Danis is Indigenous, 10 years old, and in grade 5. When I start teaching at the school she attends, she sullenly agrees to sit in my room but refuses to participate in program activities. When she is encouraged to work instead on assignments from other staff at the school, she refuses to do that. It is impossible to predict what will set her off; a seemingly innocuous comment will create a firestorm of irritation that usually ends with her getting up from her seat and exiting the room to sit in the hallway. Asking her what I can do to help only makes her angrier and more upset. It takes a full eight months for Danis to agree to take part in any of the projects underway in my classroom.

On my first day at the school Danis attends, one of my colleagues tells me "Good luck" in a resigned and slightly amused tone of voice. There are supply teachers who won't accept assignments at this school, and when I tell a colleague — an Indigenous woman herself — that I am applying for the position, she tells me, "Oh, you don't want to work there." There is a persistent negative psychological atmosphere within the Indigenous community at this school that permeates daily life, a palpable sense of dis-ease that is noticeable to outsiders but normalized by the community itself. I see beauty, strength, goodness, and exceptional intelligence in my students every single day, but those qualities exist in spite of, and underneath, layers and layers of negative emotion that have been handed down to them as a legacy of colonialism. This negative emotion is generated partly by the actions and emotional projections of the adults around them and partly by the children's own responses to the chronic trauma that surrounds them.

Danis and her classmates experience and are exposed to violence, domestic violence, adult arguments, sexual abuse, emotional abuse, physical neglect, street gangs and other criminal activity, substance abuse, and the repeated loss of adult caregiver or attachment figures due to frequent moves, incarceration, and partnership/friendship breakdown. They have witnessed injury, suffering, and death, sometimes repeatedly. They experience racism and discrimination on a daily basis, and they are subjected to systemic and institutional control through the school's attempts at behaviour management, which do not address the chronic trauma they have experienced or the neurophysiological changes these traumatic experiences produce inside the children's brains and bodies. The adults around them — themselves the survivors of chronic trauma — are intensely focused on their own issues, which makes them emotionally unavailable to their children.

The human body-mind grows and develops as people interact with their environment and learn how to function within it. When a baby cries and their distress is met with food or comfort, the interaction teaches the child that the world is a safe place filled with people who will help them when they ask. They learn that it is necessary to communicate to others how and what they are feeling. Because they are communicating these ideas, they learn a language that helps them categorize and understand what is going on inside their body-mind. When they are soothed, a child also learns that the intense emotions they feel when they are in discomfort can be changed through subtle but deeply significant actions: the touch of a hand, a whispered word, a look of concern. Their feelings are validated, and they learn that seeking connection — to their bodies and to other people — helps them move through intense emotions to get to a place where they feel better and more in balance. When a child learns these things, they develop a sense of self and are able to adapt to diverse conditions, becoming well-rounded adults.

Babies who do not get responses to their cries, or children whose emotional distress is unacknowledged or met with abuse, learn different lessons. They learn that the world is an unsafe place and that no one will ever help them. They learn that there is no point in communicating what they are feeling, because no one ever responds. Because they are not communicating what they are feeling, they do not learn how to describe or categorize what is going on inside their body-mind. As a result, they fail to develop a sense of connection to their inner selves. They become incredibly distressed, living in a never-ending state of fear, resignation, betrayal, rage, and defeat. Because they are never soothed, they do not learn how to move through intense feelings to get to a more balanced place, so they begin to ignore what they feel (their emotions) and what they perceive (their thoughts). Their mental and physical distress leads some children to dissociate from their body-mind and other children to act out their pain in an aggressive manner. As adults, they will seek external methods of controlling their distress, which may manifest as addictions or a need for control.

Because their feelings are never validated, these children feel isolated and misunderstood. They live with the expectation that every experience will turn out to be traumatic or painful, so they prioritize their survival mechanisms — the freeze, fight, or flight responses — in order to anticipate, prevent, or protect themselves against danger. Instead of acquiring new learning and creating relationships with others, they become suspicious, distrustful, and inflexible, which will have negative effects on every aspect of their adult lives.

When a parent is focused on their own pain and living in survival mode, they become emotionally unavailable to their child. Emotional unavailability is a form of emotional *neglect* — when the child's need to feel loved, wanted, safe, and worthy is not met. Emotional *abuse* occurs when a parent or caregiver attacks a child's sense of self by constantly insulting or humiliating them. Emotional abuse includes name-calling (telling the child they are stupid or bad) and also occurs when the parent constantly complains about the child. These actions harm a child's sense of self-worth and self-confidence.

After my mother divorces my father in 1978, the two of us move back to Vancouver from northern Alberta, leaving my other family members behind. We rent a one-bedroom apartment in the West End, where we share a bed. My mother is 41 years old, and her anger colours every aspect of our shared existence. My mother tells me that I am a terrible child, that she "never had this problem" with my half-siblings, and that she is going to put me into foster care. "Would you like that?" she yells one day while we are doing the vacuuming. "I'll put you in a foster home, and you can go and live with another family, and then they'll see what a rotten child you are." On one occasion, on our way back from a walk-in clinic late at night, my mother points and screams at me: "I cannot believe I had to come here this late because you have an ear infection again. This prescription will cost me money! Why can't you just be normal? This is the last time I am dealing with this!" I hear it, but I don't say anything back, because I just detach and go somewhere else. Somewhere Else is a good place to be, because when I'm Somewhere Else I don't have to engage with my mother, and I don't feel the pain in my ear anymore.

The fights my mother starts with me — a 10-year-old child — are re-enactments. She is fighting with me in a repeat of her relationship with my father. By re-enacting vicious fights that vilify my very existence, she is attempting to emerge as the victor this time. My mother is stuck inside her traumatic story — the one where my father punches her, pulls her hair, stomps on her, drags her around the house, and tells her she's ugly and fat — and this story forces me to organize my personality around the emotions she projects onto me. My mother often tells me, "You are just like your father," and this idea begins to shape my sense of self. She hates him, so she must hate me — and I must deserve it.

When a distressed child is soothed by a parent or caregiver, the child develops a bond with that person — a deep emotional and psychological attachment that involves a need for regular contact with the caregiver and a feeling of distress when separated from that person. Being attached to an adult caregiver allows a child to explore the world with the knowledge that they can return to that safe place at any time for care and comfort, especially when they feel threatened or frightened. When children form secure bonds in childhood, they learn the basics of social interaction. The responsiveness and emotional availability of the caregiver teaches the child how to create reciprocal relationships and how to manage their own internal emotional states. However, when a child is attached to someone who abuses them, it creates lifelong issues of trust, autonomy, and initiative.

A securely attached child learns to trust what they feel and how to use what they feel to understand the world around them. They learn to rely on their thoughts and feelings to respond to everyday situations — and then they learn how to apply that knowledge to new situations. This helps them develop a sense that they can withstand change and effect change on the world around them. In the words of Bessel van der Kolk, a securely attached child learns that they are "capable of making good things happen." Children who are not securely attached do not have this sense, which contributes to their feelings of isolation and powerlessness.

When I am 11, my mother and I move back to Alberta and into a family member's house, where we share the basement bedroom. I develop a cough that refuses to go away. Every night for a week, my mother yells, "Stop coughing! I can't sleep! You're keeping me up!" before turning over in a huff. I learn to swallow the coughs as much as I can, and when I can't, I apologize. After a few weeks, she takes me to the doctor. He prescribes cough syrup that tastes like glue, and my mother's sleep is restored. My health and comfort is not part of the equation. Whenever I ask my mother for a hug, she pushes me away and says, "Get away from me. What am I, a public leaning post?"

I lie awake in bed at night, and I play movies in my head: I am holding a knife, and I stab my mother over and over, and there is blood everywhere. Over and over, I destroy the person sleeping two feet away in the bed next to mine. Expressing my distress as rage makes me feel better for a while, because it gives me a way to control the emotions that I feel but do not have the skills to understand. Mostly, I just detach from reality, because I can't afford to acknowledge my anger.

In order to avoid their unbearable reality, an abused or neglected child learns to separate their physical sensations, emotions, and thoughts into disconnected fragments. This is a coping mechanism — an attempt to master, minimize, or tolerate the stress of feeling an intense emotion that the child has not learned to manage because of the lack of emotional connection shown to them by their parent or caregiver. By not having to live the actual reality of their situation, they are able to detach from the devastating truth that it is the attachment figure who is their abuser. Although this coping method helps the child survive, dissociation also causes what van der Kolk calls a "breakdown in their capacity to process, integrate, and categorize" what is happening to them at other times, even when they are away from the abusive figure.

A dissociated child cannot bring together what they feel and what they think into a cohesive whole. As a result, they experience life as a fragmented narrative within a fragmented self, with no real access to their feelings or memories.

Danis exists in a constant state of distress, and she will go to extreme lengths to avoid any experience that brings up the emotions she feels deeply — sadness, rage, fear, defeat — but does not have the skills to understand or move through. She approaches every situation with an aim to minimize her feelings of helplessness and the threats she sees. It doesn't matter that getting angry and fleeing the classroom does not help her be understood and does not protect her from further hurt. The power of "no" is the only power Danis has. Danis's angry outbursts and tendency to run away are coping mechanisms she has developed to help her feel safe and in control.

One afternoon, I am in the school office when I see Danis and her mother walking in. The principal has asked Danis's mother for a meeting. Danis's mother has sciatica, so she is leaning over to one side and using her daughter as a crutch. Despite nearly falling over from the weight, Danis has a huge smile on her face. This is the only time I have *ever* seen her smile, and I note that her happiness occurs when she is asked to play a caretaker role for her mother.

Danis is smiling today because she knows that her mother will show her love and connect with her because she is meeting her mother's needs. She's angry the rest of the time because her mother isn't meeting her needs. Danis will never show her mother the anger she feels, however, because she is desperate to secure her mother's love and approval. In order to maintain loyalty to her mother, Danis projects her anger onto the other adults with whom she interacts. Her unending distress and the lack of adult emotional connection means that Danis is learning to organize her behaviour around her mother's actions. When Danis enters adulthood, this will translate into an inability to make autonomous rational choices.

I recognize my younger self in Danis. When my mother and I live in Vancouver, my mother has debilitating back pain. She is often prescribed muscle relaxants, which make her nauseated and drowsy. Whenever she takes the pills, I navigate the buses we have to take to get to various appointments and to my weekly ballet class — counting the fare from the coins in the kitchen jar, making sure to get transfers, getting off at the right stops, finding a plastic bag and a parking lot when my mother has to throw up, watching over her when she falls asleep in public, and helping her put one foot in front of the other when we have to walk somewhere.

When children are forced to become caregivers to their parents, they become extremely resilient — but they also develop an intractable sense of hopelessness and inadequacy. Children simply do not have the life experience or coping skills to deal with adult problems, so the effort it takes to act as a parent to their own parent leads to constant feelings of futility and failure, which are compounded by their lack of sense of self. In some Indigenous communities, this sense of hopelessness and inadequacy manifests as suicide crises (as children seek some sense of control over their lives) or as chronic underachievement (as children are crippled by fear of failure). At Danis's school, the children are reluctant to experiment. Instead of working through a problem, they say, "I don't know" or "I can't." They are convinced they will fail before they even try.

In my second year at Danis's school, Danis responds to the behavioural consistency and openness of my classroom and happily tackles a new project: sketching a still life using objects from the schoolyard. The aim is to connect the students to the natural world, open up a discussion on how the urban environment connects to Indigenous cultural teachings, and then connect those

Art by Danis, grade 5

cultural teachings to the curriculum. When we return to the class-room, Danis sets up her still life as instructed, but then chooses to draw only one end of the log that is the main part of her display. What emerges is an abstract form that reminds me of Edvard Munch's *The Scream*. When I ask Danis what she is saying with this picture, she can find no words to explain what she's done.

When I look at Danis's drawing, it represents to me her utter inalienable aloneness, her silence, and her inability to connect with others. Within the abstraction, there is a floating head, with eyes and a mouth, but with the mouth so small, like an afterthought, positioned at the end of what looks like an untied balloon shooting up to the ceiling. The drawing represents the round end of the log in its basic shape, but during the process of capturing this moment, Danis has rendered a depiction of her own identity, elemental and hidden, rising up and away from the forces that power her existence. The image and the monochromatic colour scheme show the trauma-related beliefs that currently define Danis's life: *I am alone, and no one will help me.* The image is also a foreshadowing of the distress-related self-centredness and lack of empathy that will come to define Danis's adult life if her emotional needs continue to be unmet: *the log is about me, this moment is about me, everything is about me.*

Despite her mother's inability to connect with Danis emotionally or show Danis unconditional love, Danis will undoubtedly fit the pattern and continue to seek connection with her mother in any way that she can. This is a common phenomenon in children who experience chronic trauma: what is familiar is experienced as safer, even if it is a predictable source of anger, terror, or grief.

Danis and her classmates have learned to accommodate abuse and neglect early in life. They normalize it, because it is their daily reality. This is why media stories about Indigenous youth who profess their unhappiness and discomfort at relocating from on-reserve communities to urban centres to attend school must be read with at least two degrees of skepticism. First, because these stories rely on the age-old myth that Indigenous peoples are incapable of surviving in the so-called modern world — when in fact Indigenous peoples have been moving into urban areas since at least the 1950s and leading successful lives — and second, because the journalists writing these stories are not applying a trauma-informed filter to what they're hearing from their interview subjects. While there is undoubtedly some culture shock involved in relocating from a small community to an urban centre — I did it myself when I was nine, and again at 15 — the reality is that these youth are uncomfortable in their new surroundings because they have experienced developmental trauma, which means they lack the skills that enable them to manage everyday stressors. So they pine for the safety they see in familiarity, even if that familiarity is the chronic trauma they experience in their families and home communities.

Children who normalize abuse and neglect will grow into adults who do not recognize kindness or safety. This will prevent them from developing an awareness of danger, placing them at risk for further victimization. This is clearly the case with at least some of the Indigenous students who died in Thunder Bay, Ontario, who drank alcohol by the side of the river in winter, placing themselves at risk of predation, accidental death, or suicide resulting from feelings of anger, isolation, and lack of self-worth that they did not have the skills to manage.

The ineffective coping strategies that a child with a history of developmental trauma uses to manage or avoid intense emotion will also create discord in adulthood, as they respond to perceived threats through confrontation or by releasing frustration. In many cases, these actions will lead to involvement in the criminal justice system. Children who experience chronic abuse learn to expect trauma as part of daily life, so as adults they will behave in ways that anticipate that trauma. This is why so many adult survivors of childhood trauma sabotage employment opportunities, loving relationships, and domestic stability — they expect bad things to happen, so self-sabotage eliminates the possibility that they will be hurt in the future.

Childhood attachment experiences provide children with mental models for future relationships. An abused or neglected child is focused on survival, which means their relationship model looks like this: *Don't upset people because they will hurt you. Shut down to avoid pain. Don't trust others to help you or to keep you safe. Control what you can. Get whatever you can get. Reject others before you are rejected. Fight your battles yourself. Charm and recruit and manipulate others to get what you need. Make sure you have backups in case you lose an attachment figure. Always be ready for danger.*

A child who has a strong, secure attachment understands how to create relationships, which means their relationship model looks like this: *I can expect care and protection from caregivers. I can trust my family to be there for me. I want to be near my parent/family — not because I seek the safety of familiarity, but because I look to my caregivers for safety, guidance, and validation when I am unsure. I communicate feelings and needs to my caregivers and those feelings are validated. I co-operate and share and can expect my caregivers to do the same. I can handle pain and stay calm in response to any upset. Connection, touch, and interdependence feel good.*

To have a successful relationship with another person, an individual must be able to share their thoughts and feelings: about their life, the world around them, their past, and the future. Dissociation, mistrust, hopelessness, and fear of the future undermine a person's ability to relate to others, preventing relationships from forming and destroying relationships already in progress. A child whose emotional needs are never met will grow up to see other people as sources of terror or pleasure — people who might control them, or people who might look upon them with favour if they are "good" — but they will not see other people as individuals with their own needs and desires. This disrupted pattern of attachment will also have damaging effects when they attempt to parent a child.

My father tries his best to create what he never had: he buys me a bicycle and teaches me to ride it. He starts a business and buys a house in the newer part of town. He takes me to concerts at the community hall, where he uses his arm on the back of my chair as a booster seat so I can see. When we run through a park in Vancouver, he carries me along by my arm but lets me think, *I'm running as fast as Daddy!* He loves me as best he can. But the dream of love and home and family lasts exactly seven years before it collapses into domestic violence, bank fraud, and a sheriff's auction in which the business he creates is sold out from under him. Despite his remarkable intelligence and resiliency, my father's life is marked by grief, loss, and continuous discord.

From a medicine wheel perspective (using grandfather/elder Michael Thrasher's framework), a person who is consistently sad or angry is stuck in the western quadrant of the wheel, where emotion lives. That's why we make art in my classroom: because making art helps the children show what they are feeling. Once they access their feelings, then we start connecting those feelings to their experiences, which helps them make meaning and balances their emotion with reason. Once we have that, then we can begin to move past the ineffective coping strategies they've been using to create new patterns of thinking and behaviour, bringing them into the northern quadrant of the wheel. We use this foundation to support all the social, emotional, spiritual, and cognitive learning the students must do on an everyday basis at school — starting in the east and moving again (and again) around the wheel.

During our time together, the children routinely disclose ongoing traumatic events: the older brother who was recently released from prison, who barricades himself in the family apartment with a knife "and then the police came"; the mother unconscious on the living room floor after being assaulted by her boyfriend "and she had poop on her bum"; the father who knocks over the fish bowl during an incident of domestic violence "and I saw it but he kicked me out and I couldn't help the fish and they died." And then they ask me what's for lunch today and if they can have some more glue. The students in my classroom are amazingly adaptable and resilient. But resiliency is not the same as healing. If these children are to emerge as the leaders of tomorrow, then my classroom program must address the effects of chronic trauma on their development.

One of the key principles of social justice education is that the personal is political. When Danis and her classmates are able to link their individual daily experiences to a larger context of Indigenous experience — both pre- and post-contact — they are able to explore the forces that affect their lives. In this classroom, we talk a lot about power: who has it, who does not, and why. Then we talk about how we can change the situation. After a few months of this, one of my students, who is closed and silent when I first meet him, begins greeting me whenever he sees me in the hallway, loud enough so his non-Indigenous classmates can hear him: "Good morning, Ms. Methot!! How are you today?!!" He is announcing our presence to the world, he's making himself heard, he's taking up space — and he's clearly practising his PR skills. By our second year together, he starts saying that he wants to be prime minister one day.

The Indigenous children I teach aren't "bad kids." The work we do aims to get underneath the surface behaviours — the adaptations and coping mechanisms these children have developed in order to survive — so that we can construct a critical understanding of Indigenous identity, apart from the labels that have been applied to us. In this classroom, we create a counter narrative to the myths and stereotypes that position Indigenous peoples as inferior or as problems to be solved. In this classroom, we ask *Who are we? What has happened to us and to our communities?* And perhaps most importantly *What has the world made of me that I no longer want to be?* In this classroom, the children learn that they can create their own sense of self. They begin to understand that they do not need to engage in a power struggle with other people in order to feel in control. They begin to understand that they feel in control when they control *themselves*. This places them at the centre of the medicine wheel — the place of human agency, where manitow converges to create sacred being — instead of isolating them and making them feel like they are to blame for the lack of guidance and support they receive from traumatized adults in the community.

When I am teaching at Danis's school, school board statistics show that Indigenous students have the highest rates of suspension in the city. They also have a higher absenteeism rate, a higher dropout rate, and require special education at more than double the rate of non-Indigenous students. Given these stats, it is clear that the education system is not responding to their needs.

The consequences administration devises for Danis and her classmates when they exhibit trauma-related behaviours — recess detentions, lunchtime "reflection hall," sitting in the administration office, being banned from lunchtime groups — are standard educational practice. Some of these practices, such as sitting in the office, do help students feel calmer, because they are no longer in the vicinity of the trigger or stressor that caused their reaction. And for many children, being in the office is the only opportunity they have to spend time with an adult who is actually connecting with them on an emotional level. However, the majority of these practices are ineffective for children who have experienced trauma, because they are blaming. They do not address the root harm that has been caused to the child; they do not restore damaged relationships; they do not build self-awareness; and they do not build a sense of safety, identity, or personal autonomy within the children. The school system sees the children's behaviours as a reflection of an inherent, biologically determined imbalance or failing — the "What's wrong with you?" model that reflects common myths and stereotypes about Indigenous peoples. In my program, we use the "What happened to you?" model, with frequent present-moment "What's happening for you?" check-ins that model healthy reciprocal relationships. The children I teach aren't *choosing* to come into conflict with authority — they are simply a product of their traumatic circumstances.

We finish the drawings we make as part of the still life project, but Danis does not take her drawing home. A few weeks after she draws the picture, administration makes a report to the Children's Aid Society. Danis is removed from her home and placed into care on the other side of the city, far away from her home community and the school in which I work. They do it during the summer, so when teachers return to school in September, Danis is gone. I leave her work folder on the communal classroom shelf for a long time, thinking that her classmates may want to talk about her absence, but no one raises the issue. It's just one more thing the children have normalized: that children are taken away from their parents, never to be seen again. Eventually, I take the folder away and put it in the filing cabinet.

Although Indigenous children make up only 7 per cent of the total population in Canada, they make up 48 per cent of all foster care placements in the country. Most are placed in non-Indigenous foster families. For that reason, many Indigenous people call foster care the new residential schools or the new Sixties Scoop. However, this narrative is problematic.

The contemporary Indigenous narrative centres on laying blame for all the horrors of chronic trauma. In this version of the story, Indigenous peoples are good people who suffered under colonialism and the policies of the colonial government — policies and practices that continue to affect the lives of contemporary

Indigenous peoples. This story is true. But when it comes to understanding intergenerational trauma, it's also an oversimplification. The truth is intergenerational trauma has created patterns of abuse and neglect within many Indigenous families and communities. This abuse and neglect disrupts the development of countless Indigenous children, allowing the cycle of chronic trauma to perpetuate itself.

When it comes to Indigenous children, there are two stories that need to be told. The first story is historical, and it's about how genocide, land appropriation, and the imposition of colonial systems destroyed Indigenous social systems. The second story is about how the processes of colonization and the chronic trauma of colonial control has affected Indigenous families and the parenting abilities of Indigenous peoples in contemporary society. If we want to talk about healing and change within Indigenous communities, then Indigenous peoples can no longer focus only on the first story while ignoring the second.

The school does not receive a request for Danis's provincial student record for several months, so we know she is not enrolled anywhere else after she is taken into foster care. I remember the eight long months it took her to trust me, and the various oppositional and defiant behaviours she used in my classroom to manage the intense emotions she was feeling. I can only imagine how shut down and angry she must be in her foster home. The delay must mean that her caseworkers are arranging for her to receive therapy or help with anger management before she is enrolled in school. After a few months, we receive the records request, so we know she's back in school. But that's all we know until almost a year later, when I am reading the results for a girls' track meet in a different school board, and I see Danis's name. There she is, no longer gone — and she has placed 16th out of 181 students taking part in a long-distance running event. That's my girl.

Like so many of my students, Danis has taken the judgments and labels of the school and internalized the idea that she is a "bad kid" who isn't worthy of love. In the absence of any sense of self, this has become her only identity, and she acts the part. I can only hope that her stellar performance in the sporting event means that Danis is emerging from a place of anger, fear, and self-blame to a place where she recognizes her strength and goodness and makes her mark on the world.

Becoming fully human is about risking connection. When we emerge from the spirit world at birth, we need to be surrounded by a strong network of relationships based on respect, responsibil ity, and reciprocity. These relationships teach us the skills we need to learn in order to know ourselves, know others, and take up our responsibilities in the world. If we do not have that network in childhood, then we have two paths: we can spend a lifetime repeating the disconnection that we have inherited, or we can seek change through connection.

When we connect with our inner selves — with what we think and feel and with the experiences that created those thoughts and feelings — we build a sense of self. When we find a voice, we become brave enough to share that self with others. When we connect with others, we unlearn the normalization of trauma. We unlearn our belief that the world is unsafe and that no one will help us, and we learn instead how to express what we need. We unlearn the internalized hatred that stems from self-blame and our consequent feelings of inadequacy. When we connect with others, we begin to believe that we are lovable and worthy. We begin to imagine a future.

DEVELOPMENTAL TRAUMA DISORDER

EXPOSURE

The child or adolescent has experienced or witnessed multiple or prolonged adverse events over a period of at least one year beginning in childhood or early adolescence, including:

- direct experience or witnessing of repeated and severe episodes of interpersonal violence (e.g., abandonment, neglect, betrayal, physical assaults, sexual assaults, threats to bodily integrity, coercive practices, witnessing violence and death)
- significant disruptions of protective caregiving as a result of repeated changes in primary caregiver, repeated separation from the primary caregiver, or exposure to severe and persistent emotional abuse

AFFECTIVE AND PHYSIOLOGICAL DYSREGULATION

The child exhibits impaired normative developmental competencies related to arousal regulation, including at least two of the following:

- inability to modulate, tolerate, or recover from extreme affect states (e.g., fear, anger, shame), including prolonged and extreme tantrums, or immobilization
- disturbances in regulation in bodily functions (e.g., persistent disturbances in sleeping, eating, and elimination; over-reactivity or under-reactivity to touch and sounds; disorganization during routine transitions)
- diminished awareness/dissociation of sensations, emotions, and bodily states
- impaired capacity to describe emotions or bodily states

ATTENTIONAL AND BEHAVIOURAL DYSREGULATION

The child exhibits impaired normative developmental competencies in their sense of personal identity and involvement in relationships, including at least three of the following:

- intense preoccupation with safety of the caregiver or other loved ones (including precocious caregiving) or difficulty tolerating reunion with them after separation
- persistent negative sense of self, including self-loathing, helplessness, worthlessness, ineffectiveness, or defectiveness
- extreme and persistent distrust, defiance, or lack of reciprocal behaviour in close relationships with adults or peers
- reactive physical or verbal aggression toward peers, caregivers, or other adults
- inappropriate (excessive or promiscuous) attempts to get intimate contact (including but not limited to sexual or physical intimacy) or excessive reliance on peers or adults for safety and reassurance
- impaired capacity to regulate empathic arousal as evidenced by lack of empathy for, or tolerance of, expressions of distress of others, or excessive responsiveness to the distress of others

POST-TRAUMATIC SPECTRUM SYMPTOMS

The child exhibits at least one symptom in at least two of the three PTSD symptom clusters (see page 57).

FUNCTIONAL IMPAIRMENT

The disturbance causes significant distress or impairment in at least two of the following areas of functioning:

- relationships with family members
- relationships with peer group
- education
- vocational (for youth involved in, seeking, or referred for employment, volunteer work, or job training)
- legal (policing and justice systems)
- health

Text excerpted and adapted from the developmental trauma disorder diagnosis developed by Bessel van der Kolk and the National Child Traumatic Stress Network Task Force.

CHAPTER 4

THE ANGRY INDIAN AND A CULTURE OF BLAME

Roland, an Indigenous man in his 20s, is one of my colleagues at the school Danis attends. After we make decisions at meetings, Roland has difficulty hitting our agreed deadlines and scrambles around at the last minute to get things done, a process that usually means changing the plans and failing to inform anyone else of the changes. This creates problems and considerable stress for other staff at the school. Yet he never asks for help. Roland routinely ignores administration's requests — for example, he doesn't write anything about his program for the school newsletter, even after I suggest that we co-write an entry. Then he tells administration that I refuse to work with him. I ask Roland for his plans so that we can coordinate our classroom activities, but I don't receive them.

When we are asked to report on the children's progress, I provide Roland with my comments, because he's in charge of generating the final report. But then he doesn't complete his own reporting. When administration asks why the reports are late, Roland tells them he is waiting for me. During my time at the school, other staff members disclose that they have problems working with Roland and talking with him about any issues that arise. On two occasions, I try to speak to Roland as part of an informal problem-solving process but he becomes angry, talks over me, accuses me of "being on their side" (meaning, the non-Indigenous teachers), and walks away.

Roland frequently misunderstands people's actions and statements and projects his own emotional distress onto the students. On one occasion, after a child returns to school after being away for several weeks for a family funeral in another province, I greet the student in Roland's room and say, "Wow, where have you been?! We've missed you!" and receive a smile from the child in return. At lunchtime in the staff room, we all agree that this student seems to be dealing well with the death in the family. Later that same day, Roland appears at my door, almost in tears, with his arm around the shoulders of this student, and says, "Ms. Methot, she was away at a funeral." Roland informs me of something every staff member already knows because he's taken my original comment as finding fault with the child. When Roland tells her, "Come on, it's time to go," the student looks up at him anxiously and arranges her face into an expression that matches his distress.

During my second year at this school, Roland and I are in his classroom discussing our timetable when he gestures to a group of students and says, "Well, you can have these guys, any time you want." I understand from this comment, as do the children, that he does not want them in his room, as they have very specific learning needs. Their body language and the looks on their faces indicate their reactions to his comment: some of the children look sad, some look down as if ashamed, and others shutter their faces and shut down. None of them look shocked: they've all heard it before, from many of the adults and family members around them.

My other Indigenous colleague, Cassandra, is unapproachable, uncommunicative, and conveys only negative comments. In meetings, she frequently cuts others off and shouts them down, once verbally attacking a project even though the plans have already been approved. Cassandra constantly berates me in public, and instead of communicating with me in person or in writing via my staff-room mailbox, she once posts a hostile note — in which she accuses me of failing to complete an assigned task — on the *outside* of my classroom door for everyone to see. She also makes snide remarks about my teaching practice in front of the children. At one point, Cassandra says that Indigenous cultural "laws aren't being followed" in my program — but when I ask for specifics, she cannot tell me, because she hears it from a parent who does not himself provide any details. Later, I find out from Roland that the complaint originates from a parent whose spouse applied for but did not get my position at the school.

At this school, all the Indigenous staff members sit on a committee that deals with Indigenous-specific programming, including special events. The committee meetings have no agendas or minutes. There is a lot of shouting and emotional outbursts and I am often uncomfortable. One day I raise the issue with the principal, and she tells me, "Suzanne, you just have to accept certain things, like their stoic expression. It's who they are." I'm not sure what's more offensive: a white woman trying to explain Indigenous culture to me; her assumption that anger, divisiveness, emotional reactivity, disorganization, and an inability to create and maintain relationships are somehow characteristic of Indigenous cultures; or the fact that the principal doesn't know that my colleagues show her a much different face than they show me. She doesn't see their terror, anger, fear, and grief, because they don't show it to her. They only show it to me.

One day, I visit the *Where Are the Children?* website to research a lesson plan. While I'm there, I land on a list detailing the everyday impacts of intergenerational trauma. I've never heard of this before. As I read the list, I see all the issues facing our students, all the behaviours shown by the parents in the community, and all the behaviours of me and my colleagues. This gives me the information I need to finally understand what's going on. Now I can look at Roland, Cassandra, and myself and understand that we are enacting trauma-related behaviours. This allows me to step out from my role in this drama — the role of silent victim, convinced that I am not worthy of love or respect, believing deep down inside that I'm doing something to deserve this treatment — so that I can ask for help.

The mediation process is supposed to be confidential, but I walk into a stairwell one day and hear Roland complaining to one of our colleagues about how I'm trying to get him fired. Then I start getting dirty looks from some Indigenous parents at the school, which tells me that Roland is also talking to them. Soon after, a parent complains to administration about me. When she tells other parents in the community to pull their children out of my program, many parents comply. Other parents, however, make a special effort to call or attend the school to tell administration how much they appreciate the program. The school superintendent investigates the complaint and deems it to be without merit. Then he asks me what we should do to bring the community together. I suggest a feast as a first step toward involving parents and caregivers in program planning. He agrees, and we shake on it. But when administration runs the idea past the Indigenous-run office that funds my program, I am told that there will be no feast and no change in how the program is run. So administration plans a community meeting instead — but I am not invited. No elder or facilitator is present to help guide the discussion, and my union rep tells me later that there is a lot of yelling and finger-pointing. During the meeting, when the superintendent says he's going to reassign me to another school, the parent who complained about me says they will "follow" me and then threatens me with physical harm. As soon as the threat is made, administration places me on home assignment to protect my safety — and the children lose another adult that they have come to love and trust. It is yet another traumatic loss in their young lives.

When a group of people has been marginalized and oppressed, they often turn on each other. Their fear of punishment for insubordination makes them unable to express their anger to the oppressor (or control figure), so they direct their anger laterally, across peer groups. They feel powerless to fight back, so they fight among themselves.

According to the Native Women's Association of Canada, lateral violence is a learned behaviour that has roots in colonialism and patriarchy. As a result of this oppression, many Indigenous peoples have replaced their own philosophies of respect, responsibility, reciprocity, and relationships with patterns of social interaction that are psychologically violent and emotionally abusive. This means that Indigenous people who have survived colonization — and the everyday impacts of trauma — are now causing pain and suffering to each other.

Lateral violence is not the same as workplace bullying (although it can look similar in some ways). Lateral violence is a phenomenon that sees Indigenous people oppressing each other in the same ways that they have been abused by the colonizer. It is related to internalized racism and is also connected to the effects of trauma on personality development. Colonization violated physical, mental, and spiritual boundaries, and Indigenous peoples continue to act out those distorted boundaries on each other.

Rod Jeffries, a Kanienkehaka from Tyendinaga Mohawk Territory who conducts workshops on lateral violence across the country, says that lateral violence takes many forms. Gossiping, undermining, sabotage, lack of respect for lines of authority, back-stabbing, lack of accountability, blaming, and nepotism are all common to lateral violence — and very common in Indigenous communities and workplaces. These behaviours create chaos, which Jeffries says is related to Indigenous experiences of colonization.

Jeffries says that racism, discrimination, and other tools of colonization have caused many Indigenous peoples to become "chaos junkies." The chaos that some people create in the community or in the workplace is related to the fact that they grew up experiencing chronic trauma. Chronic trauma is normal to them: it's something they've learned and something they know how to survive. As adults, Jeffries says these survivors will create chaos in order to feel normal. When it gets quiet and they are alone with their thoughts, they will create crisis in order to return to a place they feel able to navigate. Psychiatrists and other medical doctors — such as Bessel van der Kolk and Gabor Maté — agree with this take, pointing to the ways that trauma impacts brain development and behaviour. When people engage in lateral violence, it is because they are repeating a pattern that they recognize. They're not deliberately trying to be mean or malicious.

Colonization robs Indigenous peoples of agency — and feeling powerless creates a fertile ground for lateral violence. When someone creates chaos in the workplace by sabotaging a project or holding on to information they should be sharing, it's their way of enacting control. It's their way of getting the power they feel they don't have elsewhere in their life.

In many cases, lateral violence is related to fear and an unwillingness to change. Indigenous peoples have been forced to change under colonization, and that experience has left many with the idea that change is always negative. When change happens — for example, when a new staff member is hired in an organization — the fear of what will happen can lead people to attack the new person in the hopes that they will quit or be fired and everything will return to normal. This is what happens at Danis's school: I am the new hire, coming into Roland and Cassandra's territory.

Lateral violence is a cycle of anger, blame, and retribution caused by traumatic experiences, fuelled by unresolved emotions, and sustained by a fear of confronting the actual control figure. Incidents of lateral violence are often used by the dominant society as "evidence" to justify racism and colonialism, serving to show how Indigenous peoples are — at least in the colonizer's mind — primitive and uncivilized.

Indigenous peoples have been used as plot devices for settler stories since contact and colonization. When settlement began in what is now Canada and the United States, it was imperative that Indigenous peoples be portrayed as the Savage Indian, so that they could be seen as something to be feared (and thus destroyed). To prop up the myth of Western progress, Indigenous peoples then became the Vanishing Indian, doomed to the dustbins of history, replaced by a "superior" culture carrying out Manifest Destiny. Then, when it was convenient — after Indigenous peoples had been killed, relocated to reserves, and denied a place in the political, institutional, and economic structures of the Americas — settler culture invented the Noble Savage. The Noble Savage was still uncivilized but in a childlike, Adam-and-Eve sort of way, serving to illustrate the goodness of humanity when people were free from the rules of social development and organization (things Indigenous cultures were believed not to have).

Over time, these genres and archetypes have been continually reinvented and reworked by the dominant society. In the 1960s, hippies invented the Fashion Indian so they could appropriate fringed buckskin jackets and headbands. In the 1970s, the environmental movement invented the Crying Indian (or Ecological Indian) of the television public service announcement created by the Keep America Beautiful campaign. In the 1980s, New Agers created the Spiritual Indian and the "sacred workshop" so they could pay to learn the secrets of the universe. After the standoff at Kanehsatake (Oka, Quebec) in 1990 and the publication of the famous Canadian Press photo of Canadian soldier Patrick Cloutier and Anishinabe warrior Brad Larocque, the media created the Angry Indian. The Angry Indian made his first appearance in the Quebec newspaper *La Presse*, which described Cloutier as "the little soldier staring unblinkingly at the angry Warrior." The Angry Indian — who is closely related to the Savage Indian — was a frequent presence in media coverage of later acts of resistance and protest, including the 1995 Ipperwash Crisis in Ontario. In that instance, residents of the Kettle and Stony Point First Nation occupied Ipperwash Provincial Park to protest the appropriation and forced surrender of their territory by the federal government in 1928 and 1942. The unarmed occupiers were portrayed as violent by both media and provincial police and described as being in the park "illegally," although they were on land they had never willingly surrendered.

When Indigenous peoples are defined and understood by these settler projections, they cease to be real people and become stereotypical *Indians* instead. And as every Indigenous person knows, an Indian is anything a non-Indigenous person wants them to be. When an Indigenous person becomes an Indian, they cease to be a player in their own story and become actors in a story told from the settler perspective.

The Angry Indian label is often applied to Indigenous peoples when they resist colonial control. When Indigenous peoples react to being invisible in the dominant society, answer back to stereotypes or hatred, or otherwise voice any kind of opinion, they are immediately labelled as an Angry Indian so that they can be demonized and what they say can be ignored.

Some Indigenous people are subverting the Angry Indian label by reclaiming it. Inuk filmmaker Alethea Arnaquq-Baril's 2016 film *Angry Inuk* presents an Inuk perspective on seal hunting and talks about the Inuit tendency to express anger in a quiet way. Iqaluit, Nunavut, mayor Madeleine Redfern regularly posts her thoughts on various issues via her Twitter account, where her play-on-words handle is @MadInuk. Artist Jay Soule, from the Chippewas of the Thames First Nation, uses the name Chippewar to declare war against the dominant society's most cherished symbols — including paper money and the Canada 150 logo — by committing acts of reverse appropriation that mash up iconic Indigenous images and settler pop culture. These Indigenous peoples are using their platforms to reclaim images of their own making, refashioning the warrior as truth teller.

The key to this kind of work is the resurgence, or reappropriation, of the Indigenous story. These artists and politicians aren't objects in a settler story. They're living their own story, rewriting the colonial script. This is Angry Indian version 2.0, a superior, Indigenous-made version of the colonizer's original concept, repositioned and repurposed as a tool to highlight the colonial agenda.

Unfortunately, Angry Indian version 1.0 is still around. But something has happened to this invention of the dominant society. Whereas Angry Indian 1.0 was once a stereotype — a tool used by the control figure to marginalize Indigenous voices — this Indian has now become a self-fulfilling prophecy, created by the colonizer but perpetuated by survivors of colonial trauma.

The Angry Indian 1.0 might sometimes talk about the colonial agenda, like Clay, a man I know from my work with an Indigenous agency's street patrol van, who stabs the air with his index finger one summer night in 1993, gets in my face, and spits, "They. Don't. Know. Why. We. Dance." The Angry Indian 1.0 might also sometimes undertake the business of reclamation, like when I see Clay a couple of months later at the health centre, clean and sober and attending the programs. Generally speaking, however, the Angry Indian 1.0 is in a perpetual state of rage. Sometimes the rage is understated and comes across as continual criticism or constant frustration and irritation at everyday occurrences. Sometimes the rage is explosive, like the Indigenous man I see standing in the middle of the Queen and Bathurst intersection in Toronto in August 2017, shaking his fists and screaming at no one and nothing in particular. Sometimes the rage is directed inward, as with the mother of one of Danis's classmates, who weighs more than 300 pounds and continues — like so many survivors of childhood sexual abuse — to eat herself into oblivion in an attempt to make herself invisible.

Anger is a justifiable response to an actual or perceived injustice. Rage is a response to extreme anxiety, a way to reduce the uncomfortable emotions associated with feeling helpless and powerless. So although the Angry Indian 1.0 is big and loud and might seem threatening, they're actually anxious and scared. They're stuck in an old story — the traumatic story of terror, anger, grief, and loss.

The Aboriginal Healing Foundation states that in the aftermath of the genocide in the Americas, Indigenous peoples are now "recreating trauma as a way of life." The lateral violence committed by the Angry Indian 1.0 is a prime factor in this way of life.

Like countless other Indigenous people, Cassandra, Roland, and I have all experienced traumatic episodes during childhood. The way they treat me reminds me of events in my family, triggering me to enter the "freeze" response I learned as a child. When I start shutting down, it reminds them of the hatred they carry for their own perceived weakness, triggering a "fight" response that positions them as the strong ones who don't have any needs. We are responding to each other using childhood survival strategies, which are all connected to a deeply buried sense of distress that shapes how we interact with one another.

By the time I meet Roland and Cassandra, I have spent 15 years clearing my own anger by taking part in healing circles, ceremonies, and political activism. They are both much younger than I am, however, and have not yet had this opportunity. When Roland and Cassandra are triggered, they become overwhelmed with feelings they cannot categorize and do not understand. To someone viewing the situation from outside, unaware that the current event is triggering an association with a childhood event, their reactions and behaviours seem inappropriate and exaggerated. But if we look at their anger through a trauma-informed lens, then we see that Cassandra and Roland are living in survival mode, prone to hypersensitivity and aggressive behaviour as a result of the traumatic events they experienced as children. In essence, they are adult versions of Danis: unable to transition out of intense feelings, frozen at the time of their trauma, prisoners of an old story and the maladaptive coping mechanisms they have developed to survive that story.

Some time after I leave this school, I learn from a colleague that Cassandra is a former foster child who is reclaiming her culture. The principal assumes that because Cassandra is Indigenous that she has cultural knowledge to share, but Cassandra was raised apart from her community. To help manage the fear and anxiety that often results from the principal's assumptions and the lack of institutional support she is offered, Cassandra directs her anger toward others in an attempt to mask her feelings of inadequacy.

Although her aggression toward others colours her interactions with both staff and students, Cassandra is noticeably more aggressive with Indigenous colleagues and students. This makes sense when we consider that her fear and anxiety are connected to her cultural identity and her relationship with her birth parents.

After I leave the school, I hear an education official describe Cassandra as "lazy," but this is a misunderstanding that perpetuates common stereotypes about Indigenous peoples. Adults who have experienced childhood trauma often deal with everyday situations and manage their feelings of distress by employing the freeze, flight, or fight responses central to survival mode. When Cassandra isn't fighting other Indigenous people, she's frozen or in retreat from everyday interactions.

During our time working together, Roland tells me that his parents attended residential school. In fact, given the history of his reserve community and the date the school opened there, it's possible that up to five generations of his family were sent to residential school. That history is spelled out in Roland's disproportionate emotional response to everyday situations. His parents and grandparents are accomplished people working in highly specialized professions, and Roland is a university graduate, powwow dancer, and artist. However, because Roland's parents experienced chronic trauma as children, they were unable to meet his needs, which means that Roland did not learn how to modulate his feelings of distress or create emotional bonds with other people. When he works alone, my colleagues and I surmise that it is because Roland is uncomfortable responding — or does not know how to respond — to other people and their needs.

When an individual experiences a traumatic event (or chronic trauma), it increases their biological and psychological stress responses. Stress hormones trigger physiological changes in heart rate, breathing, muscle tension, digestion, and, if the individual is a child or young adult, in the developing brain. The individual then becomes highly sensitive and hyper-responsive to threat. They exist in a state of constant agitation, primed for a freeze-fight-flight response at the first hint of danger. This distress leads to an inability to focus, concentrate, and process information. It also has negative effects on the individual's ability to interact with others in a social context. Survivors become anxious, with a tendency to withdraw from others, and prone to defensive aggression. In the Indigenous context, these disrupted patterns of connectivity are a huge factor in lateral violence.

Roland's distress and distrust make it difficult for him to create relationships. Instead of meeting the children's emotional needs, Roland makes his relationships with the students about him and his fragile ego. Instead of working alongside his colleagues, he makes negative comments about them in order to keep them at a distance. Roland is a product of his upbringing, and his relationship style mirrors the parenting style of his mother and father.

As Murray Sinclair has said, "You cannot take a child, and raise that child in an institution, and expect that child to be able to function well and provide a loving or caring environment to his or her family. You cannot separate that child from any adult of any importance to them and put that child in an environment where they don't see a loving and caring family, and then ask that child to return and become a parent and expect them to be able to function properly. We know the effect of that institutional situation is not going to be immediate, because the first generation of children still have their parents living back home to help them when they return. Even the second and third generations would have their grandparents and great-grandparents to help them. But eventually, those who are not tainted by the residential school system begin to die off. As each generation returns, the previous generation becomes less and less able to maintain a stable and balanced influence for them. So we begin to see the impact of it all after five, six, even seven generations in the families."

Research in the field of epigenetics has shown that the neurobiological changes created by chronic trauma and an individual's heightened stress response can be passed down to the survivor's children. Roland and Cassandra are both high-functioning people, working in important jobs, but they still bear the mark of their early (and inherited) experiences.

Avoiding accountability for their actions is a common instinct for people who have experienced trauma, because they are unprepared to see themselves as perpetrators. Their unresolved emotions mean they are stuck in an old story — that of their victimization — and projecting those emotions is the only way these survivors know how to communicate their distress. Their emotional reactivity and exaggerated stress responses are actually attempts to get others to see and hear their own pain. What they often don't understand is that these behaviours also victimize other people.

If children have caregivers who meet their emotional needs, they are able to grow into adults with a sense of their own individuality. An adult with a healthy sense of self has stable self-esteem that enables them to engage in accurate self-appraisal. They learn to see themselves as a good person with some flaws. When they make a mistake or act in a way that hurts someone, they accept the consequences and undertake the process of learning from the experience. An adult who has never developed a sense of self can't admit mistakes or admit that they should change, because they don't see themselves as individuals with agency — they see themselves as victims who are constantly under threat. Across a community, this leads to widespread mistrust and a culture of blame.

In my work with adult clients in community-based, direct-service environments, I have noticed that one of the ways in which survivors of trauma cope with the everyday ups and downs of life is by maintaining a fixed view of the world. This insulates them from the feelings that arise during such situations, feelings they are ill-equipped to deal with because they are focused on managing danger and protecting their victimized self. Instead of accepting the uncertainty of their own perspective — because uncertainty is dangerous to a person who has felt unsafe since childhood and continues to feel unsafe in every adult situation — adult survivors of childhood trauma tend to be rigid in their viewpoints, with a low tolerance for differing perspectives. This translates into an inability to comprehend and appreciate the experiences and motivations of other people. This also feeds the culture of accusation and blame that exists within some Indigenous communities.

People who have experienced trauma often avoid being alone with their own thoughts. They fear the intensity of their emotions, because these feelings remind them of the traumatic experience. By blaming someone else for whatever situation they find themselves in, or whatever they are feeling, they make everyone else the problem, erecting a barrier that protects them. Although Roland complains about my perceived failure to work alongside him, the truth is he is only comfortable when he works alone, because when he works alone he doesn't have to deviate from his own point of view or his own way of doing things, and he doesn't have to consider any uncertainty in his perspective.

Roland's lack of flexibility is an expression of his need for control. Like so many others who experience chronic trauma or trauma in childhood, he is used to relying only on himself, making his own snap decisions on what is safe and what is not. By maintaining a position in which he is always right, he compensates for the lack of control he felt during the original traumatic experiences and the lack of control he feels as an adult with unresolved emotions. Unfortunately, Roland doesn't connect his rigidity to the fact that his colleagues find it difficult to work with him. He sees himself as a victim, and any request for flexibility and accountability is further proof that the outside world and other people are not safe.

Because people with complex post-traumatic stress disorder (CPTSD) lack trust but still crave the emotional connection they have never or rarely experienced in their families and communities, they tend to swing from one extreme (dependent and aggressively seeking connection) to another extreme (distant and avoidant) when they interact with other people. Survivors are terrified of abandonment, but their anger over being controlled means they are also terrified of domination. They approach all relationships through a life-or-death lens, swinging between extremes of intense attachment and terrified withdrawal, or, as trauma scholar Judith Lewis Herman describes it, "abject submissiveness and furious rebellion."

On my first day, Roland asks me to include him in my program activities. Then he withdraws from every opportunity for collaboration. After I help plan and execute the school powwow, we ride home on the subway together, and he tells me, "I couldn't have done it without you." Then the next day he denigrates my work and mocks me in front of his students.

The human personality functions on two levels: the self and the other. When an individual has a well-functioning personality, they have a complex and well-integrated inner world based on a positive sense of self that adapts to daily experiences and the learning that comes from mistakes and self-reflection. They show a range of emotions and can regulate their emotional states. This gives them the capacity to engage in fulfilling relationships that are reciprocal in nature and defined by empathy and an appreciation for different perspectives. When an individual has experienced chronic trauma, they have an impoverished, disorganized, or conflicted inner world based on a weak or maladaptive self-concept, a tendency toward negative emotions, and an inability to engage with others or adjust their social behaviours in diverse conditions.

The Aboriginal Healing Foundation's list of intergenerational impacts clearly outlines how personality development contributes to chronic trauma and intergenerational transmission of trauma within Indigenous communities. The Angry Indian 1.0 is that person: the individual who projects their negative emotions, doesn't learn from experience, and refuses to be accountable — and who destabilizes the community in the process.

According to a model developed by the American psychologist Abraham Maslow in 1943, human beings can only fulfill their true potential when their basic needs are met and they can begin to find higher meaning in life — a process Maslow called "self-actualization." Maslow's eight-stage developmental model begins with physiological needs such as food, water, warmth, and rest; safety needs such as security of the body, security of resources, security of the family, security of health, and security of property; belonging needs including friendship, family, and sexual intimacy; and esteem needs including confidence, achievement, respect by others, and respect for others. When a person's physiological, safety, belonging, and esteem needs are not met, they live their lives from an anxious, self-centred perspective that leaves little room for the needs or perspectives of others. Instead of self-actualizing, people whose basic needs have never been met engage in behaviours that are aimed at fulfilling those needs.

Maslow identified the last four needs in his model — cognitive needs such as knowledge and understanding, aesthetic needs including the beauty found in the natural world, the need for self-actualization, and the need for transcendence — as "growth needs" that constantly motivate the individual to seek knowledge and develop into the best person they can possibly be. Healthy people create healthy communities. In this way, self-actualized people are the foundation of community and community well-being.

MASLOW'S HIERARCHY

Transcendence
Becoming motivated by values that transcend the personal/self

Self-Actualization
Realizing personal potential, self-fulfillment, seeking personal growth through transformative experiences

Aesthetic Needs
Beauty

Cognitive Needs
Knowledge, understanding, curiosity, exploration, search for meaning

Esteem Needs
Respect, self-esteem, recognition, feelings of accomplishment

Love and Belonging Needs
Intimate relationships, friends, family, sense of connection

Safety Needs
Security, safety, resources, health, personal objects, support of community

Physiological Needs
Food, water, shelter, warmth, rest

When people think of basic needs, they often think of the physical aspects of survival, such as food and shelter, and fail to consider safety, love and belonging, and esteem. While it is certainly true that economic disadvantage increases an individual's level of distress, conceptualizing basic needs as representing only food and shelter is reductive. People also need an orderly world — with familiar, predictable events and a reasonable expectation of fair outcomes — in order to get their safety needs met. They need to have emotional relationships with friends and a supportive and communicative family in order to get their belonging needs met. They need to feel respected, accepted, and valued for their contributions to the community in order to get their esteem needs met. When human beings do not have consistency or predictability in their surroundings, it leads to feelings of doubt and a sense of constant failure instead of autonomy and a sense of control. When they do not have supportive relationships, they tend to develop negative emotions such as anger and shame. And when they do not feel valued, they develop feelings of inferiority and worthlessness.

In the 2007 *Maclean's* story "Canada's Worst Neighbourhood" — which is about North Central Regina, where a significant segment of the population is of Indigenous ancestry — University of Regina researcher Kathy Donovan said, "Regina is the only place I've ever heard of where they steal the food out of people's freezers during break and enters." While it's true that most people will not be able to work on self-actualization if they're hungry or tired, chronic trauma within Indigenous communities also stems from a lack of safety, belonging, and esteem. So it's not just material poverty that creates the challenges that lead to chronic trauma. These challenges are also caused by a poverty of mind, body, spirit, and emotion. To assume that Indigenous peoples living in material poverty are the only ones dealing with intergenerational trauma or chronic trauma is a grave error in thinking, as well as a biased assumption that pathologizes people who lack class privilege. Chronic and intergenerational trauma are issues in all Indigenous communities, across a spectrum of economic and material circumstances, driven by both internal (lateral) and external (colonial) forces.

Maslow described self-actualization as being "fully alive" and self-actualized people as capable of being good to themselves and to others. Because Indigenous peoples and communities experience chronic trauma that interferes with individual and collective safety, and because colonial policies, systems, and institutions have had negative effects on Indigenous families and other structures of belonging, it is impossible for many Indigenous people to arrive at a place of esteem. When an individual lacks confidence and a sense of self-esteem, they cannot engage in a reciprocal exchange with other people. This absence of reciprocity drastically affects social and family relations within Indigenous communities, contributing to a negative psychological atmosphere — and interfering with an individual's ability to self-actualize and reach their full potential.

There are stone medicine wheels across Alberta (the place where I am from), built by the Niitsitapi and the Nehiyawak. Each medicine wheel is unique, but they generally feature a central cairn or rock pile, one or more surrounding circles, and two or more stone lines radiating outward from a central point. Many of the wheels use a tipi ring as the central circle — simple circles of stones constructed to hold down the edges of the buffalo skins used to create the tipi homes of the Plains Nations.

To the Nehiyawak, the tipi is not just material culture — it is a framework for understanding connection and balance and responsibility. When people sit inside a tipi, they sit in a circle. Everyone is equal, and communication is face to face. The circle of the tipi ring, therefore, denotes equity and consensus. One half of the tipi circle is for women; the other half for men. This represents the balance of active and receptive energy in the universe, the balance between masculine and feminine. Inside a tipi, people sit on the earth, grounded in a literal way. This grounding is balanced by the opening at the top of the tipi, which allows for constant visual and energetic contact with the sky world. This is the place where human beings sit, where they learn how to relate to other people, connect with the world around them, and know themselves as beings in balance. The tipi is home, representing the influence of parents and family on an individual's development. Placed at the centre of the medicine wheel — the place of human agency — the tipi ring reminds individuals of their connection to the cyclical workings of the earth and the cosmos and of the necessity for transformation.

Little-known historical fact: Maslow visited the Niitsitapi people at the Siksika First Nation in southern Alberta in 1938, during the time he was working on his model. Reason why this matters: Maslow's triangle is not a pyramid — it's a tipi. Maslow used one of the central frameworks of the Plains Indigenous cultures to illustrate his model.

Before Maslow worked with the Niitsitapi, he believed that individuals in any society naturally seek to dominate others, and he was creating a model for human development based on that idea. (This way of seeing the world was undoubtedly influenced by the fact that his parents, who were Jewish, fled Czarist persecution in Russia. According to Maslow's biographer, Edward Hoffman, after the family settled in New York City, Maslow was often chased by anti-Semitic gangs who threw rocks at him.) After his studies with the Niitsitapi, Maslow discovered that there was another way of being and that this way of being created societies based on generosity and collaboration. Indigenous models for human development vary by nation — not every nation uses the tipi or the medicine wheel — but they all match Maslow's model in that they stress the need to develop a healthy sense of self as the foundation for community well-being.

In Indigenous cultures, the human experience is defined by the extent to which an individual establishes meaningful relationships with other people and with the world. According to Maslow's model, there are two ways of thinking about the world. The first is deficiency cognition, where an individual focuses on themselves, what they don't have, and how they might get it. The second is being cognition, where a self-actualized individual focuses on the world outside of themselves, pursuing knowledge on and living according to the principles of justice, wholeness, aliveness, goodness, beauty, and truth, among others. These "being values," as Maslow called them, are very similar to the Seven Sacred Teachings of the Indigenous Plains Nations.

For Maslow — and for Plains nations including the Nehiyawak — the being values/Seven Sacred Teachings represent healthy human functioning and serve as a framework for human society. Maslow believed that self-actualized people are capable of feeling harmony within themselves and their surroundings because they are reality-centered (able to differentiate between the genuine and the unimportant), problem-centred (they treat difficulties in life as problems that can be solved), and comfortable being alone (and alone with their thoughts). The Seven Sacred Teachings help individuals achieve this harmony by providing them with core values that can be used to understand actions and events, solve problems, and engage in reflection and accurate self-appraisal.

When an individual's needs are not met, they exist in the selfish and competitive space defined by deficiency cognition, trying to get their needs met and hostile to the needs of others. When we look at how Indigenous peoples and communities functioned before colonization, and how they function after colonization, we

SEVEN SACRED TEACHINGS (NEHIYAWAK VERSION)

LOVE

To know love is to know creation. Connecting to creation helps you love yourself. If you cannot love yourself, you cannot love another person. The Eagle represents this teaching, because it flies highest in the sky and has the gift of vision. Love requires vision and the recognition that each individual is part of a greater whole.

RESPECT

Showing respect for others is about sharing your spirit. The Buffalo represents this teaching, because it shares every part of its being with the people, providing shelter, clothing, tools, and utensils. The sustainable relationship the Plains people had with the buffalo — never wasting anything — shows us that reciprocity is part of respect.

COURAGE

Living as your own true spirit is a great challenge. It takes mental, spiritual, and emotional strength and also requires integrity. The Mother Bear represents this teaching, because Bear is gentle by nature but ferocious when defending cubs. Living through your heart and spirit is difficult, but the Bear shows us how to face danger and keep ourselves and those around us safe.

HONESTY

Being honest means keeping your promises to other people, to creation, and to yourself. Long ago, the giant creature Kihci-Sabe walked among humans to remind them to be honest. Kihci-Sabe was a giant not because they were big in size, but because they demonstrated greatness by earning the trust of other people.

WISDOM

To build community, people must offer their gifts and skills to the world and use them in a good way. The Beaver represents this teaching because it uses its teeth to cut trees and build dams, lodges, and wetlands. If Beaver does not cut trees, its teeth grow too long, becoming useless and preventing them from eating and doing the things they need to do to survive. If human beings do not use their gifts and skills, they also become weak. But when they use their talents in a good way, they help create a peaceful and healthy community.

HUMILITY

Living in balance with creation and accepting that all things are equal teaches us humility. Considering the needs of others before ourselves demonstrates humility. Wolf represents this teaching by living in a pack and working as a team. Humility is about living without arrogance.

TRUTH

To know truth is to know and understand all of the Seven Sacred Teachings and remain faithful to them. Grandmother Turtle represents this teaching through the 13 sections on the centre of her back. Each section represents a lunar cycle, and together these 13 moons represent the Earth's yearly rotation around the sun. The 28 sections around the edge of Grandmother Turtle's shell represents the lunar cycle as seen in a woman's monthly cycle. The human body reflects the truth of creation.

see clearly how Indigenous values of balance and interconnect-edness have been replaced in many cases by deficiency cognition. Indigenous people who are hungry for community or family (belonging needs) are drawn to gangs. Indigenous people who crave mastery and competence (esteem needs) work hard to excel at anti-social tasks even when it lands them in prison. Indigenous parents who are trying to get their own needs met cannot meet the physiological and safety needs of their children. The anger that underpins all of these deficiency cognition behaviours is terrifying — and it stems from the six-year-old children and the 10-year-old children whose needs were never met, now living in 25-year-old, 40-year-old, and 50-year-old bodies. As Katharina Patterson, a Haida woman, says in the radio documentary "Reserve Judgement," which ran on the CBC program *Ideas* in 2014, living in an Indigenous community today is "like living in a war zone," where chronic trauma and complex post-traumatic stress disorder (CPTSD) are ever-present realities.

The behaviours that result from a deficiency cognition frame-work are a result of the Angry Indian 1.0's struggle to establish emotional boundaries. When an individual has healthy internal boundaries — when they know their feelings and when they under-stand that they are able to transition out of intense emotions and responsible for the process — then they are able to communicate their feelings and needs to others. When an individual does not have this internal boundary as a result of experiencing trauma in childhood, they tend to blame others for the way that they feel and take no responsibility for transitioning out of intense emotions. The Angry Indian 1.0's weak emotional boundaries lead to an extreme reactivity: they take every comment personally, and when bad things happen, they react as if they are re-experiencing the original trauma. When the Angry Indian 1.0 tries to communicate their distress, they often pick random targets, and they see all people as somehow responsible for their pain.

When 33-year-old Darcy Allan Sheppard, a bicycle courier, is killed during an altercation with Michael Bryant, the attorney general of Ontario, in 2009, he becomes a symbol for aggrieved cyclists dealing with the bike-unfriendly streets of Toronto. This is, however, a misreading of the situation. Sheppard was an Angry Indian 1.0, and what happened on August 31, 2009, was a result of childhood trauma.

Born into a Métis family in Alberta, Sheppard was the eldest of his mother's eight children. According to research conducted by Daniel Dale and Robyn Doolittle at the *Toronto Star*, Sheppard's mother was addicted to alcohol, and Sheppard was removed from her care when he was a toddler. He was adopted at age four or five but was back in foster care within five years. As Sheppard's younger half-brother Dave Sheppard puts it, "We probably had one of the hardest lives growing up. A lot of foster homes. Broken-down families." At the time he speaks with the *Star*, the younger Sheppard is serving a sentence in Stony Mountain Institution, a federal multi-security facility near Winnipeg, Manitoba.

In the bike courier community, Darcy Allan Sheppard is known as a charming, generous man. But his adoptive father says Sheppard constantly put himself at risk. As a child, Sheppard would often refuse to attend school, so his adoptive father would leave him home while he went to work. When his father returned home at the end of the day, he'd find the house trashed, with holes in the drywall where Sheppard had punched and kicked the walls. In an interview with the *Star*, Sheppard's adoptive father said, "Darcy Allan had an especially difficult time. He was medicated with Ritalin from infancy and spent two separate one-year stays in closed-custody psychiatric treatment, once when he was around 11 and again when he was around 13. What always struck me is how little the psychiatrists and the psychologists . . . seemed to know about what they were doing." As an adult, Sheppard has trouble holding down a job. After spending time in jail and living on the street, he moves to Toronto in the early 2000s. According to one source, Sheppard was "a Métis who wanted to be seen as white."

By the time Sheppard throws his backpack at Bryant's car and jumps onto its hood, he has already been in contact with the police on the day of the incident. He arrives at his girlfriend's apartment intoxicated, and a neighbour calls 911 after hearing what he thinks is a domestic assault. There is another alleged assault outside the apartment building after Sheppard is asked to leave. Sheppard then cycles down to the intersection of Yonge and Bloor, where he is seen throwing a traffic cone into the street and screaming at an SUV. A few minutes later, Bryant and Sheppard have their altercation. Sheppard dies of blunt impact head trauma after being dislodged from Bryant's car and hitting either a fire hydrant or the sidewalk curb. His blood alcohol limit at time of death is 0.183, or two times the legal limit. As Richard Peck, the independent prosecutor brought in from BC to try the case, says in his decision, Sheppard "did not deserve to have a criminal offence committed against him, regardless of prior conduct." But Sheppard's "propensity for aggressiveness or violence . . . is relevant to considering whether the accused [Bryant] was attacked by the deceased and to show the probability that the deceased was the aggressor in the altercation." Peck withdraws the charges against Bryant, saying that Sheppard was "agitated and angry and acted without any provocation."

When we look at Sheppard's behavioural patterns, we see that his primary coping mechanism is to project his anger outward in whatever situation he is in. If we consider this behaviour through the lens of childhood trauma theory, then we can draw a direct line from lack of parental emotional attachment during his early childhood years to Sheppard's lack of opportunity to master the skills he needs to describe and categorize his feelings and transition out of intense emotions. He learns early in life that asking for help is a useless exercise because the traumatized adults — and agents of the state — around him will never respond, so he feels alone and misunderstood. He is in constant distress. In 2009, that distress — and Sheppard's lifelong propensity to put himself at risk while expressing that distress — costs him his life.

Although it is Toronto cyclists who get the Sheppard story wrong, Canadians as a whole seem uncomfortable discussing the phenomenon of the Angry Indian 1.0 — especially lefty, social justice types who need to see Indigenous people as perfect victims but not as complex people with resiliencies that have helped them survive and resist colonization.

When a group of Indigenous people from Attawapiskat First Nation in northern Ontario book a press conference on Parliament Hill on June 29, 2017, they invite media to engage with them as they speak about their frustration with the federal government's National Inquiry into Missing and Murdered Indigenous Women and Girls. About 10 journalists attend, including Julie Van Dusen of the CBC and Glen McGregor of CTV. When Van Dusen asks the group to explain how their reference to youth reported missing or found dead in Thunder Bay, Ontario, connects to the Trudeau government, two of the women from Attawapiskat become extremely angry. One of the women says, "Excuse me? Did I just hear you correctly? 'How can he be blamed for that?' Excuse me, don't speak to us that way. That's not acceptable. Stop it right now. Step out." When Van Dusen refuses to leave her place of work, the woman from Attawapiskat says, "Then I don't want to hear from you," and proceeds to stop Van Dusen from speaking by saying, "Stop. *Stop*," in a long, drawn-out manner. McGregor then repeats Van Dusen's question but with a clearer focus: "I'm asking how Justin Trudeau's record compares to Stephen Harper's record. Do you think he's improved the situation?" It's a good question, one that gives the Attawapiskat group a chance to examine how past and present colonial government policies play a role in the high mortality rate of Indigenous people, including murdered Indigenous women and the youth in Thunder Bay. Instead of answering McGregor's question, however, one of the women responds with "You know what, white people? You've had your voice here for 524 years — 524 years you've been visible, white lady! Look how fast your white man comes and steps up for you. Where is everybody else to come and step up for us?" The woman then makes a few general statements about residential schools and the Sixties Scoop before calling the press conference to a halt after only a few minutes.

The women from Attawapiskat become angry when they are asked to explain their views and to engage in conversation — which is, after all, why they booked the press conference in the first place. Something about Van Dusen's question and McGregor's follow-up question frightens them, so they become the Angry Indian 1.0, using anger as a defence mechanism. By shutting other people down, the women avoid the conversation, thereby avoiding any examination of their competency as speakers, their knowledge of the subject, or their feelings of distress. The comment about "your white man comes and steps up for you" is also a clue to the one woman's distress: she feels isolated and misunderstood, alone and unsupported. But instead of engaging in conversation with 10 journalists who are there to hear what she has to say, the woman blames them, projects her anger onto everyone present, and allows her feelings of distress to sideline the aim of the press conference and the issue under discussion.

As Iqaluit mayor Madeleine Redfern later says via Twitter, "Screeching & blaming 'white people' on nat'l tv is going to undermine garnering or keeping political / societal support." Although

Redfern states that "there are problems with race & systemic relations," she also states, "It is blatantly unfair to blame Julie Van Dusen & all 'white' media or all white ppl."

That's exactly what Darcy Allan Sheppard does during his altercation with Michael Bryant. After leaving his girlfriend's apartment and cycling down to Yonge and Bloor, he finds himself near the upscale shopping district of Yorkville and the wealthy residential neighbourhood of Rosedale. Then, instead of working through his emotions, he proceeds to project his rage onto the wealthy strangers around him — people he sees as somehow responsible for his pain.

The Angry Indian 1.0 does not live in the present: they live in the moment of the traumatic event. For the women from Attawapiskat, it is the deaths of Indigenous women, girls, and youth — and perhaps the times when they themselves were at risk. For Sheppard, it is the moment when he sought connection with his birth mother and did not receive it, or when he could not make himself understood to the psychiatrists and psychologists Sheppard's adoptive father believes failed him. For the Angry Indian 1.0, anger is a reliable tool when fear and frustration become overwhelming and vulnerability is not an acceptable option.

For someone with a history of chronic trauma, vulnerability represents the difference between life and death. To be vulnerable in the present day is to return to the moment of the traumatic experience in an emotional sense, the time when the survivor faced injury, violence, and possible death. Vulnerability and openness to others is not something that feels safe.

When I am 20 years old and working as a banquet waitress at a convention centre, I am a sometime visitor to the Plate Room where all the side plates, dinner plates, and dessert plates are stored. There are thousands of each, piled on ceiling-high open shelves accessed by wheeled stepladders, enough to serve a banquet for

1,700 people downstairs and various meetings and smaller events on upper floors. I'm a good employee: reliable, observant, and detail-oriented. I get extra shifts at the eighth floor members-only club, and, unlike my colleagues, I don't steal scallops when I'm transferring them from the heated storage carts to the serving trays we use when we circulate around the room. But every once in a while — when I can't figure out what to do or how to be — I go into the Plate Room, where I pick up large dinner plates and hurl them against the nearest surface (floor or wall, doesn't matter). After two or three plates, I feel better, and I walk back to my station. I only get caught once.

Indigenous people living in the midst of chronic trauma learn early in life that expressing emotion is either useless or unsafe. As a result, episodic anger becomes the only recourse when they feel distress later in life. When I am in the Plate Room, I have no idea that I don't have a sense of self. I have no idea that I am experiencing the past as if it is the present. I have no idea that other people are sources of terror or pleasure (but never reciprocal exchange), and that when I feel terror, I freeze or flee. I have no idea that I have a negative view of myself and, as a result, often blame myself for normal, everyday experiences of human conflict that could be solved by genuine communication. I don't know that I resist being vulnerable because I live in constant fear. I don't even know that I'm angry. All I know is that I am frequently overcome by something inside of me, something I can't describe, something that feels like when I look down into the ocean from the ferry: too vast to even consider and frightening in its depth. The Plate Room makes me feel like I'm in control again.

I recognize the same forces at work when I'm hired at an Indigenous-run magazine 10 years later, in 1998. The magazine is a quarterly, and it's weeks behind schedule. I do some interviews, write a bunch of stuff, pull together and edit a bunch of other articles, and get the magazine out on time. But my work doesn't elicit any compliments from the publisher. He calls me into the meeting room and says, "I know what you're doing." When I ask him what he means, he starts yelling and stabbing his finger at me. He accuses me of trying to "steal" his magazine. He says, "You think you're so good. But who the hell are you?" He screams and rages, and when I get up to leave, he yells, "Don't let the door hit you on the way out!" Perhaps the most amazing thing about this "meeting" is that both he and I know he's not firing me. These kinds of exchanges are standard in Indigenous workplaces in 1998 and in 2018. When I report to work the next day, the publisher and I proceed as if nothing has happened. I've gotten used to it over the years, working for Indigenous organizations. Yelling, snide comments and remarks, gossiping, bosses who make themselves purposely unavailable for meetings (after which they blame the other person), colleagues and bosses withholding information or purposely giving the wrong information, supervisors not giving staff enough work so that they feel excluded or out of the loop, bosses complaining to employees about their coworkers (and to the coworkers about them) — I've experienced it all.

Trauma specialist Eduardo Duran, who works with Indigenous communities in the U.S., says that lateral violence is part of a process whereby Indigenous people externalize their self-hate and attempt to destroy the colonized archetype of the self. When the publisher enacts his self-hate with me, it combines with lessons I've learned from my mother and the dominant society: how to be a silent victim, how to continue seeking validation from an abusive control figure out of a need to be seen, and how to argue away or defend the abuser's behaviour out of the sense that somehow it's all my fault.

Until one day, when I stop being that person. Maybe it's what I've learned at the healing circle, or the elders' conferences, or from other community members. The next time the publisher pulls his finger-pointing rage routine, I find my voice. I stand in front of him in the archway between production and editorial, cut him off in mid-sentence, and I say, "Dude, I do not have to put up with this. You're just jealous because I do the work and you don't. Why don't you figure out what you're meant to do, and work at being good at that." It's a justifiable response to his unfair treatment, but looking back I can see the dynamic that underpins lateral violence: I'm quiet and I take the abuse, but I also observe and measure. Then, when I see my opportunity — a space in public where it's safe to use my voice and he's surrounded by people from whom he seeks respect — I raise myself up by dressing him down. Although I enjoy short-lived fame within the community for calling out the publisher, my response isn't professional. This time, we both know I'm fired.

According to Abraham Maslow's biographer, when Maslow worked with the Niitsitapi in southern Alberta, he was amazed to find that 80 to 90 per cent of the Niitsitapi population was as high in ego security as "the most secure individuals" in settler society, who Maslow believed made up perhaps 5 to 10 per cent of the settler population "at most." This ego security and deep sense of self paved the way for respectful relations with (and empathy for) other individuals, and it was the result of Indigenous child-rearing practices.

In pre-colonial Indigenous societies, children were often carried in cradleboards or moss bags strapped to their mother's backs. They were in constant contact with a warm human being, able to detect their mother's heartbeat, wrapped tightly in her smell and her energy field — her particular and individual manifestation of manitow. The child was joined but separate. In this manner, children were safe but also very independent, as the mother might not turn around or take the child out of the cradleboard/moss bag for many hours. Cradleboards/moss bags were also used to calm a child (and keep them safe) when the mother was busy with her daily routine. Strapped into a cradleboard/moss bag and propped up somewhere near the mother, the tight embrace of the cradleboard/moss bag generated a feeling of security even when human touch was not available. Indigenous peoples also used ceremonies and the structures of their society — clans, moieties, and ceremonial societies — to socialize the individual and create individual identity within a collective philosophy. This balance has been destroyed by the trauma of colonialism, leading to generations of Indigenous people who lack a sense of self and are, therefore, unable to connect in a meaningful way to anyone else. This lack of ego security and lack of empathy has obvious negative effects at the community level.

The publisher doesn't know how to see other people as allies. In the absence of a self-actualized sense of identity, the publisher sees the world through a deficiency cognition framework, where he must battle to get what he does not have. The publisher is also enacting the sexism that Indigenous men have learned through Christianization and the Indian Act. He's known for targeting and abusing women who intimidate him and remind him of the sense of powerlessness he feels as an Indigenous man unable to fulfill his pre-colonial roles in the community due to the fact that he's been stripped of land, culture, and a sense of self by the process of colonization. The Angry Indian 1.0 often uses this sexist framework to project their anger on to others. In the Parliament Hill case, even the woman from Attawapiskat chooses to attack the "white lady" — CBC journalist Van Dusen — while ignoring the male CTV journalist.

According to Pia Mellody, who lectures and writes on childhood trauma, there are two types of stories that define the lives of trauma survivors: a disempowering narrative, which tells the survivor that they are unlovable, alone, helpless, and unsafe; and a falsely empowering narrative, which tells the survivor that they are grandiose and entitled in order to compensate for feelings of inferiority and worthlessness. Survivors with falsely empowering narratives are often irresponsible, blaming, judgmental, disdainful, righteously indignant, and preoccupied with settling scores and getting revenge.

In the Indigenous context, it is not necessary for a survivor to have either a disempowering post-traumatic narrative or a falsely empowering post-traumatic narrative. Many Indigenous survivors of chronic trauma have both. In some cases, the falsely empowering post-traumatic narrative becomes a protective front for a fearful individual who carries a disempowering post-traumatic narrative at their core. These narratives are not good or bad — they are simply a manifestation of complex trauma and the survivor's attempt to regain control. When I call out the publisher, I falsely empower myself to make up for the disempowering narrative I carry at my core. I also gain strength in a very real way by using my voice and refusing to accept any further abuse. It's not who I am or how I would act today, but it was who I was — and needed to be — at the time.

There are complicated cultural politics related to grief and post-catastrophic memory within Indigenous communities. As Gail K. Gus, the crisis care and wellness coordinator for the Tseshaht First Nation on Vancouver Island tells *Maclean's* in 2015, "When you live in a community full of lateral violence like ours, you are taught to bury or deny what happened." If any party refuses this directive by calling out the destructive behaviour, the other parties are enraged and attempt to settle the score and take revenge. The dynamic is fraught with the learned behaviours, unresolved emotions, and power narratives of the colonized. When it comes to lateral violence, there are no perfect victims, and the perpetrators are not monsters.

Métis scholar Patti LaBoucane-Benson, the director of research and evaluation for Native Counselling Services of Alberta, has a theory on why lateral violence has become so common in Indigenous communities. LaBoucane-Benson says that Indigenous peoples used to live in tipis and small houses, which meant that adults had to watch what they said. They couldn't put their children in another room because there was no other room. The multi-roomed homes of today mean that contemporary Indigenous adults do not have to learn any self-discipline. They can talk about others, gossip, and act in a critical, judgmental fashion. Once they become comfortable with these behaviours, it creeps into daily life, and children in the community learn it and replay it.

LaBoucane-Benson says that ending lateral violence starts with the individual. As she said in a presentation to North Central Alberta Child and Family Services in 2013, "We are responsible for cleaning our own space."

Ending lateral violence also depends on effective leadership. To create kind, respectful, and caring workplaces, LaBoucane-Benson says that leaders must be knowledgeable about lateral violence, create policies and consequences for those who engage in lateral violence, and offer trauma-informed conflict resolution services that create lasting change in the individual and the organization. Finally, leaders must be able to deal with perpetrators of lateral violence with both kindness and authority. They must not allow themselves to be bullied or allow the perpetrator to circumvent the system, but they must also be compassionate. This compassion comes from understanding that the perpetrator is also a survivor: of colonialism, of intergenerational trauma, and of the lateral violence they have witnessed, experienced, and learned.

CHAPTER 5

INVISIBLE ROOTS

My mother is born in 1937 in Nelson, BC. Her parents, Thomas and Thelma, are the deputy warden and matron of the Nelson Jail, which, in addition to locking up those in conflict with the law, is busy locking up Doukhobors, Indigenous peoples, those who refuse orders in BC's Second World War internment camps, and anyone else deemed deviant, unnatural, or in need of the civilizing forces of Canadian society. My mother tells me that when she is born, no announcement is made in the Nelson newspaper. This is odd, as her parents are prominent members of Nelson society. A birth announcement is certainly published when my mother's sister is born a few years before. Twenty years later, when my mother fills out the paperwork for a driver's licence, she discovers that not only is her birth never announced — it is never registered. She does not have a birth certificate.

Eventually, Thomas and Thelma move to Burnaby, BC, where Thomas becomes the deputy warden of the Young Offenders Unit at Oakalla Prison Farm. When Thomas and Thelma have dinner parties, my mother is kept in the kitchen with my great-grandmother, Thelma's mother, whom we call Little Gramma. When her parents entertain, they introduce my mother's older sister as "our daughter" and invite her to play piano for the guests. My mother is not introduced to the guests. She is a shadow child, unloved by an emotionally distant mother and unclaimed by a father-in-name-only who, when my mother is a teenager, throws her belongings onto the lawn, saying she is a whore and does not belong in this house. My mother's black hair and dark eyes are a constant reminder of his wife's extramarital affair with a Nehiyaw man in Nelson and of his wife's mixed ancestry, courtesy of two of my great-grandfathers, who were born in New Brunswick. My mother's half-sister is fair-skinned, showing none of the New Brunswick Peskotomuhkati ancestry. She is also the product of Thomas and Thelma's early years, when they were first married and in love.

From my mother's diary: "How do you grow up in silence? You don't exist; you're there but no one acknowledges your presence. It's like I am invisible. I can't eat, she sits there staring at me with that stick from the wood box always set there as if it's part of the table setting, ready to crack my hands if I happen to talk. Why does she hate me? Why is she always hitting me? I retreat into daydreams, into my fantasy world. I lie under my bed all day, so silently no one can find me. Sometimes I hide in the basement in the coal bin. It's nice and dark in there and I can stay for hours not moving or speaking."

By the time she is a young adult, my mother is incapable of

relating to anyone, especially strangers. As she writes in the diary, "I am always afraid of other people. I am afraid of the very idea of life. I can't speak up when it is my turn in a store to buy something. My mind is on hold and I am not able to help myself." This inability to be open to other people and to the world will eventually turn into an inability to be vulnerable or emotionally honest. This, in turn, will have devastating consequences on my mother's adult relationships and her parenting skills.

From the diary: "I do not ever receive hugs or kisses or any warmth from my parents. I do receive verbal abuse daily, and physical abuse from both my mother and father on occasion. The verbal abuse is the most damaging. My sister is looked upon as good. She is always praised and told how smart she is. I am bad. I am told I am lazy and will end up doing nothing worthwhile. The last time my father beats me up, I become oblivious to physical pain and acquire the ability to put on a mask of indifference. Never after that time do I ever cry in front of them again. Mommy and Daddy cease to exist. In my mind, they become 'them.' Them to avoid, them to retreat from, them to not listen to. Them to hate."

When she is in elementary school, my mother comes home one day and finds her father with his hands around Little Gramma's neck, banging her head against the kitchen wall. Another time, she sees that one of Little Gramma's arms is black and blue with bruises. Thomas often says that he's "just waiting for the old bag to die," so he can inherit her house and her money. Thomas and Thelma live with Little Gramma in her big house on Gilmour Avenue in Burnaby.

From an early age, my mother discovers that the only way she gets any attention from Thomas and Thelma is when she is a problem. Play hooky from school, and Thelma has to come home from work to look for her. There might even be a meeting with the teacher. Steal things from the five-and-dime store, and the store owner calls Little Gramma. Throw up in public, and

My mother's diary

Thomas and Thelma have to show concern. Even if they hit her when they get home, it's still worth it, because in the moment when my mother vomits, they are embarrassed and my mother finally has some control. My mother begins to use that need for control as a primary way of functioning. She also begins to equate negative attention with love.

From the diary: "Grade 3, what a wonderful year for me. Mrs. Muir is really strict and gives spankings to kids. Strict is good for me. I have a real sense of rules in her class. It is a quiet and orderly place and I love Mrs. Muir. I never get to go to the front of the class and get a hit on the behind, though."

My mother does experience some joy early in life, from the inmate trustees in the Nelson Jail — men convicted of non-violent offences who mop floors, do laundry, paint walls, and perform other unpaid duties in exchange for privileges and the chance to work throughout the jail with little or no supervision. My mother's experience with the trustees leads her to equate happiness with the acceptance and affection she gets from men.

She writes in the diary, "My earliest recollection is of the jail trustees. These young men are my babysitters and the only ones who are affectionate to me, probably because they are lonely and welcome the chance to be outside their cells during the day. They do the housework and dishes, etc., and of course I am always underfoot. I am two or three years old." I see from our family photographs that there are also plenty of Indigenous women at the Nelson Jail, both visitors and staff. Although my mother never speaks of it, I'd like to think that these women loved her, too, and that they told her about her real father when Thomas and the trustees weren't around.

My mother marries three times in her life. She first marries a man who is a few years older than she is, who chooses her at a teen dance at the Anglican church hall in Burnaby and whose friends become her friends. His stepfather is an alcoholic, so Bob spends a lot of time away from home. The second time, she marries my father, who is as isolated and angry as she is. The third time, she marries a man recently retired from the Royal Canadian Navy, who spends his childhood under Nazi occupation in Vichy,

The author's mother as a child at the Nelson Jail, circa 1939, Nelson, British Columbia

France, during the Second World War. These men all have a history of unresolved childhood trauma, and my mother recognizes in them the modes of communication and methods of interaction she has learned within her childhood home.

My mother gets pregnant at least half a dozen times during her first marriage, but most of the pregnancies end in miscarriage. Finally, my mother carries a son to term, but she knows nothing about her body, and she thinks the baby will come out through her belly button. When he is born, my mother finally feels a sense of accomplishment. She tells me later that she dislikes how the baby's ears fold over when he sleeps, so she tapes the tips of his ears back with black electrical tape for the first year of his life. This family member has perfectly shaped ears as a result. Two years later, a daughter is born with jaundice, which is the result of my mother's Rh-negative blood type. My mother tells me that the baby screams constantly and is allergic to formula. My mother tries everything (except breastfeeding, which the doctor discouraged) until she finally discovers that the baby will tolerate powdered skim milk. The child survives.

My mother does her best to negotiate her way through motherhood in the absence of any positive parenting knowledge passed down by her own mother. She is good with babies, who have clearly delineated basic needs and who make her feel good; as research shows, babies time their smiles in order to make their mothers smile in return. But my mother has no idea how to create, nurture, or maintain relationships with her children as they age and begin to exhibit more complex emotional needs. My mother's own emotional needs were never met in childhood, so meeting her children's emotional needs and helping them develop strong identities is uncharted territory.

My mother is devastated when her first husband leaves her after seven years together and one year of marriage. He visits his son occasionally, and after one such visit, my mother discovers she is pregnant. Her estranged husband denies that the child is his. They do not reconcile, so my mother is divorced, alone, and pregnant in 1960 — a time when women who get pregnant out of wedlock are considered little better than prostitutes and other so-called fallen women. She gives birth to her second child in 1961, and because there is no maternity leave in Canada at the time, she is forced to quit her job and reapply again a few months afterward, starting again at the bottom of the seniority list — for the second time, because she had to quit and reapply when she had her first child, too.

While she is home in the months before and after the birth, my mother has no income, no family support (because Thomas and Thelma refuse to help), and there is no unemployment insurance program in Canada at the time. She has no money for food, so she gets unlabelled canned food from a nearby church basement. She is so poor that she cannot buy oil for the oil stove, so she goes out back of the house she rents in Burnaby, collects firewood, then loads the wood into the oil stove and lights it. She takes her children outside in case the house catches fire and sits in a rocking chair, waiting in the backyard for hours as the chimney emits thick black smoke. When it starts burning clear, she returns inside to a wood fire. My mother is capable of creative problem-solving when circumstances require it, and she passes this resiliency on to me.

Out of necessity, my mother dates men who can provide for her and her two young children. She tells me that when she goes on dates with "Professor Norman Young" — she always calls him that, using his title — she only eats half her restaurant meal and brings home the other half for my half-siblings. She tells me about her lover, Dino Gerussi, a musician who buys my mother Oil of Olay face cream when he is touring the U.S. and brings it home to her in Canada. She asks Dino to leave his wife and marry her because she doesn't want her children to think she is a "whore"

— whenever she tells me this story, she uses her father's word (*whore*) — but Dino refuses, and the affair ends. Around this time, my mother is date-raped by a third-year law student she is introduced to by friends. For years, she tells no one about the rape, because she is afraid the courts will take away her children and "what about my friends who introduced me to him?"

When my mother meets my father, she tries again to create a family and to gain a sense of belonging. But my mother's efforts to fix my father fail, as any effort by one human being to fix another human being always will. And my father, imprisoned not by Catholic nuns or Corrections Canada this time but by his silence about his past, struggles under the pressure of maintaining a business, creating professional relationships, and fulfilling the roles of partner and father. My mother gets regular phone calls from girls and women, claiming that my father promised to marry them, impregnated them, then left. And then there's the matter of my father's first family, which my mother thinks she can fix, too.

My father was married before he met my mother, and he has two children with his ex-wife. During the 1970s, my mother maintains a department store credit card for Loretta, his ex, because my father won't pay child support and the law doesn't force him to. She also arranges for Joseph and Maurice, my half-brothers from my father's marriage to Loretta, to visit us one summer. They come all the way from another province, but they are older and hang out mostly with older family members.

My father is mean to Joseph, because he is quieter than Maurice and a convenient target. One evening during dinner, my father asks Joseph, "Did you wash your face before coming to the table?" "Yes," Joseph answers. "I used the cloth hanging over the tub." To which my father thunders, "What? You used the cloth someone used to wipe their crotch? On your face? What kind of pig are you? We have clean cloths!" This isn't really about Joseph — it is about my father re-enacting his own abuse at the hands of the nuns (*you are stupid, you are a pig*). It is also about my father's sense of inadequacy, which in this case means the kind of home he is providing (*we have clean cloths*). It is about the script that runs inside my father's head and his choice to identify with the oppressor's tactics as a way to gain the power he has never had. But none of us realizes this then. Joseph looks down at the table and we eat in silence. My half-brothers do not visit us again.

To an individual who has experienced trauma — whether inside the family context or outside of it — the family can either be a source of support and healing or a source of additional harm.

Even if everyone in a family is exposed to the same event at the same time, each member of that family will react to the trauma differently. People have differing degrees of resilience, and they rationalize the experience of trauma differently depending on their beliefs, perceptions, frames of reference, and how they respond emotionally to an event. Family therapy exists in part to help families figure out a way to exchange perspectives, which will enable them to understand, accept, and adapt to the reactions of other family members. This creates a supportive family environment, which is key to resolving the experience of trauma.

Different people have different ways of coping with trauma and stress. Some will employ emotional strategies, such as crying, humour, or anger; others cognitive strategies including denial, distraction, anticipation (planning for the next stressful event), or needing to "know" or figure out what happened. Some people will use social strategies, such as reaching out to others for attention or performing altruistic acts as a way to forget their own troubles. Most people use a combination of strategies, with one or two forming the main part of their response. Most children learn their coping mechanisms from their parents, although as the nature-nurture debate shows us, individuals also have an inherent way of being that is uniquely their own.

My own response to trauma and everyday stressors combines emotional and cognitive strategies. I cry or get angry, then I reflect on every aspect of the event in order to figure out what happened. I never use denial or distraction, and I rarely use anticipation. In my 20s and 30s, I do not reach out to others; in my 40s, I learn how to ask for help from the people in my support system. I sometimes use humour, depending on the situation, but never as an attempt to distract from processing the incident. These responses put me at odds with other members of my family, who tend to use denial as their primary coping mechanism. As a result, they do not understand, accept, or adapt to my perceptions of the events that take place. Not only are they unable to provide a supportive environment to me as the youngest child, they also mock and deride me for those perceptions, which silences me. This has created a great deal of mistrust on my part toward other members of my family.

The Fairbanks Native Association (FNA) says that healthy families share certain characteristics. In a healthy family, problems are talked about and solutions are found, everyone is free to express their thoughts and feelings, the perspectives of each person are valued, and communication is honest and direct. People are free to be different, roles in the family are chosen, and these roles can change over time. In a healthy family, everyone can get their needs met, parents are self-aware about the ways in which their past experiences have affected them, and they deal with that past (and the effects) in an honest way. If I measure my family against the FNA's checklist, we completely strike out.

In the 1950s and 1960s, psychologist Silvan Solomon Tomkins described the relationship between affect (biological responses to signals in the brain), feelings (awareness of an affect), emotions (a feeling plus prior memory of a feeling), and personality. Tomkins identified nine affects that categorize the expression of human emotion.

THE NINE AFFECTS

Affect	Description	Inherent Feeling	Purpose
Distress-Anguish	The cry for help	Punishing	Signals to our caregivers/support system that all is not well
Interest-Excitement	The pull toward mastery	Rewarding	Motivates us to learn
Enjoyment-Joy	The social bond	Rewarding	Creates a sense of familiarity and trust
Surprise-Startle	The reset button	Neutral	Stops us from continuing so we can pay attention to something new
Anger-Rage	The demand to fix it	Punishing	Signals that something is "way too much"
Fear-Terror	The signal to flee or freeze	Punishing	Focuses our attention on survival
Shame-Humiliation	The self-protection signal	Punishing	Hiding
Disgust	The need to expel	Punishing	Helps us get rid of toxic things/people
Dissmell	The avoidance signal	Punishing	Helps us push away (or pull away from) harmful or unpleasant people/things

Tomkins Institute, via http://www.tomkins.org/what-tomkins-said/introduction/nine-affects-present-at-birth-combine-to-form-emotion-mood-and-personality

Most human beings are motivated to seek positive (reward-ing) affect and reduce negative (punishing) affect. But in order to maintain this balance, an individual has to be in a place where all the affects can be expressed. When people are unable to express affect — because they are in survival mode or under someone else's control — they remain unaware of their feelings and unable to form the memories that help them categorize and understand their emotions. Having a flat affect or expressing only some of the affects (such as Anger-Rage, Fear-Terror, or Shame-Humiliation) has negative impacts on relationship building and the stability of families and communities.

Human beings need to experience both positive and nega-tive affect. Experiencing Enjoyment-Joy alongside other people creates a sense of familiarity, trust, and commitment. These are the bonds that tie families and communities together. Although Shame-Humiliation is a negative affect, it presents the individual with opportunities to reflect on (and change) whatever is getting in the way of belonging and mastery.

Shame is associated with many of the everyday impacts of trauma as defined by the Aboriginal Healing Foundation. According to researchers at the Tomkins Institute, when people feel shame, they react by exhibiting one or more specific behaviours: Withdrawal (isolating oneself, running, or hiding), Attack Self (self putdown or masochism), Avoidance (denial, abusing drugs/alcohol, or distraction through thrill-seeking), or Attack Others (turning the table, lashing out verbally or physically, or blaming others). These behaviours play a large part in chronic trauma as well as in the persistent negative atmosphere found within many Indigenous communities. Shame and its associated behaviours also explain why so many Indigenous families are fractured, lack-ing even the most basic of emotional bonds.

In October 2010, I am awakened at 2 a.m. by the doorbell,

which I ignore. Then I hear loud knocking that continues until the young woman in the first-floor apartment opens the door. Turns out, it's our neighbour Tyrell, the Anishinabe guy who lives in the bachelor apartment next door to me. He's lost his keys, so he climbs the stairs to our shared landing and proceeds to try to break into his own apartment. As I listen to him repeatedly kick his all-metal fireproof door, I also hear him talking about his dilemma in a running dialogue with himself. This is a trauma-related form of communication I've seen in many Indigenous clients in direct-service environments: he needs help, but he doesn't know how to ask for it, so he talks out loud, hoping that I'll hear and come to his rescue. So I lie there and consider my options: I can't bring him the phone because the cord isn't long enough to get to the door (this is before I have a cellphone). I can't call the landlord, because calls to that number always go straight to voicemail. One thing is clear: I sleep in a space off the living room, converted from the old second-floor sleeping porch, and the space doesn't have a door — so I am not letting a 300-pound drunk man into my house. Tyrell won't be comfortable on the hardwood landing, but it's warm and dry in the hallway, he's safe, and if he needs to use my phone in the morning to call a friend, or the landlord, he can. And if he needs to pee, we have a front yard. So I let him bang and mumble, and after a half-hour or so, he quiets down and I drift back into sleep.

An hour or two later, I'm awakened by the thud-thunk-thump of Tyrell falling down the stairs. The house has 13-foot ceilings, and the staircase is long. I dial 911, then I hear a soundscape of voices, both cop and paramedic: "Hey, buddy. You've been drinking tonight, eh?" "Let's get your pants back on. Oops, looks like you had an accident." "Yeah, we're gonna need a blanket from the truck." "Come on, settle down, we gotta get something on your head. You're bleeding." I watch through my bedroom window as the paramedics lead him to the truck wearing an ambulance blanket around his waist to replace the urine-soaked pants he removed in the hallway. After they drive away, the silence of night descends once again. When the landlord calls the next day, he says Tyrell will be leaving the house. Several weeks later, Tyrell returns to remove his belongings. When he is done, he stands in the hallway and bangs his door open and shut — which is noisier than it sounds, because the house is old and none of the doors fit into their frames properly. As he bangs and bangs, shuddering the very foundations of the house, I hear him shout, "Seven years I lived here. Seven years! But you know why I'm leaving? Because of you. Because of *you*." Tyrell doesn't even know that I'm home, but he talks to me anyway, putting the energy he carries into the universe in a very Indigenous culture–related response.

Tyrell's anger is a classic "attack others" shame response. I had nothing to do with Tyrell's current situation, but rather than reflect on his actions on that evening, or the reasons why I might have chosen not to let him into my apartment, he protects himself by blaming me.

Blame is used as a frequent tool in my family. Sometimes it's a defensive cover for internalized shame, used by family members when they want to deflect attention from themselves. At other times, blame is used to shift the conversation and avoid talking openly and honestly about an issue.

Exhibit A: When we move back to northern Alberta from Vancouver, my mother and I move in with a family member, in the house they buy during the oil boom. The plan is that they will give the tenant in the basement apartment notice, and we will move downstairs. Although we sleep together in the basement bedroom, however, my mother lives upstairs, claiming a spot on the couch across from the TV and cooking and eating meals in the upstairs kitchen. One day in 1982, I trundle in the front door with my bass guitar and amplifier, because it's the Christmas school break and I have to practise. When the family member sees it, they yell something about "So I'm going to have to listen to that?" and storm out of the house. Instead of having a conversation with my mother about the arrangement — her lack of respect for the boundaries they have attempted to set, or the way they benefit from my mother buying the groceries and she and I doing all the cleaning and cooking — my 24-year-old family member attacks me, projecting all their anger over the invasion of their space onto 14-year-old me.

Exhibit B: Sometime in the early 1980s, my mother gets angry and blames me for forgetting to buy bread on the way home from school. In response, I mumble "bitch" under my breath as I walk up the stairs from our basement bedroom to the kitchen. A family member hears me, says, "What did you say?" and punches me in the face, bloodying my nose. Then he tries to joke as he takes me to the bathroom and helps me stop the bleeding with a wad of toilet paper. This family member will never speak the truth about our mother, the control figure in both our lives. But he will always punish me for doing so.

Families need to have narratives. Storytelling helps the family put their experiences into a shared context that each member of the family can understand. Family stories pass along ideas and help define the family's past, present, and future. When families tell stories, it provides members of the family with the opportunity to build shared history and cement the bonds of affection. As children grow in healthy families, they begin to participate in the family story/history-making, finding their individual voices and solving issues in a nonthreatening way. The teller decides what to tell, how to tell it, and what kind of emotions they want to associate with events. The listener accepts another individual's facts and emotions. In that sense, storytelling is a form of family therapy: it allows a family to create a coordinated perspective and engage in the co-regulation of affect.

While not every story told in a healthy family needs to have a healing subtext, these same skills are important for sharing, and recovering from, traumatic experiences. Well-functioning families are able to guide each family member toward a "healing story," where they help reframe traumatic experiences in a way that leaves them with hope for the future; able to make peace with what has happened and the effects of that event and able to once again see joy in life.

My family doesn't tell stories about what happened to us. When I try, there is little tolerance for the narrative or for my perspectives. I am only able to start making meaning in my life when I surround myself with chosen family who listen to my stories and share their own. Trauma experts all agree: memory management is key to recovering from PTSD and CPTSD. To heal, a survivor must recall, manage, restructure, and reframe the information they carry within themselves. If they cannot or do not engage in this process, there is less chance that they will successfully achieve biological, psychological, and social recovery from a traumatic experience.

A couple of months before my neighbour's bad night, I notice that he isn't going to work anymore. The company truck is parked out front, and he isn't getting up in the morning. His girlfriend has also stopped visiting. Then one day, I hear someone knocking on Tyrell's door, which is followed by a knock on my door. I answer it expecting to see the landlord or the downstairs neighbour, but instead I see two Indigenous people I don't know. A woman says, "Can you tell me if you've seen Tyrell?" I don't know who they are or how they've managed to get into the house, and the woman's breath smells like alcohol at 10 in the morning, so I say, "Are you family?" The man next to her says, "She's his mother." So I say, "Well, I actually haven't seen him lately. Maybe you could try calling him?" The woman replies, "We've been calling, but he doesn't answer." After they leave, I remember something that happens the first summer I move into the house: Tyrell, walking up the front stairs after work, saying hi to his half-brother, a white guy who does work on the house for the landlord, and the white guy looking down and saying nothing back. A week after his mother leaves my door, Tyrell puts one of his two cats out into the hallway and refuses to let it in again. A neighbour down the street adopts it after she sees the cat prowling around outside, looking for food.

If Tyrell's behaviour is viewed through the lens of trauma theory, his story would look like this: for a while, Tyrell's girlfriend functions as his missing parent or missing family, the person who is supposed to give him unconditional love. When she leaves, it confirms his belief that he is a bad, unlovable person. His avoidance and withdrawal response to this and his "attack others" response to being evicted are related to the shame he feels over both situations. So, because he cannot challenge the control figure — either his mother or the girlfriend-as-mother — he punishes the cat.

Children who grow up in dysfunctional environments where they are unable to share affect, where their feelings are never validated, or where no one ever meets their needs grow into adults who think that they are to blame for their loneliness and pain. When they enter into adult relationships, they are overwhelmed by and unprepared for the complex demands of intimacy and relationship-building. When they become parents and their children ask them for validation and connection, they are often overwhelmed by — or triggered by — the task of meeting their children's emotional needs. Tyrell doesn't answer the door when his mother knocks because he knows it is unsafe to do so. People who drink behave unpredictably. If Tyrell makes himself vulnerable and goes to her for comfort, he cannot be sure of her response. The anger, frustration, disappointment, sadness, loneliness, and abandonment he feels after his breakup are the same feelings he carries from his relationship with his alcoholic mother. So he acts to protect himself.

In the wake of colonization and intergenerational trauma, toxic shame is a core aspect of many Indigenous families.

Toxic shame is a pervasive feeling of being fundamentally flawed and inadequate as a human being. It is handed down through generations and is connected to the effects that residential schools, racism, discrimination, chronic trauma, and the everyday impacts of trauma have on the family system. When individuals do not receive love in their families, they often grow into adults who are self critical and who think they are unworthy of having meaningful relationships with other people.

Shame is not the same as guilt. When people feel guilty, they feel bad about the things they have done. When people feel shame, they feel bad about who they are as people. This shame becomes toxic when it becomes a core part of an individual's sense of self. This happens when Indigenous peoples are marginalized or mistreated by the dominant society and when Indigenous people are made to feel inadequate by their own families. These feelings of inadequacy often lead individuals to think they are somehow responsible for the traumatic events that happen to them. When they catch themselves thinking that maybe they are good people who deserve love, these individuals believe that there is something wrong with them for even having these thoughts. Once this cycle of self-criticism and toxic shame begins, an individual is living their life through a distorted shame-based lens.

Because they have such negative feelings about who they are, people who are shame-based are terrified of intimate relationships or of letting other people really know them. As a result, they tend to push people away, sabotage relationships, or put up barriers to creating new relationships. Although this is done on an unconscious level, the individual senses that their relationships are lacking in authenticity and trust. This makes them feel even more isolated and alone, which compounds their sense of shame. We see these same patterns enacted in the workplace.

When shame-based people become parents, they cannot meet their children's needs, because the child's emotional needs interfere with the parent's search for love and acceptance. (In her diary, my mother says she decided to "make my own family so I could be loved.") As a result of these clashing needs, the parent will shame the child whenever the child is needy or speaks about their true feelings.

To correct the dysfunction in the family, children will take on roles in an attempt to bring the family back into balance. If a child is not wanted — as my mother was not wanted — they will try to balance the family by not being troublesome. This means they will take on the role of Helpful or Super-Responsible or Perfect or Invisible. My mother became Invisible, and I become a combination of Super-Responsible and Perfect. This Super-Responsible and Perfect version of me never shows her true feelings and takes care of other people instead of taking care of herself.

Because the members of a shame-based family are trained to hide their feelings, one member of the family — usually the most sensitive person (the one who does show their feelings) — is assigned the role of Scapegoat. Blaming the Scapegoat helps other members of the family lessen their pain and manage their feelings. I'm the Scapegoat in my family, blamed for wanting to talk about our secrets and blamed for trying to create authentic relationships with people who do not want to be known.

As a young adult, my experiences growing up in a shame-based family lead me to re-enact my childhood roles in many adult relationships. I enter into friendships with people who bully and mock me. In romantic relationships, I choose people who are angry and blame me for everything. When I get rid of the shame, my ability to set boundaries improves because I finally have a positive sense of self.

People who struggle with toxic shame often have difficulty setting boundaries because they react to everyone else's thoughts and feelings and they think these thoughts and feelings reflect on them — so they believe them and internalize them, or they become defensive. Years ago, at a meeting at an Indigenous workplace attended by all program staff, I say something (no one at the meeting can remember what), and the Indigenous supervisor responds by getting up from the table and fleeing to her office to cry. When no one comes after her, she returns to the table, only to see that the group has managed to get everything done in the 10 minutes she's been gone, whereas we hadn't been able to accomplish anything while she was there. This compounds her sense of shame, and my status in her eyes changes from favoured employee in whom she can confide to threat that she must neutralize. When shame-based behaviours are replicated in the workplace, it often leads to lateral violence.

Every individual needs to feel that they have access to safety, trust, esteem, intimacy, and control in their relationships. An individual's ability to demonstrate these things to others and seek these things out in their relationships with others is shaped by their childhood experiences. The good news is relational skills can change as a result of healing from a traumatic experience. To unlearn the dysfunctional patterns that are so often transferred into the workplace and other adult relationships, the survivor must explore the experiences they have had in their family and find the connection between those experiences and the patterns they enact with other people. I eventually learn this — and develop skills in demonstrating and seeking out safety, trust, esteem, intimacy, and control — through a practice relationship with Celina, my traditional Chinese medicine (TCM) practitioner.

Celina looks like a mad professor. She has unruly hair and is the type of person who puts her pen behind her ear, then forgets it's there while she walks around looking for her lost pen. She is sometimes late for her appointments — like, still-on-her-way-to-the-office late — and also forgets appointments on occasion. She is, however, a gifted TCM practitioner and my only health-care provider for six years.

The first time Celina forgets about me, I am ambivalent. I separate myself from my emotions so that I don't have to feel abandoned. The second time it happens, I am compliant. I say it's fine when we talk about it, but secretly I am furious. The third time, I'm angry and I show it, because (a) it's the third time and (b) I know I can. There is safety here: I know she loves me for who I am and that this love is unconditional. The fourth time, I'm standing next to the front desk when she arrives, 45 minutes late, and I think, *What a brilliant little freak.* So I smile and say, "Glad you could make it," and her face changes from pensive to relaxed, because she, too, knows there is safety in this relationship. My family does not teach me what it means to be loved unconditionally or to love someone unconditionally. I learn that with Celina.

Over weekly acupuncture sessions for six years, Celina takes on many roles in my life, depending on what new skills I'm learning, which unresolved emotions are surfacing, and which behavioural and communication patterns I'm unlearning at the time. Sometimes, she acts like my mother, ready to defend me against all outsiders, sure that the person who just blamed me for a breakup is wrong, wrong, wrong. Sometimes she acts like my best friend, who, when I mention that I've finally signed up for online dating, waves me over to a private spot in the reception area and leans in while we sit on cushions on the floor and I tell her all about it. Sometimes, she acts like my partner, saying, "Hey, sweetie," when I show up with a new haircut.

Over six years with Celina, I learn what mutual empathy looks like. I learn what it's like when someone hears, sees, and understands how I feel. I learn how to be honest about what I think and what I feel, because Celina never punishes me for those thoughts and feelings and never turns away from me. I learn what mutual respect feels like: what it's like for someone to recognize my brilliant, flawed humanity and what it's like for me to love someone because of their brilliant, flawed humanity. I learn what it's like to establish an emotional connection with someone based on the qualities and capabilities we admire about each other, while still being honest about (and working through) our shortcomings.

When I'm waiting for a writing grant and I'm so broke I can't even buy toilet paper, Celina says matter-of-factly, "We have toilet paper here." I learn what it's like to be honest about what I need and how to accept help, instead of coping alone. Celina listens to me, even when our appointments go long. Over the years, the various roles she plays in my emotional life allow me to revisit the relationship skills I did not learn as a child. Being seen and heard — and accepted — by Celina undoes the shame that I carry.

One day, during an open-house celebration at the clinic, I also learn how to set boundaries. Celina and I are talking, then someone goes by and Celina turns — and places her hand on my hip. I think about this for a long time afterward, and I decide that Celina won't punish me if I pay more attention to how touchy-feely and familiar we're getting. So I draw back a little, try not to be so *out there* with her, while still maintaining all the other aspects of our relationship. And it works: I draw back, our relationship stops raising the eyebrows of her colleagues, and she still respects me and is there for me. This is the first time I have ever felt control in any relationship. When Celina asks if she can start the treatment each week, I learn that it is my right to say yes or no.

I learn some valuable skills in my family. Needing to be alert for changes in my mother's mood teaches me to be observant of the minute details of word choice, subtle body language, and tone of voice — skills that benefit me to this day. And although my father pressures me to function at a level far beyond my years, having to answer questions about his diagrams and installation plans leaves me with the sense that I must pay attention and learn everything I can about the world around me — an inclination that also benefits me to this day.

Patti LaBoucane-Benson, writing about the pre-colonial Nehiyawak worldview, says that before residential schools, "the family was the all-encompassing unit — a mediator between the individual and the social, economic, and political spheres of a larger society." However, colonization and government efforts to assimilate Indigenous peoples have now "deprived [Indigenous] children of the principal agency that helps them make sense of the world. . . . The loss of connections and communication between children and their parents and grandparents severely damaged essential family relationships, blocking the transmission of cultural, ethical, and normative knowledge between generations." The intergenerational consequences of these damaged family relationships have led to what Nehiyaw elder Fred Campiou describes as "sinning against your children," creating what he calls "conflict, division, hardship, animosity, and resentment."

The hardship that Campiou refers to is partly the hardship caused by isolation. Many of the difficulties experienced by Indigenous peoples are caused by isolation: the lack of family, friendships, and other relationships (such as with teachers or mentors) that provide guidance and support in moments of need and offer an individual the chance to share their pain and joy. Indigenous people often lack these circles of support, and the resulting isolation can have a profound effect on self-esteem, sense of belonging, achievement, daily survival, and an individual's ability to work toward growth and change. Family breakdown caused by the everyday impacts of trauma is one factor behind this isolation, along with residential schools, foster care, adoption, and high rates of incarceration.

As the work of Judith Lewis Herman tells us, healing from trauma is about reconnection. It would seem to follow, then, that Indigenous peoples should pursue family connection as part of the path toward healing from intergenerational trauma and the effects of colonization. However, many of the everyday impacts of trauma — such as physical abuse, emotional abuse, and toxic communication patterns — are experienced by the individual within the context of family. For some survivors, seeking connection and creating circles of support outside of the family context is key to healing and change.

Throughout my life, my mother continually tells me that I am crazy. In Vancouver, she takes me to a child psychologist, who asks me to draw something. I draw a single candle with a flame, in shadow on one side, because I know it's an image I can draw well. I don't remember what he asks me, or what I tell him, but on the way home, my mother is angry and tells me that he "doesn't know anything," and we never go back. At 15, she takes me to a therapist in another city, and when he tells my mother in a family session that she could put up a curtain in our shared bedroom to give us each some privacy, she tells him she will but doesn't. Then she tells me that I am abusing her.

When I am 15 and my mother takes two vintage tops out of my closet for cleaning — exactly half of the four shirts I own — I ask her a week later if they're back, and she says, "What tops?" So I remind her, and she says, "Oh, those things? I gave them away." When I ask, "What am I going to wear now?" her answer is, "You never wore those." Weeks later, when she loses the last two shirts I own in the laundry room dryer, she tells me that she'll replace them, then screams at me and demands that I give her half of every paycheque because I cost her so much money. Then she asks me to "lend" her the money to join the dating service where she meets her third husband.

When I move to Toronto at age 22 and begin creating circles of support for myself, I finally realize that the world is not how my mother sees it, and that the things my family tells me about myself simply aren't true. I learn how to hold on to my own reality alongside my mother's interpretation of events, to a point where I start feeling less unsafe around her. And I never give up hope that someday she will find her healing.

In 1994, when my name finally comes up on the waiting list at a housing co-op in Toronto, I give my mother my spot and then spend the summer painting and fixing up the apartment for her. When she has a housewarming party, I invite my friends because she has none of her own. I take her to the friendship centre and the Indigenous health centre, and when she tells me that she's going to talk with the elder next month, I tell her that I'm happy for her. So when I walk away from my mother in 1996, it's not because I don't care. When I walk away, it is because I finally realize that my life is my own. I have my own healing to accomplish, and I cannot do that work when I am part of a toxic family system. When I walk away from her and then from other family members, it is an act of self-preservation. I save myself, because I cannot save them.

In my family, it was never safe to grieve what happened to us. Once I leave them behind — because their paths are theirs to take — I am able to work through the anger I feel toward my mother. This allows me to reveal the fear that underlies that anger. When I get rid of the fear, I can feel the grief. Then I can mourn, and create something new.

CHAPTER 6

FRACTURED NARRATIVES

All my life, the images are in my head. They're disjointed, and they don't tell a story. They are flashes, scenes, disconnected bits of experience without context or meaning. They feel like clues. They will not go away.

Scene #1: I am sitting on the floor of an empty apartment. I am in the kitchen, against a wall. The walls are white. The kitchen is in the back of the building. I am sitting, and I reach over to pull up my sock. I took a family member's socks the other day, without permission. They're knee socks, with orange and white horizontal stripes. The first time I wore them, I took a pair of scissors and cut the elastic at the top just to see what would happen. Now they're falling down on one side, and I know I'm going to be in trouble. I am sitting on the floor in the kitchen. I am pulling up my sock.

Scene #2: I am sitting on the floor in the kitchen, and my father is with me. He has a camera in his hand. He opens the sheer drapes on the window with one hand, sweeping right to left, and looks into the back parking lot. We are on the second floor of the building. We are waiting for someone.

Scene #3: A family member has taken me to the hospital. I fell off my bike this morning, and my hand hurts, so she thinks something might be broken. There is a man, a doctor, sitting in a chair in front of us as we stand there. I see a messy desk and a window into the rest of the building, not outside, and it's weird to be taller than the doctor. The doctor says he needs to examine me. I say, "Do I have to take my shirt off?" He laughs and says, "No, I don't think that will be necessary." All day, this family member complains about how weird I am. "Why did you say that?" she says.

Scene #4: It's 1975, and we are driving to High Level, Alberta, in my father's red Econoline van. My father is driving, my mother is in the passenger seat, and I'm bouncing around in the back. They're talking about the new store they're opening in High Level. My mother says it's a dumb idea, and why did my father buy this building anyway? It's the only time we travel there as a family. The store never opens.

Scene #5: My father is driving me to his friend Maggie's house. She doesn't live with her husband anymore. I tell him I don't want to go. He tries to convince me, saying, "I'll drive you there, then I'll pick you up and we'll go home, okay?" In my four-year-old mind, I think this means that we will drive there and then turn around and go home again. So I agree, and I am glad that I don't have to go to Maggie's. When we get there, he gets out of the van, and I ask him why we're not going home. "You said you would drive me home." He laughs and says, "No, pumpkin, that's

silly. You stay here for a while and I'll come and get you after —
then we'll go home." I walk inside. I am betrayed. I eat cereal in
Maggie's kitchen, coloured sugary stuff my mother doesn't allow
us to have.

Scene #6: Maggie is at my parents' store on Main Street in Peace
River, Alberta. We are in the staff area, in the back. Maggie reaches
across me and unplugs the electric kettle. She picks the kettle up,
and when she moves it toward her mug, the water splashes out of
the spout and onto my leg. My mother says, "You did that on purpose!" Maggie replies, "I did not." Maggie doesn't apologize and
my mother doesn't ask if I'm okay. I don't cry or complain. There
is a scar on my thigh for years afterward, a pattern of four dark
brown circles, each one smaller in size than the last.

Scene #7: Maggie lives in the low rentals now, with her three
sons. When my father leaves me there, I usually go out back in
the alley and play by myself. But sometimes I hang out with her
son Harold, who is older. We play ballerina sometimes, and he
likes to lift me. I don't like how his hand feels, holding me up by
my crotch, but it's part of the game. I like it better when we play
dress-up and he puts makeup and clothes on me.

Scene #8: We are in the yellow bedroom in the two-storey
house. Someone older tells me we are playing a game. He tells
me to put my arms around him and to roll across the beds with
him. There are two single beds in this room, which he pushes
together. Then he tells me we're going to practise kissing. So
we roll across the bed again. His mouth is all wet. I do it because
he tells me to.

Scene #9: Another time, nighttime, and we are sleeping in the
yellow room, on our sides so we both fit on one bed. I feel his hand
on my bum. I don't like it, and I say, "Your hand's on my bum." He
takes his hand away, but he tells me he's disappointed that I would
say such a thing. He says, "I wasn't touching you."

Scene #10: This one isn't a solitary image or scene. It's more like a thematic series. I can be walking down the street, or standing at a bus stop, or watching traffic go by my window. In my mind's eye, I see myself falling and breaking a leg. I see a car plow into me from the traffic outside the bus shelter. I see cars hitting each other outside my window. These things never happen. The world doesn't disappear. I see these things on top of what I already see, like it's something I can expect at any moment.

Scene #11: It's 2014, and I am in the kitchen of my rented apartment in an old house in Toronto. I've repurposed an old closet that doesn't have a door and made it into a pantry/storage space. I walk past it toward the fridge, and I see a severed head inside, below the metal IKEA shelves that hold my laundry soap and clothespins. I immediately look away, frightened. Then I stop. I say in my head, *Well, that's clearly not possible.* So I walk backward, retracing my steps so that I am once again across from the pantry/storage. I turn my head to the left, and I make myself look again. What I see this time is a 40-pound bag of cat litter, orange and white with some light shining on it from the window. The top is cut ragged and rolled down in a haphazard way. That's my bloody severed head: just a bag of cat litter, not rolled up properly and out of place. I stand there a minute. I'm okay. Then I walk to the fridge.

Some people who experience a traumatic event have a continuous memory of it. Other people have fragmented flashbacks. Still others have complete amnesia in relation to the experience. Two main factors influence memory in an individual: the nature and frequency of the traumatic events and the age at which they occur. A single traumatic event, such as assault or witnessing a murder, is more likely to be remembered. Chronic trauma, such as ongoing domestic violence or repeated torture, often results in memory disturbance. Adults are more likely to remember traumatic events than children. The younger a child is at the time of a traumatic event, the less likely the event will be remembered.

There are three stages involved in forming memories: encoding, when the brain processes the event by changing it into a picture, sound, body feeling, or meaning; storage, which is when the individual's body-mind decides where the memories will be stored and for how long; and retrieval, which is the act of remembering. The way we encode information affects how we retrieve it. Traumatic memories are encoded differently than ordinary memories, because when the brain is under stress, events tend to be stored in the part of the brain that processes emotions and sensations but not speech or reasoning. This is why survivors of trauma may live their lives with sensory knowledge of an experience that they cannot consciously recall. They recall the terror, anger, and sadness of an event, but they cannot create a narrative — a story — that explains the feelings they carry with them on a daily basis. They may have mental photographs, but they are not able to construct a coherent story out of those visual pictures. When present-day sights, sounds, smells, or other associations create distressing feelings, the survivor is unable to connect them to a past event that helps make sense of what they are feeling. In some cases, the survivor will act out in anger as a way to control these overwhelming feelings. In other cases, survivors respond by dissociating from what they feel, creating a separation among mind, body, and spirit that protects them from having to confront the traumatic memory.

Survivors with sensory knowledge but no narrative memory of a traumatic event often engage in re-enactments. This is why so many Indigenous survivors of trauma come into conflict with the law for interpersonal crimes such as assault or sexual assault — because they are re-enacting what they themselves have experienced. Other survivors re-enact by engaging in risky behaviour in which they attempt to change the outcome of the original event — but which only puts them at risk for further violence and exploitation. This is a huge factor in the phenomenon of missing and murdered Indigenous women and girls.

When survivors of trauma do not have, or are unable to create, a coherent narrative of their traumatic experience, they are unable to create meaning from it. As a result, they carry a sense of victimization, helplessness, and betrayal that they constantly try to avoid, or for which they constantly try to construct explanations. The problem is these explanations bear little or no relationship to the original traumatic event. They don't help the survivor create meaning from their experience, to learn and recover from it, and they often disrupt the survivor's relationships, employment, and life in the present day.

Carrying a sense of victimization, helplessness, and betrayal often creates deep, unexplained feelings of shame and guilt in the survivor. During the traumatic experience, the individual first feels anxiety, because they are facing death. Eventually, however, the survivor must accept that they can no longer resist, so they shift from anxiety to passivity and surrender. This often leads to feelings of guilt for somehow failing to fight back or prevent the traumatic situation. To survive daily life with these feelings of shame, guilt, and self-blame, survivors often engage in psychic numbing, where they display a diminished capacity or inclination to feel. This numbness also helps them live with the unnamed, unassimilated, and often terrifying images that they carry.

When these fragmented bits of sensory memory intrude on the present day, survivors can enter a dissociative state, where they lose awareness of who they are and where they are, essentially returning to the time of the original trauma. In this dissociated state, they often re-enact the events of the past without conscious knowledge of what they are doing or why.

Although I don't know it at the time, I re-enact the sexual abuse I experience as a young child over and over in my adult life. At 15, I give the driver on the bus route my phone number when I get off at my stop because he looks at me in the rearview mirror. At 16, I talk to my friend Shauna's dad like we're the only two people in the car as he drives us to a choir gig, playing to the eyes in the rearview mirror. At 21, I let the Aussie guy on the staff camping trip invite himself into my tent. When I leave to brush my teeth the next morning and return to find he's done a disappearing act, I feel a flood of immense relief and a terrible abandonment. At 30, the contractor guy who's been hired to fix the radiator in my apartment seems nice, so I get into the shower even though he's there and parade through the apartment in my bathrobe. At 39, I allow myself to be cornered by a predator super-intendent in the bathroom of an empty apartment I'm viewing on St. Clair Avenue West in Toronto, and instead of running, I become passive, because that's what I learned to do to survive childhood abuse. When I get home, I kick my clothes under the chair in my bedroom. The mound is like some sort of symbol, and I spend a week looking at it every morning when I get up and then every night when I go to sleep. I'm trying to make sense of this part of the story — trying to figure out why I do things I don't want to do — but I haven't yet made the necessary connection to past experience that will help me understand. I still don't have a coherent narrative of my traumatic experience.

Individuals who have learned to use dissociation to manage the overwhelming feelings associated with their original traumatic experience often use it as a coping mechanism in daily life. This reliance on dissociation often makes it impossible for the survivor to connect emotionally with other people in any capacity, making intimacy and adult relationships — whether platonic or roman-tic — impossible or problematic. It also means that the survivor is disconnected from their own feelings and sense of self, which leads to self-blame when bad things happen.

I do not date as a teenager, in my 20s, or in my 30s, because I am terrified of other people and convinced that I am unlovable. I do get involved in situations where I am preyed upon or treated as an object, however, usually in one-time-only encounters but a few times in repeat circumstances with people I might know casually from a workplace or the Indigenous community. Many times, they do not take the bait (like the bus driver, Shauna's dad, or the contractor). I initiate these re-enactments because at some level I know they won't respond, which makes it safe to look for the love I am searching for. With others — like the Aussie and the predator superintendent — I do not initiate but also don't do anything to get myself out of the situation. These patterns of behaviour are a repeat of the trauma I experience as a child, and some men are very good at recognizing it. They see my brokenness and they use it to get what they want. In other cases, I re-enact with Indigenous men who are themselves the survivors of sexual abuse, not because I'm attracted to them but because it is expected. Dissociation makes it easy for people to do things without actually having awareness of what it is that they are doing, or why.

In 2017, 62-year-old Dale Stonechild is sentenced to 15 years in federal prison for killing 84-year-old Victor McNab in Regina, Saskatchewan, in 2013. According to Stonechild, the two are hanging out at McNab's house when McNab makes a comment about a prior relationship he'd had with Stonechild's mother and calls himself a "rude old man." The comment enrages Stonechild, who says at trial that he stood up to confront the older man but doesn't remember anything else after that. According to the testimony of a forensic pathologist, McNab dies from blunt and sharp-force trauma after suffering 16 stab wounds, at least 30 blows to the head and face, and a broken back.

According to the pre-sentence report, Stonechild is a valued member of the community, an accomplished dancer and artist who studied fine art at university. He is also a survivor of the Gordon Residential School, where he was sexually, physically, and emotionally abused for seven years, then expelled and assigned to live at four different foster homes. He was first convicted of a crime in 1972; most of his convictions are for violent crimes. Stonechild was clearly triggered by the mention of a man "being rude" (having sex) with his mother. The subsequent blackout indicates a dissociative state, a coping mechanism Stonechild likely returns to time and time again in order to manage the distressing feelings created by his own traumatic experiences, for which he has no coherent narrative.

To heal from a traumatic event, the survivor needs to create a coherent story that helps them understand that *something has happened to them*, and that this event, or series of events, is the reason why they feel the things they feel. Creating a narrative also helps the survivor see who or what is responsible for that event, which helps them understand that they were the victim and are not to blame for the original event. As the survivor becomes more aware of the various elements of the traumatic narrative — what happened, when it happened, who was responsible, who was a bystander, and the effects the event has had on their thoughts and feelings — then they are able to see how the traumatic event has impacted their behaviours and their choices in life. As a result of this process, the survivor begins to mend the separation between sensory knowledge, memory, and their concept of self. The survivor can then build a new sense of who they are inside and who they are in relation to other people. This sets the stage for living in the present, instead of recreating the sensory memory of the past.

When trauma is unnamed and unassimilated, the imprints and effects can be passed down from parent to child, demonstrated in daily interactions that allow the parent's psychic state to take root in the child's unconscious.

In my mother's diary, she writes about her family history of sexual abuse: "My father made it very clear to me, both by words and actions, that I was not his child and I was to stay away from him. Maybe because of that I was saved the most damaging effects. My sister was not so lucky. She was sexually abused by our father. He used to sit my sister on his lap all the time and hug her. As young children my sister and I would bathe together, but I was hurriedly dried and told to get out and my father would go and lock the bathroom door, telling me he was going to wash my sister. I thought that Father loved my sister and didn't love me. Sunday morning my sister was always anxious to go downstairs and get into bed with Mommy and Daddy. I would be left standing at the bedside, asking if I could please come into bed, too. As we grew older, our father took to taking his girls to the park on Sunday afternoon. Stanley Park is well known for its lovely wooded areas and nature trails. What transpired was for me a confusing and unhappy time, as we always seemed to walk farther and farther into the woods. Father would tell me not to wander away and he and my sister would disappear. I spent most Sunday afternoons alone on a trail waiting for Father to return and tell me we would now be leaving for home. I learned by grade 3 or 4 how to create a world right inside my own head. I was good at letting my mind go wherever I wished to go. I was oblivious to pain and acquired the ability to put on a mask of indifference. I didn't know how to act or get along with anybody."

After I leave babyhood, my mother never hugs me or demonstrates any affection toward me whatsoever. My father, on the other hand, dotes on me and shows immense delight in everything I accomplish. He often takes me out of school, so I can accompany him on his service calls. He uses up roll after roll of film taking pictures of me. In many photos in the family album, I am posing for my father's camera and my mother is behind me in the frame, looking at the two of us intently but without any emotion on her face. Because she does not have a coherent narrative of her childhood experiences and how they have affected her adult life — both in terms of the men she marries or the way she parents her children — she is living out her childhood experiences in the present day, competing with me for my father's affection. I become her sister, and she projects this hatred on to me.

From the diary: "Sister: I don't know who you are. You're my enemy, someone who lies in wait for me, waits to catch me doing something wrong so you can go and tell your mom or dad. You never have to do any household chores, instead you practise your piano lessons. I know I can play the piano better, but I just can't compete with you for affection. It's always you who is asked to play for company, it's you who is praised for your talent."

My mother could have an identity as an artist (she paints with oils), a pianist (in 1950, she records two 78 rpm audio discs at recording studios in Vancouver), a model and actor (she is a catalogue model in the 1950s and works as a film extra and print model in the 1990s), a business owner, or any number of other things that she has accomplished in her life, but she doesn't talk about these things. She is so numb and dissociated that she doesn't realize that she's repeating her past in our shared current reality. Her lack of a coherent narrative also prevents her from seeing her own mother's trauma, and how those experiences have affected her mother's parenting. There is a reason why Thelma marries an abusive man, why she drinks too much, and why she takes to her bed and does not call for help when she develops gangrene in her leg (which is amputated as a result). But my mother's distress-related self-centredness prevents her from seeing her own experiences as part of a larger story.

My mother says her mother "passes through life as in a dream, avoiding all reality, staying only within her selfish little world she has created. Doing her hair, always doing her hair, spending her time before the mirror. Going to work, work she doesn't have to do, but a nice safe job to help escape whatever she imagines she must escape from. Mother going out in the evening. What words can I use to describe this woman. Selfish, yes. Stupid? I don't know, maybe she was just not capable of orderly and clear thought. Uncommunicative certainly, unfit to be a mother definitely."

When I read my mother's description of Thelma, I see that most of it also applies to her. Although her economic circumstances are different — my mother helps with my father's business and also takes outside jobs to make ends meet — they both share a tendency to dissociate and to reinvent reality when they are asked to be accountable. But because she has no coherent narrative to help her make meaning of past events and current realities, my mother sees herself only as a victim, not as a perpetrator. As a result, my own narrative and sense of self are altered, and I become confused by the reality of my own experience. I begin to minimize or deny my own point of view in order to adapt to my mother's distorted sense of who I am. This leaves me at risk for further abuse, as I consistently undermine my own thoughts and feelings in order to make room for my mother's projections.

Creating a coherent narrative after surviving a traumatic experience (or chronic trauma) is not merely an intellectual process. Because traumatic memories are encoded as sensory knowledge, they can't be retrieved in the same way as everyday memories. The process of remembering — of creating a story — requires the survivor to have a sense of their physical self: how they felt at the time of the traumatic event, how they feel now, the links between how they felt/feel and how that mediates their response to everyday stressors, and the ways in which they respond to reminders of the event. I don't have a coherent narrative for the first 40 years of my life because I also don't have any sense of my physical body. This is a common phenomenon for survivors of childhood sexual abuse, who tend to dissociate at the time of the original trauma in order to survive the experience.

When I am in grade 4, one of my stories is published in the school newspaper: "We lived on a beautiful planet, but Martians invaded it and blew it to pieces. My family and a few friends are the only survivors. We have been travelling in space for a century. I am 2,000 years old. We wear spacesuits outside but inside we wear skirts, and we all have beautiful long blond hair. My planet is all girls. My planet is a peaceful planet. We have no weapons: but that will soon end. Gazoo, from Venus, and Gonzo, from Neptune, will come to my planet. They will capture me." When I find this story in a scrapbook at the age of 40, I laugh at (and then cry for) my 10-year-old two-spirit self, fantasizing about living on a planet full of girls while still parroting my mother's insistence that I wear long hair and a skirt. But I still don't see the rest of what I'm writing about — the trauma narrative that I'm unable to properly retrieve — until a couple of years later, when I'm working with Celina.

One day, Celina taps acupuncture needles into my back to correct my alignment, and I feel my body shift: a leg dropping and my hips straightening out. It's the first time I actually feel my body from inside. When I lie down in bed that night, I feel longer somehow, flatter, the entire length of my body on the mattress. I notice it because it's different. My lower back is touching the bed. I feel my whole body, from top to bottom, grounded. So I try to imitate what it was like before, because I need to compare, to understand the difference. I don't know how to do this exactly, but as soon as I move, my lower back moves up and away from the mattress. My body knows this position, and now that I am aware of it, I know what it means: I was arched away from him, from them, my entire life, *no no don't* my way of being in the world. Thirty years after I write the grade 4 story, I realize what it means: they did capture me, but now I'm free. And you don't have to be blond to be safe or beautiful. Retrieving the memories of sexual abuse — why I spend my life arched away from the perpetrators — only becomes possible once the encoded images stored in my head and the encoded postures stored in my body coalesce into a coherent narrative.

Prior to colonization, every Indigenous community in the Americas had customs of behaviour that communicated social norms and embodied moral codes and notions of justice. Trickster stories illustrated the consequences of going against accepted norms and codes. And many Indigenous nations had strict social customs that prohibited — or strictly regulated the conditions for — communication between siblings or family members of the opposite sex. There were boundaries and codes that taught people how to think of other people, how to interact with other people, and how to understand the sacred nature of sexual connection. When colonization broke those boundaries and codes apart — through cultural genocide, the residential school system, and the resulting everyday impacts of trauma — behaviour between people and within families began to change. Today, Justice Canada reports that sexual abuse committed against children is "quite prevalent" within Indigenous communities, with studies showing that up to 50 per cent of Indigenous women are victims of sexual abuse as children (compared to 25 per cent within the non-Indigenous population). Some studies indicate that sexual abuse in Indigenous communities is most often committed by someone in the victim's immediate or extended family, while other studies have found that sexual abusers also come from a wide circle of people outside the family, such as friends, neighbours, and peers. The numbers are sure to be distorted by the fact that many survivors do not have a coherent narrative of their childhood trauma, making it impossible for them to report the abuse.

The Department of the Solicitor General refers to the sexual abuse of children in Indigenous communities as a "family system disease." In many families, children are abused in the exact same way in which the perpetrator was themself abused as a child. This family system disease has disastrous effects on children and youth, leading to feelings of shame, self-blame, and depression. Children are dependent on their parents and caregivers, so they will protect that relationship and maintain an idealized view of the family member no matter what that person does to them. There is no room in their worldview for a caregiver that harms them, so children often come to believe that they have done something to deserve the abuse, or that they are unworthy of attention and care. This then becomes the only narrative they have.

A 2012 study conducted in northern Ontario clearly shows the connection between the sexual abuse of children and the suicide crisis in many communities. As a study participant says, "There were nine [youth] suicides in . . . [our community in one year] and 100 attempts. . . . A healer was hired . . . to deal with these kids having suicidal ideation. One hundred per cent of the girls and 60 per cent of the boys had been sexually abused at home." Sexual abuse is also behind much of youth substance abuse. According to Jason Smallboy, the deputy grand chief of the Nishnawbe Aski Nation in northern Ontario, "If somebody's addicted to alcohol or drugs, there's a reason — and probably 80 per cent, 90 per cent, is related to sexual abuse."

However, despite the widespread nature of sexual abuse in many Indigenous communities, much of the abuse remains secret. This culture of silence not only prevents survivors from creating a coherent narrative of their own — due to a lack of support and few or no opportunities to share their experiences with others — but also prevents the community from creating the collective narrative necessary for confronting the painful legacy of colonization and beginning the process of healing.

"Sexual abuse is not talked about," says Laura MacKenzie, a former president of the Rankin Inlet, Nunavut, women's shelter. After MacKenzie testifies at the National Inquiry into Missing and Murdered Indigenous Women and Girls in Nunavut in 2018, she makes a plea to her community on APTN National News: "Let's quit turning a blind eye to this. Too many family members stay silent."

The silence is not limited to Indigenous communities, however. There is a resounding government silence around the subject of sexual abuse of children in Indigenous communities. When a House of Commons committee releases a 2017 report on youth suicide, Liberal MP and committee chair MaryAnn Mihychuk says, "We have heard and we know that there is significant sexual abuse in Indigenous communities," before also saying that the issue was raised "lightly" due to the sensitive nature of the topic. This reluctance to directly confront the issue has major implications for policy and program development, as well as for public and media discourse.

To combat the silence around sexual abuse, some people in the Anishinabek community of Hollow Water, Manitoba, have created "abuse family trees" as part of their healing journey, showing the names of family members and the different impacts of everyday trauma they have each experienced. By mapping out the legacy of abuse within their families, survivors in Hollow Water have begun to understand that perpetrators are also survivors, and that what they have experienced at the hands of those perpetrators is part of an intergenerational cycle created by the impact of colonization. This helps the Hollow Water survivors create their own narrative, so they can make meaning not only of their experiences, thoughts, and feelings but also of the experiences of their

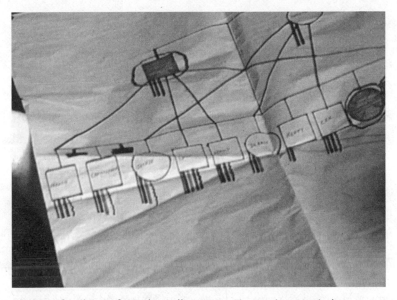

An abuse family tree from the Hollow Water First Nation, Manitoba

(*Hollow Water* © 2000 National Film Board of Canada)

ancestors. This connection to an ancestral narrative is important, because lateral violence within Indigenous communities has negative effects on cultural identity. Survivors often carry a deep mistrust of their own community and the people in it.

Sexual abuse in childhood has negative effects on an individual's personal identity, including their sexual identity. Survivors frequently have difficulties developing intimate relationships, engaging in sexual relations, and discovering who they are as sexual beings. Survivors who were abused by someone of the same sex often find themselves engaging in same-sex re-enactments, even when they know that they are heterosexual. Survivors who were abused by someone of the opposite sex often find themselves engaging in opposite-sex re-enactments, as I did, even when they know they are gay. Developing a coherent narrative is key to overcoming feelings of helplessness and developing a sense of agency.

When I'm 12 years old, I spend entire evenings staring at the *Bad Habits* album cover by The Monks. I can't take my eyes off the woman's legs, or her black stockings. When I'm 14, some girl asks me if I'm a lez, and I say no because I know that's bad, but I spend a long time afterward staring at a picture of Rough Trade singer Carole Pope, as if there's a message there for me to decipher. At 17, I'm reading *Vanity Fair* with my friend Nancy on the bus, and I'm not interested in any of the pictures she points out. But then I finally see a boy I like, so I say, "Oh, wow, look at this guy! He's so hot!" and Nancy says, "Oh my god, Sue! That's a girl!!" At 29, at the Pilot on Dyke Night, dragged there by a friend, sitting at a table with all these beautiful women, not dancing, I don't ever go back, but I start saying to some people that I guess I like girls or something. But since I still don't have a coherent narrative, I spend another 10 years re-enacting my abuse and embarking on relationships with straight girls who like the flowers and attention but don't ask for sex. When I hook up with a custodian at the school where I teach, I get quiet and withdrawn, and he says, "Are you into this?" because he thinks I don't like the DVD he brought. Finally, after a few months of acupuncture with Celina, the day comes when my mind, body, and spirit start telling the same story. I leave a meeting with a colleague and I say in my head, *Uh oh. She likes me. So . . . this again* — and I actually hear myself. I stop dead in the street, annoying everyone because this is Toronto and sidewalks are for walking, and I say to myself, *What do you mean, "This again"? What's this? Did you not come out over a decade ago?* Then: *So why have you never been in a relationship with an actual lesbian?* And I finally know what it is to hear myself in my own lies, in the silence that means I don't have to feel.

The powerlessness felt by a survivor of childhood sexual abuse can, in many cases, propel them to seek control and power over others. When a survivor-perpetrator connects with a victim, they imagine the victim as devalued, worthless, and dirty — all feelings they have about themself — which allows the survivor-perpetrator to project their helplessness, shame, rage, and self-hatred onto the victim. By projecting these emotions onto the victim, the survivor-perpetrator feels powerful once again. When the victim is forced to play a central role in the survivor-perpetrator's re-enactment of their own traumatic experience, these emotions then become part of the victim-survivor's unconscious life. This forces the victim-survivor to be in a relationship with the survivor-perpetrator long after the abuse has stopped. Instead of living their own story, victim-survivors end up living in the context of the survivor-perpetrator's story.

When the survivor creates a coherent narrative for themselves — creating a story with details about who, when, where, how they felt then, and how they feel now — they are able to name the traumatic event(s). This helps them externalize it. By separating themselves from the event — placing it outside themselves — they are able to separate themselves from the survivor-perpetrator's story, the beliefs they have internalized, and the explanations they have created to help them make sense of their feelings. Once the individual has externalized the event, they are able to see that any difficulties they may be experiencing in life are not rooted in who they are but in what they have experienced. This, in turn, makes it possible for them to imagine change — whether they are the survivor-perpetrator or the victim-survivor.

The justice system in Canada recognizes the impacts of chronic and intergenerational trauma on offenders, as well as the necessity of creating a narrative about those experiences. In an effort to deal with the overrepresentation of Indigenous peoples in the criminal justice system, section 718.2(e) of the Criminal Code allows judges to consider the life history of the offender during sentencing. Under this section, which is known as the Gladue decision, offenders can be diverted from prison and into programs — such as transitional housing, addiction- or anger-management sessions, a life rehabilitation program, sessions with elders, and sweat lodge ceremonies — that aim to help the offender. A Gladue report takes into account the offender's life history and experiences, including whether they attended residential school, grew up in a home where there was poverty or domestic violence, were physically or sexually abused as a child, whether they were removed from their home by the child welfare system, or have developmental, medical, or mental health issues such as fetal alcohol spectrum disorder (FASD) or addictions.

The Gladue decision isn't about Indigenous offenders getting off easy. It's about getting to the root causes of why an individual is in conflict with the law and then applying sentences that aid the offender in the kind of self-discovery and personal change that will keep them from returning to prison. A Gladue report externalizes traumatic events. When offenders are given the opportunity to think about the events that have created them — and the patterns of behaviour they have developed in response — they are also given an opportunity to begin a journey of self-discovery that can lead to healing and real rehabilitation. When offenders understand how the events of colonization have affected their lives — and when they understand that there are reasons why they do the things they do — they can begin to build an identity that disrupts their feelings of shame and self-blame, concentrating instead on their resiliency and their strengths, and how they might use those skills and those aspects of their personality to make changes in their lives.

As Senator Murray Sinclair said in a speech to the Aboriginal Justice Learning Network, "We have not been able to give our young people their sense of identity. . . . Each and every young person who comes before me in court is weighed down by that burden, and when I look at the options available to me as judge,

I think, *Well, I can impose a fine. Now, if I fine him $50, is that going to give him his sense of identity?* Well, no . . . So how about if I put him on probation and make him go and report to a white probation officer downtown, will that give him his identity? Well, I don't know, maybe it would. It would depend on the probation officer. . . . Maybe if I send this person to jail . . . maybe that will give him a sense of his identity. The sad reality is there is an awful truth to that. . . . The reality is that some of our men and women do find their answer through learning their culture while they are incarcerated."

Jerry Adams, a member of the Gitlaxt'aamiks First Nation and the CEO of the Circle of Eagles Lodge Society in Vancouver, BC — a halfway house that works with formerly incarcerated men from across Canada — says that most of the lodge's clients are products of violent, abusive homes. "We get the end results," Adams told the CBC in 2016. "They murdered somebody, sexually assaulted somebody. We see the worst part of who they are. But if you talk to them, they're people who have many regrets about what they've done. We try to change their lives around to reintegrate them into the community."

Reintegration into community is a critical function of creating a coherent narrative. When formerly incarcerated people are able to create an externalized narrative, they are able to gain the kind of insight that makes them better able to connect with other people, create intimate relationships, and make meaningful contributions to their communities. Adams thinks that Indigenous communities should reintegrate sexual offenders, rather than ostracize, punish, or banish them. As Adams says, "They've got stories; they need to tell that to the community. 'This is what I did. I don't want my nephews and nieces doing what I did.'" When individual narratives are understood as part of the collective narrative, it helps people create meaning on both the individual and collective levels. This meaning-making helps create healing. Ostracizing and banishing survivor-perpetrators only leads to further silence around the issue of sexual abuse, because it erases the stories that can help create understanding about intergenerational cycles of trauma.

As Sinclair points out in his speech, "For most Aboriginal people, criminality is often a forced state of existence, a direct result of their inability to function as individuals, as human beings in society." Creating a coherent narrative is a central pillar in becoming functional and connected to something other than the traumatic experience.

After 22-year-old James Clifford Paul attacks and sexually assaults a seven-year-old girl on the Paul First Nation in Alberta in 2014, he is sentenced to 10 years in prison: four years for sexual assault and six years for aggravated assault. Paul admitted that he lured the girl away from her family and sexually assaulted her, leaving her naked in the snow. When the girl follows him and begs him not to leave her, he beats her until she is unconscious and throws her in a bush. At a sentencing hearing in 2016, after reading Paul's Gladue report, the judge states, "Given his tragic upbringing . . . it's no surprise to see Mr. Paul, at such a young age, before the court. But the offences here are of unspeakable violence. . . . I struggle with the nature of this offence, notwithstanding his background and the difficulties Mr. Paul had growing up. I struggle with how he got to the heinousness of this offence on a young child."

To those who work with survivors of trauma, the offence (perhaps a re-enactment, perhaps a survivor seeking power over another) and Paul's choice of victim (someone who, given his actions, he clearly sees as devalued, worthless, and dirty — which is likely also how he sees himself) are actually unsurprising. As Paul's family says in a statement, the community is dealing with "drugs, alcohol, violence, threats, abuse, and more and more suicides." After Paul is arrested, his family, including his parents and eight siblings, are forced to move away from the community after threats are made against them. This response robs the community of a narrative they could use to make meaning — and create change. To achieve healing and decolonization, Indigenous communities must create new narratives characterized by compassion and understanding instead of anger, blame, and revenge.

I see and hear fractured Indigenous narratives every day, all around me, in work and in life.

The Indigenous man on the Spadina streetcar in Toronto, smelling like mouthwash, talking out loud: "Why? Why? You tell me why." Then: "Time to go to sleep now. Go to sleep. Time to go to sleep." Then: "You're under arrest." The first is said with outrage, as if he is asking the people on the streetcar to be accountable for the myriad issues of colonization — or as if he is asking why he has experienced the things he has experienced in his life. The second comment could be the words of his abuser, or the words of the one person who protected him, loved him, and made him feel safe. He says the last comment to a child on the streetcar, and I'm willing to bet that this child is him and that he thinks he's responsible for his own traumatic past.

The Indigenous student at school who pulls up her sleeve to show me her upper arm: "Ms. Methot, have you ever had a big bruise? Look at mine." When I look at her arm, I see three or four small circular bruises in a fan shape. They look like finger marks. "Wow, how'd you get that?" I say. She looks down at her arm, squints her eyes, and hesitates before replying, perhaps because she is trying to remember, perhaps because she wants to protect her abuser. "I don't know. I think I fell and hit my arm." She has a fractured narrative and no sense of the story that is creating who she is in the world.

Pierre Gregoire, a 28-year-old Innu man who ODs on heroin and fentanyl in the bathroom of a KFC on Queen Street West in Toronto in 2017. At age three, he is taken from his home community of Sheshatshiu, Labrador, and put into foster care in the home of a loving family on the Kahnawake Mohawk Territory. He is raised with a pool in the backyard, dirt bikes, guitar lessons, family vacations, and spots on the hockey and lacrosse teams. He says his foster family are "amazing" parents who live their culture and love him "with all their hearts." But he keeps returning to Sheshatshiu, to his biological mother, searching for a reunification that is not possible due to her substance abuse and the unresolved trauma she carries as a result of her own past in the foster care system. It doesn't matter what his foster family in Kahnawake does, how much love and care they show him. Gregoire's narrative is "I am not lovable." He blames himself for his mother's inability to parent him, writing poetry that says, "So sorry, so sorry," and "It hurts / To know I can't be better."

Whenever I need some strength to continue, I think of the words of my colleague Marcel Petit, a Métis filmmaker, photographer, and playwright who works with Indigenous youth in Saskatoon, Saskatchewan. After our panel concludes at an arts education conference in Calgary, Alberta, in 2012, I meet Marcel on the sidewalk as we walk between the hotel and the conference venue. We stand in the snow for quite a while and talk about our families and our work. At some point, Marcel says, "I do this work because everything is not all right." His words remind me that the eastern quadrant of the medicine wheel is about vision. We have to see the whole story in order to create movement and change.

In my 40s, I create a coherent narrative out of the disconnected bits and pieces that have always been in my head. The story I manage to organize out of the visual fragments, intrusive images, everyday childhood memories, family photos, and facts my mother supplies is this: my father builds a darkroom in the basement of our house in Peace River. My father grooms me. There are pictures of me all over the family album, posing in different outfits, on the picnic table, on the swing, hamming it up for the camera. My mother finds pornographic photos of Maggie in the darkroom, taken in a sauna alongside other adults, having group sex. The kitchen is in the empty apartment above my father's store in High Level, the one that never opens. He brings me there to take pornographic pictures of me. There are other adults and other children involved, maybe the same people in the pictures with Maggie; that's who we're waiting for that day. Maggie's son Harold fondles me. It goes on for years, in the multiple places that Maggie lives. The person who denies touching me is surrounded by dysfunction. My father routinely has sex with my mother with the bedroom door open and even engages people in conversation while he is on top of her. The person who touched me is responsible for what they did but is not to blame. Their behaviour is a result of their experience, just as my father's behaviour is a result of his experience in the Duplessis orphanage. Understanding this fact allows me to let go of this story. They were victims, too.

The fragmented visual images go away once I create a coherent narrative. The scariest intrusive images — the car crashes and falls — also go away. One minor intrusive image still flashes in front of me sometimes, at times when I am facing an extreme stressor in my environment, so I think of it as a contrary-style protector. It reminds me to take care of myself.

Creating a coherent narrative isn't limited to stories of childhood sexual abuse or intergenerational trauma. In the wake of colonization, Indigenous peoples need to make (or remake) many narratives. One of the first coherent narratives I create — long before I am able to face the story of sexual abuse — is my identity narrative.

All my life, I am accepted by other Indigenous people as an Indigenous person, but as a child, I have no family stories that help me make sense of this. When I am young, my family story centres on our glorious settler narratives: Rebecca and John Scott, who arrive in Salem, Massachusetts, in 1648 before moving to Providence, Rhode Island, the brothers Samuel and Sylvanus Scott, who settle the town of Machias, Maine, in 1763 and are key players in the American Revolutionary War, and Ward Farrar, who is born in St. Andrews, New Brunswick, but enlists in the Union Army during the American Civil War and dies in New Orleans in 1862. My mother also tells me about the women: Ward's wife, Charity, and their daughter, Rebecca, who fight the U.S. government for Charity's share of Ward's war pension, and Rebecca's daughter, Bertha (Little Gramma), who volunteers in an emergency ward during BC's 1918 Spanish flu epidemic. Later, when my mother contacts the Red Cross Family Reunification program to find my father's birth mother, the narrative expands to include the French-Canadian side via Annie Charbonneau, who calls me "mon petit chouchou" and cooks me potato pancakes. Then Annie tells my mother about her parents. Turns out, Annie is actually Anna Mechenkov, and her upper-class, French-speaking, czar-supporting family had two choices in the Russian Revolution: exile or execution. I am lucky to have these stories, but none of them tell me how I am also Indigenous.

As a child, whenever I ask my mother if we have Indigenous ancestry, her standard response is "My father was Welsh. The Welsh are dark," which is inevitably followed, at some point, by "Well, my father wasn't my real father." And then my mother will say, "I was so happy when you were born. You had black hair and dark eyes, and when I saw you, I said, 'I have a little squaw baby!'" And then she puffs up with pride when we go to the Chippewas of Rama (Mnjikaning) powwow and the person at the registration table says, "Don't forget your change! Elders are two dollars." This cognitive dissonance — *we aren't, he isn't, you are, I am sometimes* — positions me within my mother's fractured narrative, unable to make sense of my own self and how I am seen by the external world. As an adult, I decide to make sense of all the pieces that aren't talked about or don't quite fit together, so that I have a coherent identity narrative of my own.

I ask the medicine person at the Indigenous health centre why I'm dreaming of bears all the time, and he says, "That's your clan. They're coming for you." Then a family member brings me a photo they take from my grandmother Thelma's photo album, showing a small band of Indigenous people on a prairie. It has no inscription, no names attached, but I get help from friends in Edmonton, the Saddle Lake First Nation, and Maskwacis, who tell me about the Smallboy Camp and the Rocky Mountain Cree. Then I receive my spirit name, and that's the final clue to my origin story. My community brings me home.

Little Gramma takes great pains to deny our family's Indigenous heritage. She marries a Peskotomuhkati man from New Brunswick but never speaks of his ancestry, and when her son, my great-uncle Bernard, marries a woman from the Skeetchestn First Nation in Savona, BC, the family narrative does not extend to include her origin story or any of her relations. And when Bernard and his wife have a son, he is raised white. Then Bernard's marriage ends and another Indigenous woman shows up pregnant at Little Gramma's door, but according to my mother, Little Gramma gives her some money and tells her never to come back. And although Little Gramma raises my mother, she never tells her anything about her father or the circumstances of her birth. But there are always people who mess with Little Gramma's agenda, including Bernard (who is dark-skinned), his out-of-wedlock daughter (who refuses to be disappeared), the

New Hampshire and California branches of the family (who tell me that Ward Farrar is also Peskotomuhkati — although they use the word Wabanaki), Thelma (who keeps the photo of my mother's father and his family, standing on the prairie), and me. I don't renounce my white people — culturally speaking, I am just as Scottish as I am Nehiyaw, and being of mixed ancestry gives me precious insider insight into more than one world — but I choose to reanimate the Indigenous narrative so that I can find the missing parts of myself. I realize the story is worth more than that when one day, my mother stops as we're walking down the street, turns to me, and says, "I think you were born to show me where I came from."

Sometime in 1993, I have a dream: a little girl in a bombed-out house, rubble, me holding her hand, taking her out, I know it's me, both of them, but I don't know what it means. For the next 20-plus years, I have recurring dreams about unknown apartments, always nonsensical, rooms and hallways that shouldn't connect, or should but don't, roundabout stairways and crawl spaces and always me, trying to find my way. Which door to use, where am I supposed to be, how do I get from one room to the other? Then I wake up one morning in 2016, and I realize with considerable amazement that the usual apartment dream has changed. In this dream, I am in my mother's apartment, and I am redecorating: hanging curtains, moving furniture, painting the door. Weeks later, I have another dream, and it's even more different: in this dream, I am in my current apartment. I am dreaming about the place where I actually live.

CHAPTER 7

WHAT THE BODY REMEMBERS

The headaches start in junior-high school. The dentist tells me he needs to take a wisdom tooth out. The headaches continue. By the time I'm 17, I can barely open my eyes when I go outside, because the light of the sun slices into my head like a machete. I am sent to a maxillofacial surgeon, who says I need the other three wisdom teeth out. After the surgery, I end up getting an infection, which means I get a cavity from not being able to brush my teeth properly. It's still the only filling I have. The headaches continue.

The headaches change as I grow into adulthood, settling themselves firmly in the back of my head. I take fistfuls of Tylenol Extra Strength tablets but nothing seems to work. It feels like someone is reaching in and grabbing the back of my head and squeezing it. Sometimes I get so angry at the pain that I slap my head, as if that might make it go away. I spend a day or two every month, sometimes twice a month, unable to function. I try to cry, but that just makes it hurt more. My medical doctor sends me for a CT scan. Nothing there except my brain.

In my last year of university, I spend most days lying in bed, punching the little metal snooze button on my wind-up clock. Every 10 minutes, I hear the racket of metal bells. And every 10 minutes, I hit the snooze button again. I have pain in my legs, pain in my head, pain everywhere. I miss lots of classes, and my 3.78 grade point average falls to 0.8, with a host of incompletes. When I go to the emergency room in the middle of the night, the nurse asks me where it hurts, and I tell her. Then another nurse asks me a little later, and I tell her. Then I hear the first nurse talking to the other nurse: "She said it was the right side. Now it's the left side. Presto change-o." They send me for physiotherapy I can't afford. The calf pain gets better but not for long.

In my 20s and 30s, I develop back problems. They come suddenly: I wake up one morning and every move I make turns into a spasm strong enough to unhinge my bones from my flesh. I am bent inward, over, crooked, stopped. Then the next day, or the day after that, I am fine. I spend days lying flat on the floor, watching the world go by outside my apartment in Toronto's Parkdale neighbourhood.

Then the digestion and elimination issues start. I eat, and then I have to spend half an hour in the bathroom. I think back: when I was young, I was always constipated. Now it's the other end of the spectrum. At an appointment, I tell my MD that the day before, I ate bruschetta at a restaurant and had to run to the bathroom in the subway station afterward. No one in their right mind uses a subway station bathroom. She says tomatoes can cause diarrhea but doesn't suggest any follow-up.

I seek care from the Indigenous health centre in the city. The old man who comes down every month from Manitoulin Island prescribes me a salve for a skin issue I've been dealing with for a couple of years. It goes away immediately and never comes back. When I tell him all my other symptoms, he gives me an herbal mixture and precise instructions: put a little bit of the mixture on the tip of the handle of a teaspoon. Right before bed, place the herbs into a bowl of warm but not boiling water. Drink it all, including the grounds. Do this for four nights. "People aren't sleeping properly," the old man says. "This will help with everything. You might have dreams." I sleep. I dream. A door opens, and the line between the everyday world and the spirit world becomes a little less defined. I begin to feel like there is something I need to know.

I have always been the sensitive one in the family. I have stomach aches as a child. I have sore throats and laryngitis. When I'm on the volleyball team in junior high, I come home from away games and puke up the host school's hot dogs. I watch my mother eat spoonfuls of brown sugar directly out of the jar and chew on Gelusil antacid tablets every night. I learn that weird food cravings and having a sore stomach is just part of every human being's life. Whenever I ask her about girl stuff — like discharge or cramps or heavy bleeding — she says, "Don't worry, it's normal." So I accept that these things are also just part of life. It will be another 20 years before I learn that she's wrong.

One night in 1994, I wake up with incredible pain in my lower abdomen. It's excruciating, so bad that all I can do is sit on the step in the hallway — the gateway between the basement and lower basement in my mouldy apartment near Toronto's Christie Pits — and rock back and forth, clutching my stomach and gasping for breath. I call my MD in the morning, and she sends me for an ultrasound. The ultrasound image reveals that I have at least 17 to 20 egg sacs attached to each ovary. The eggs haven't released, and the sacs holding the eggs haven't dissolved properly. When I ask what caused this, and what I should do, she tells me not to worry and to wait and see if it happens again. When I start having breast pain, I am sent for a mammogram. I'm only 32, and I know another test is not going to help. But I don't know what else to do. So I go and get my boobs squished between two cold machine plates. The pain continues.

This is the pattern: I complain about a negative physical experience or state, and I am sent for tests. Blood sugar, thyroid, CT scan, ultrasound, mammogram, pee bottle, more blood, repeat as necessary. Once, when I complain about heart palpitations, I am attached to a Holter heart monitor for two days. When the results are measured, the MD tells me it's nothing. It doesn't feel like nothing.

After I dislocate my left ankle while running for a streetcar — the joint spontaneously reduces while I'm waiting for the ambulance — St. Joseph's Hospital takes an x-ray, tells me nothing is broken, and sends me home. I tell them I can't walk, but they don't have any suggestions, and they don't give me a cane or a crutch. So I call a cab and hop on one leg back into my apartment, where I collapse on the couch and wail in pain. The next day, my foot is purple and blue and as big as a balloon, and my calf is swollen up to the knee. The fracture clinic at Toronto Western Hospital puts a plaster cast on my leg, just below the knee and covering my foot to the toes. By the next morning, it feels like my leg is being crushed by the cast. It is a pulsing mass of pain, and it feels *wrong*. After three days of this, I go back to the fracture clinic, but when the ortho comes in to talk to me, he doesn't ask me what's wrong. Instead, he tells me I have a walking cast and asks me why I'm not walking. I tell him he did not give me a walking cast. We go back and forth like this for a while until he finally looks at my leg for the first time during this visit. Then he glances at my chart for the first time and closes it quickly. I know he's seen his mistake, but he won't admit it or apologize to me. They take off the cast because I tell them I am not leaving until they do. After another week of hopping around my apartment on one leg, I ask the MD for physiotherapy.

When I get to the rehab clinic, it is two weeks after my fall. The physiotherapist asks me if it's okay if a student sits in on my consult. Rafael is a young Jewish guy, studying to be a physiotherapist after retiring from Cirque du Soleil ("Bone spurs in my heels," he tells me. "Too many hard landings. Surgery isn't working anymore"). Vivian is an older Chinese-Canadian therapist and Rafael's clinical practicum teacher. Before Vivian touches me, she asks Rafael, "Is this injury chronic or acute?" Rafael checks my intake chart and replies, "Chronic." Vivian says, "Actually, this injury is acute." Rafael says, "But it's been two weeks!" And Vivian says, "Don't go by the calendar. Look at what the patient presents." Vivian is my saviour.

Vivian and Rafael use what I call the Triangular Mallet of Evil to break up scar tissue and the adhesions caused by long-term hardened swelling. They put me on a wobble board and start me on gait training, and they harangue me about doing my resistance-band exercises at home. One day, when I tell Rafael that I can't make it up the steps of a streetcar using crutches, and that I'm running out of money to take cabs everywhere, he wraps my ankle using a special supertight Cirque du Soleil tape job, with strict instructions to take it off within three hours "or else." I use a cane to walk a block to the streetcar and get myself home using two legs for the first time in weeks. After several months of intensive rehab, I am able to walk again. As part of the healing process, I learn how to focus on my body and respond to the messages it sends me. I also learn that individualized, hands-on treatment is an art as well as a science.

One sunny day the next summer, I'm standing at the counter of the OK Convenience in Parkdale when I hear my spirit helpers tell me, "Buy this newspaper." As I read through it, I see an article about a sports therapist who works with one of the pro teams in Toronto. He's pioneering a new therapy in Canada, called active release technique — and he is opening a clinic of his own. When I see John for the first time, I tell him that the injury to my left ankle has left me with reduced movement in both my dorsiflex and my plantar flex, numbness in my last two toes, generalized pain and weakness, and the feeling that my entire left leg is out of place somehow. John nods, gets up on the table with me, grabs my leg, and brings it around his torso. Then he moves it around using a bunch of subtle arm and back movements. I hear ferocious cracking sounds, but there's no discomfort. Then he jumps off the table and says, "Now walk! Don't think! Just walk! And tell me how it feels." I get up, take a few steps, and start to cry. "It feels normal again," I say. "Better than normal." I don't know what the tears are about until many years later, when I learn that the left side of the body represents receptive energy in Indigenous medicine and philosophy. Joe has opened what's been blocked for so many years.

Four years later, the back pain is now ever-present. I can't sit without spasms. I can't walk for very long without getting completely locked up. I get to the point where I have to dig the cane out of the closet so that I can get around again. It's my massage therapist who recommends I see a chiropractor. She can't figure out why my muscles are so locked and rigid. She pinches my trapezius muscle using "the lobster claw" and she digs in everywhere with her elbows, but my muscles still won't release. Or if they release a tiny bit, they lock up again on the way home.

The chiropractor has a community practice: he lugs a portable treatment table around to local community centres and sets his fees on a sliding scale, which means I pay only $10. As I inch slowly down the street after one appointment, leaning heavily on the cane, I get a very concerned look from a white-haired old man who is walking down the street just fine, thank you very much. I notice his look, and it makes me wonder. I'm young, but this level of physical discomfort and difficulty is normal to me.

Then a bizarre new thing: my eyes start to hurt. I can't wear my contact lenses anymore, and I wake up in the middle of the night in agony because of the pain. When I see the ophthalmologist, he says, "Wow. Your eyes are as dry as the Sahara Desert." When I ask what's causing it, he says, "Well, sometimes it's hormones. Don't worry about it. I'll give you some eye drops. Just use these throughout the day."

I manage this way for years, with headaches and back problems and ovary pain and breast pain and an irritable bowel and dry eyes, until my digestion begins to get even worse. The bowel symptoms are now joined by constant heartburn and acid reflux. I see an MD who is an allergy specialist, and his skin tests indicate that I'm allergic to pretty much everything I eat. He gives me a list of foods to stay away from and a prescription for two EpiPens. As I'm leaving his office, I ask him why my body is doing this — I mean, I never had allergies as a child — and he chuckles and looks back down at his desk. When I realize he's not going to answer me, I turn and leave the office.

I decide not to fill the EpiPen prescription. Instead, I head to the Eastern European herbal store on Danforth Avenue. I ask Dan, the guy behind the counter, if he can recommend anything for stomach problems and allergies. He asks me some questions and then prescribes me a mixture that I am to drink as a tea three times a day. I take my first dose that night right before bed. Sometime during the night, I am woken up by . . . whatever it is that my body is doing. I can feel my esophagus and stomach pulse in a gentle squeezing action, all the way down and inside. I'm frightened at first, and I wonder if I'm about to be sick. But as I concentrate on how I'm feeling, I realize that the pulsing feels good. It's as if something is working again, or awake. The feeling passes, and I go back to bed and sleep well. I stick to my food list and I begin to feel better. For a while.

A year passes. Now I can't sleep more than a couple of hours a night. I have a constant raw cough and a constant stream of thick clear mucous draining from my nose. I ride my bike everywhere, and I go around the corner to my local Y for step class and volleyball and spin classes three or four times a week, but I'm swelling up like a balloon. I'm now 212 pounds, and none of my clothes fit me. I am irritable and easily frustrated. Even though I push myself at the Y and on my bike, the truth is I can barely lift my arms above my head to wash my hair in the shower. I am exhausted, and I'm not thinking straight at work. There are days when I can barely make it up the stairs to my new apartment. I am 39 years old, and I feel like I could lie down and die.

Then the "safe" food on my list becomes my enemy. One night, my throat closes as I'm eating. At other times, my tongue tingles and gets swollen. When I speak with the doctor on call at the clinic, she tells me she is issuing a prescription for an inhaler that she will fax to my favourite pharmacy. I say, "An inhaler? Like for asthma? But shouldn't I come in, so you can see me? I don't have any trouble breathing." She says she doesn't have to, that she deals with this all the time. I tell her I don't have a "favourite pharmacy" and that I don't want an inhaler. I hang up, and I think to myself, *This is ridiculous.* Then I remember something the other MD told me once: *I'm thinking of studying naturopathy. I want to do more to help my patients.* So I hit the Yellow Pages and make an appointment with a naturopathic doctor (ND).

The ND sends me an eight-page questionnaire to fill out before I see her. It asks me when I wake up at night, when I poop, how my poop looks, how my poop smells, what colour my pee is, the colour and consistency of my snot, when I get hungry, the consistency of my menstrual blood, if my anus has ever been itchy, if I feel cold and when, if I feel hot and when, if I am overly aware of my heartbeat, what I eat, what I drink, how many times I've been on antibiotics, whether I bite my tongue and cheeks a lot when I eat, and a gazillion other things. It takes me three days to complete the paperwork.

At our first appointment, which lasts 90 minutes, the ND diagnoses me with multiple conditions: a hormonal imbalance that has led to polycystic ovary syndrome (PCOS), candida overgrowth in my digestive tract, liver toxicity and a "heat rising" condition, chronic inflammation, and leaky gut syndrome. For the PCOS, she prescribes an herbal blend of anti-androgens and androgen antagonists to restore a healthy hormone balance. To battle the candida, she takes me off all sugar — including dairy — and prescribes a billions-per-capsule human-derived probiotic to restock my intestinal microflora. She prescribes the Heel homeopathic detox kit and a sulphur homeopathic remedy for my liver. She places me on an anti-inflammatory alkaline diet and tells me to drink a tall glass of lemon water every day to flush my liver. She explains the difference between the fight-or-flight and the rest-and-digest nervous systems and tells me I should try to chew each mouthful of food at least 30 times before swallowing. Then she shows me how to direct the flow of energy within my body by teaching me a yoga mudra (hand pose): cupping my fingers together, right hand on top of the left, with my thumbs touching. She also tells me to stop going to the gym, so I begin a restorative yoga class instead.

I begin to sleep again. My mood improves dramatically. The headaches, dry eyes, and muscle pain go away. I lose 18 pounds in the first three weeks and 70 pounds within four months. But the real change is energetic: I am happy and I think positive thoughts. I change so much that a colleague I have known for 11 years doesn't recognize me when I pass her on the street. When I stop and say, "Hey, how are you?" her face is blank at first, then it turns to shock, then she says, "Suzanne?! I didn't recognize you, except for your voice."

It's fitting that she mentions my voice. For four decades, my body has been my only voice. It spoke when I could not. For that gift of memory, I am thankful. But now it's time to understand the story my body is trying to tell. Now it's time to heal.

In a 2016 study published in the *International Journal of Circumpolar Health* and a 2017 study published in the *Canadian Medical Association Journal*, researchers in two separate projects found that the experiences of Indigenous children in residential schools set the stage for many of the negative health outcomes currently experienced in Indigenous communities.

In the 2016 project, researchers at the University of Saskatchewan analyzed historical data on the body mass index of more than 1,700 Indigenous children from Saskatchewan and Manitoba who were sent to residential schools in those provinces between 1919 and the 1950s. The data show that 80 per cent of the children were at a healthy weight when they were brought to the schools (a better rate than Canadian school-age children today). In the 2017 project at the University of Toronto, researchers studied survivor testimony from the Truth and Reconciliation Commission to determine that the typical diet in the schools delivered approximately 1,000 to 1,450 calories per day. The average child requires between 1,400 and 3,200 calories per day. According to the researchers at the University of Toronto, prolonged malnutrition "causes height stunting and a tendency to put on fat when calories are available, predisposing children to obesity, insulin resistance, and type 2 diabetes. Improper nutrition also has reproductive effects, such as a higher risk of stillbirths, premature births, and growth issues for babies." These issues are all experienced in Indigenous communities at rates disproportionate to the non-Indigenous population in Canada.

But it wasn't just the poor diet. In a 2015 study published in the *Proceedings of the National Academy of Sciences*, researchers from the University of California and the University of Chicago discovered that people who are socially isolated are less able to fight infection. In other words, being lonely has negative effects on a person's immune system, leaving them at risk for ill health. The loneliness suffered by children in residential schools — removed from their families, forbidden from speaking to siblings, away from their home territories for months or years at a time, forbidden from practising their cultures or speaking their languages, and receiving little or no affection — also set them up for a lifetime of negative health outcomes. A study of residential school survivors in British Columbia conducted by the Aboriginal Healing Foundation in the early 2000s found that all the survivors who were interviewed specifically mentioned suffering from chronic headaches. Other frequent health issues included heart problems, high blood pressure, and arthritis.

Poor health also has roots in childhood trauma and poor attachment to parents and caregivers. A longitudinal study published in the journal *Pediatrics* that followed 1,000 children in the U.S. into their teenage years discovered that more than 25 per cent of those who as toddlers scored lowest on mother-child attachment tests went on to become obese by age 15, compared to only 13 per cent of the children who were securely attached to their mothers. And a 2011 study in the *Journal of Aggression, Maltreatment, and Trauma* that used data from the 2007 Statistics Canada Canadian Community Health Survey found that children who are physically abused have a greater tendency to experience irritable bowel syndrome, chronic fatigue syndrome, fibromyalgia, and multiple chemical sensitivities when they enter adulthood, even when adult socio-economic stressors, mental health, and other adverse childhood experiences were controlled for. Researchers in the first study point to genetic reprogramming and behavioural changes as the main culprit, while the second study referenced changes in how the brain reacts to stress.

Stress reactions are a big part of the negative health outcomes within Indigenous communities. The chronic stress of colonization, forced assimilation, and racism and discrimination, along with the stress created by the everyday impacts of intergenerational trauma, is behind many of the health issues that afflict contemporary Indigenous peoples. Irritable bowel syndrome is anxiety felt in — and demonstrated by — the gut. Chronic stress also creates problems with the endocrine system, which governs hormones in the body. When the body's endocrine system is out of balance, it creates excess insulin, which can lead to insulin resistance and type 2 diabetes, along with complications from diabetes, such as kidney disease. Excess insulin also affects the ovaries, which can lead to PCOS and body-wide inflammation. The white blood cells involved in inflammation are good when they're responding to injury or infection, but when inflammation becomes chronic, it leads to a long list of disorders including arthritis, asthma, allergies, heart disease, diabetes, and cancer. According to Cancer Care Ontario's Aboriginal Cancer Prevention Team, Indigenous peoples had a lower cancer incidence and lower mortality rates than non-Indigenous people in Canada as recently as the 1980s. Before that, cancer was almost non-existent in Indigenous populations. Today, however, rates of lung, breast, cervical, colorectal, and prostate cancer are rising. The seventh generation of Indigenous peoples after colonization is much sicker than the first.

What these studies and statistics tell us is that colonization has had a negative effect on the Indigenous body. The dis-ease felt in Indigenous communities is the physical manifestation of intergenerational trauma and the metaphysical inheritance of the pain of colonial history. In the words of Nehiyaw writer Billy-Ray Belcourt, "Indigeneity is a zone of biological struggle. . . . Misery wears you down. . . . Existence is what taxes."

Physical and sexual abuse in childhood is a prime driver of chronic pain. This chronic pain is not generally understood by Western health-care practitioners, because it is a diagnostic enigma. There are no lab results to confirm the existence of the pain, and any treatments that are attempted fail to address the pain. As a result, many Western biomedical practitioners become frustrated with Indigenous patients who report chronic pain. They are often thought of as complainers, and they are often told that the pain is in their head.

The Western biomedical system cannot interpret what patients with chronic pain are saying and showing because chronic pain does not fit the disease models taught in medical school. There is no tissue damage and little or no physical evidence to support the patient's story. And that's even if they tell it. Most of the time, patients with chronic pain are seeking validation for something they feel but can't even define for themselves. They carry a feeling that things are not right, or a feeling that they are at risk of injury or death, but they often do not consciously understand — or even remember — what happened to them. But their bodies remember the story, exhibiting various signs and symptoms through a hyper-vigilant response to the stress of the original traumatic experience.

It is generally thought that human beings have two nervous systems: the sympathetic (fight or flight) and the parasympathetic (rest and digest). In fact, they have three. The third nervous system is the enteric nervous system, and it is centred in the gut:

the esophagus, stomach, and small and large intestine. The enteric nervous system has more nerve cells than the entire spinal cord, and it can act independently of the other two nervous systems, activating organs and cells of its own accord. This is why children who experience physical and sexual abuse so often grow into adults who experience chronic abdominal pain and gastrointestinal disorders: because their enteric nervous system is engaging in a hypervigilant stress response. Survivors of childhood sexual abuse also report stiffness in muscles and joints, back pain, severe headaches, vaginal or vulval irritation, locked vaginal muscles, and erectile dysfunction, as well as anxiety and anger. To cope with the anger, some survivors turn it inward against themselves in an attempt to avoid the feeling or protect the abuser, causing the anger to morph into self-blame and depression.

According to the *Oxford Dictionary*, disease is defined as "a disorder of structure or function in a human, animal, or plant, especially one that produces specific symptoms or that affects a specific location and is not simply a direct result of physical injury." Chronic dis-ease as felt by Indigenous peoples is definitely a disorder of structure or function. But because it occurs as a cluster of nonspecific symptoms that come and go among various organ systems and locations on the body — what I now call the Presto Change-o Effect, in honour of the ER nurse — and because it results from a frighteningly holistic mental, emotional, spiritual, and physical complex post-traumatic stress response, siloed Western biomedicine is ill-suited to understanding how to address it.

Symptomology is the word used to describe a set of symptoms characteristic of a medical condition or exhibited by a patient. The problem with Western biomedicine is that it rarely gets past symptomology. Even the most enlightened biomedical practitioners — those who understand the importance of looking at illness through a bio-psycho-social lens — still treat dis-ease by trying to control or regulate the symptoms. Western biomedicine believes that disease exists as a thing in and of itself, and that the way to help people is to remove the infecting agent. It's a one-size-fits-all, this-equals-that approach that reflects a mechanistic, Newtonian understanding of the universe. Indigenous science, medicine, and philosophy is based on an understanding of the universe that is closer to quantum physics. Holistic medicine sees disease as dis-ease, where physiology becomes disrupted and turns inward, against itself. The holistic practitioner asks what is causing the disruption, then seeks to address the disruption using treatments designed to return body, mind, and spirit to a state of balance. In holistic medicine, an individual's internal environment is more important in determining, and recovering from, disease than the infecting agent or pathogen itself.

Manitow circulates within the human body through meridians, accessible at certain points on the meridians. The Earth also has meridians and points where the spirit world is more easily accessed. The particles and waves that make up creation connect to each other through a constant exchange of energy that uses these points and meridians. Nehiyaw artist Carl Ray's painting *Shaking Tent* depicts that energy circulation and exchange in relation to a shaking tent ceremony: the Earth's meridians radiate below the tent. The energy of the shaman, his spirit helpers, and the transformational figures inside the tent radiate up and out of the tent and back down toward the earth as indicated by the narrow lines. The figures inside the tent exchange energy with each other and with the water or medicines inside the bowl. Shaking tent ceremonies are performed at night, so Ray has depicted the moon with radiating lines that connect all life on Earth through the 28-day lunar-tidal cycle. The figures inside the tent are drawn to show how energy moves within them, via the body's meridians and points.

Carl Ray's *Shaking Tent*, 1976, acrylic on paper, 60 x 90 cm, Thunder Bay Art Gallery, The Helen E. Band Collection, 1994

When it is functioning well and in balance, the human body works the same way everything else in the universe works: moving through cycles and engaging in constant transformation. When the human body is not functioning well and is in a state of imbalance — or dis-ease — it is stuck in time, stuck in a response, stuck in an old story that prevents transformation and change.

The movement required to achieve transformation is not accomplished in isolation. It is a product of our connections and relationships. Human health cannot be understood unless it is seen as part of a framework that includes the spirit world, the family unit, the community, and the land that supports us.

Umeek Richard Atleo, a hereditary chief of the Ahousaht First Nation in British Columbia, has written extensively on the Nuu-chah-nulth concept of *tsawalk*. Tsawalk means "one," and it refers to the Nuu-chah-nulth worldview, which sees the nature of all existence as an integrated and orderly whole that is defined by

— and maintained through — relationship. In the Nuu-chah-nulth language, the phrase *hishuk ish tsawalk* means "everything is connected, everything is one." This same knowledge is demonstrated in the cultural frameworks of Indigenous nations across the continent, from the medicine wheel of the Plains Nations to the wheel-like petroglyphs drawn by Mi'kmaq people in Kejimkujik National Park in today's Nova Scotia. The requirement for balance, however, demands that we understand the wholeness of the universe, that it consists of a system of complementary opposites including but not limited to negative and positive, day and night, active and receptive, and warm and cold. The complementary opposites within the wholeness of the universe are illustrated by Carl Ray as the divided circle that connects the transformational figures in the shaking tent.

Holistic medicine, whatever its originating culture, understands that dis-ease is the manifestation of imbalance within the whole. As a result, holistic practitioners understand that the symptoms themselves are not always the actual problem. More often than not, the symptoms point to a problem with the whole: the disconnections and distorted relationships that underlie the symptoms. That story is not seen through the lens of a microscope or in the images of an x-ray or scan that isolates parts from the whole. That story is the sum total of everything that the person has seen, experienced, heard, and understood across time.

Medical doctor and addictions expert Gabor Maté illustrates this in the approach he takes with people who have addictions: "If your addiction gives you a sense of control or power, why do you lack control, agency, and power in your life? If it's because you lack a meaningful sense of self, well, how did that happen? What happened to you?"

Part of the goal when holistic medicine tackles trauma is to bring the individual to a place where they understand the source of their dis-ease, where they can engage (or re-engage) with the world as a whole being, outside of the encoded memory of, and disconnection created by, the traumatic incident. As part of that journey, holistic practitioners teach survivors how to be more aware of their bodies, to recognize how their bodies work, and to recognize the distortions in thought they have developed in relationship to their bodies (thinking of their bodies as the enemy, for instance). Another part of the journey is learning how to recognize some of the early warning signs of impending pain and how to take steps to alleviate or minimize symptoms, thereby slowing or stopping the cycle of multiple appointments, treatments, and tests.

Western biomedicine is often a fragmented and dehumanizing process, especially for Indigenous people. The system usually positions MDs as the experts and assumes that the patient has nothing to say or contribute to the process of diagnosis and healing. By examining the physical organs and tissues at the microscopic level and in isolation from one another as systems — and in isolation from the forces of the universe and an individual's spiritual, emotional, and mental states — Western biomedicine often ends up treating the symptoms of chronic traumatic dis-ease instead of the dis-ease itself. This approach costs society in terms of tests and failed treatments and lost human productivity, and it doesn't do the individual in dis-ease much good, because it does not offer them an opportunity to get unstuck or to exercise the agency they were denied at the moment of the original trauma.

When I am working at a residential facility for Indigenous women and women-led families in 2014, we are expected to have a trauma-informed practice. So I am not surprised to find that every single one of the residents, in every age bracket, has a multitude of health problems. Particularly common are asthma, kidney issues, and diabetes.

One day, a resident named Clara asks me to look at her discharge summary from a local hospital to help her understand what it means. Her pre-admission co-morbidities are listed as "EtOH abuse" (biomedical doctor-speak for alcoholism), chronic hepatitis, chronic pancreatitis (inflammation of the pancreas caused by excessive alcohol consumption), lap cholecystectomy (which means she previously had her gall bladder removed), a laparotomy (surgical incision) she received after a stabbing two years ago, and seizure disorder. After I google the medical terms and abbreviations, translate them into plain language, and insert some explanatory language, the story on the discharge summary is this:

Clara presented to the ER with sudden onset epigastric pain, nausea, and five episodes of vomiting with no food or drink for two days. She has also had painful, difficult urination and inability to urinate for approximately one day. Abdominal examination revealed diffuse tenderness most prominent in the right upper quadrant as well as the right lower quadrant. A bladder scan showed 900cc, or nearly four cups, of urine. Initial blood work showed normal liver enzymes. Of concern was an elevated lactate of 3.1 related to liver and renal dysfunction. Abdominal ultrasound did not show any abnormalities. Abdominal x-ray showed constipation. Urinalysis was negative. Given the elevated lactate, we were concerned about an ischemic bowel — inflammation of the large intestine due to insufficient blood supply — as cause of her abdominal pain. However, a CT scan with dye contrast was negative and did not identify any other pathology that could explain her pain. Moreover, the lactate dropped to 0.5 or normal range the following day. Her pain gradually resolved. She was able to tolerate an oral diet at time of discharge. After resolution of the abdominal pain we performed a trial of voiding. However she was still retaining about 450cc, or two cups, of urine post void. Patient was seen by urology and they believed her retention to be multifactorial. Luckily, over several hours she was able to void better. Ongoing common bile duct dilatation. New tiny right pleural effusion (water on the lungs). Issue for follow-up/investigation: has had a couple of admissions for abdominal pain not yet diagnosed. No pathology iden-tified on imaging or blood work. Could be related to abdominal wall pain secondary to previous stab wounds and constipation. Diagnosis most responsible for her stay is abdominal pain secondary to constipation.

Clara is discharged with 10 medications — some new, some continuing — including an anti-convulsant, something for choles-terol, a PPI for acid reflux, an SSRI for depression, a stool softener, a laxative, and a drug that increases movement through the diges-tive system.

The Western biomedical system sees Clara as a collection of her problems. The MDs admit that the tests show nothing and that previous visits have not resulted in a diagnosis. So they pick one of the presenting symptoms — the constipation — and call that the diagnosis. She is released with a bag full of medications and given a follow-up appointment with a urologist. None of it will help her resolve her dis-ease. None of it will lead her to the reasons for her pain.

If Clara were receiving holistic health care, she would have the opportunity to proceed much differently. In this imaginary yet completely attainable world, the holistic practitioners on staff at the hospital — Indigenous medicine people, traditional Chinese medicine practitioners, Ayurvedic practitioners, and others — work with the Western biomedical doctors on staff to provide Clara with care.

The TCM practitioner examines her tongue and takes her pulses to start. From that, they immediately see which organ systems are out of balance and how the qi (manitow) is flow-ing. They connect what is going on in her body with the season (it's summer when Clara is in the hospital, which can tax the kidneys). They also use Five Elements Theory to examine how her body is reflecting and connecting to the earth, metal, water, wood, and fire that make up everything on Earth. By seeing and measuring how her organs are functioning and then engaging in questioning, they connect her physical state to any unresolved emotions that she carries by linking organ function to the emotions that they rule. The nausea could be Liver attacking Stomach (which points to Anger), but given the vomiting and urination issues, it could be that the Kidneys are struggling to circulate some stagnant qi (which points to Fear). The dilated bile duct won't be seen as such because the holistic practitioner is not examining her on the microscopic level, but it turns up when Clara is questioned about her digestion, when it shows as a Small Intestine issue. The constipation is a Large Intestine issue, which also explains the water on the lung: although that water will not be seen on the microscopic level, the TCM practitioner sees it because the Large Intestine connects energetically to the Lung, indicating excess Grief and Sadness. This corresponds to Clara's pre-existing diagnosis of depression.

While the TCM practitioner is doing their assessment, the Indigenous medicine person sits nearby, reading Clara's energy signature and engaging in ceremony — maybe shaking a turtle-shell rattle or singing softly to connect with their spirit helpers — to help them discover the source of Clara's dis-ease. Depending on their training and area of focus, the Indigenous medicine person might also read Clara's pulse to determine a diagnosis. They might use their hands to align her back and joints in an effort to realign her energy flow. Or they might remove negative energy by placing a small piece of cloth on her upper chest or back and sucking out whatever she carries.

When Clara begins to urinate again, her pain also goes away. This indicates that her Grief and Sadness are ameliorated by the care she receives, pointing to a lack of caring present in her life. The TCM practitioner and Indigenous medicine person ask her about this, to try to help Clara develop some understanding about her past experiences and the thoughts and feelings and physical symptoms she is experiencing as a result. Her constipation indicates that Clara is unable to define what is useful (and should be held on to) and what is useless (and should be let go). At this point, Clara is given an acupuncture treatment, perhaps utilizing the Ba Liao points from the famous acupuncture text *Thousand Ducat Formulas*, written by the master acupuncturist Sun Si-Miao in 652 CE. The Ba Liao points are renowned for their therapeutic effects in cases of difficult urination and defecation. Then the TCM practitioner and Indigenous medicine person consult on herbal remedies to rebalance Clara's organ systems and improve the flow of manitow/qi, relieving her physical symptoms and her emotional pain. She is also given a list of foods that will help strengthen her and bring her back into balance: foods that are cooling or warming, that strengthen certain organ systems, or that otherwise fit what the practitioners see and understand during their examination. The Indigenous medicine person might also prescribe an herbal bath and other ceremonial practices Clara should continue at home. As part of her follow-up, Clara is referred to the Indigenous shaman or energy practitioner on staff at the hospital. The shaman might rebalance her by using light and colour to adjust the frequencies that give unique characteristics to all matter, thereby powering dormant cells and activating DNA synthesis. Or they could decide to use sound — a drum or rattle — to realign her heart rate and brainwaves, boost her immune system, and trigger the repair and growth of cells necessary for unblocking chronic inflammation and spurring healing. Or they could decide to use ceremony to support identity creation and healing by making contact with the spirit world.

Holistic medicine does not see Clara as a collection of her problems but rather as a reflection of the wholeness of her existence, connected to Earth cycles, connected to the manitow/qi that powers the universe, and with each of her organ systems reflecting the story that her body-mind is trying to tell but her spirit is too afraid to confront.

Indigenous science and philosophy tells us that a person's life essence is determined at least in part by the energy we inherit from our ancestors. Their strengths and weaknesses, constructed through their own inheritance as well as through their life experiences, then becomes part of our own life essence. This life essence is held in the kidneys. A deer hide dress in the McCord Museum in Montreal illustrates this concept, as well as the concept of energetic connection. When the dress is constructed by the Niitsitapi Siksika between 1900 and 1940, the maker uses red and white beads on the bottom of the dress to outline the deer's kidneys. I can't speak for the Niitsitapi, but I have seen these same designs on Nehiyawak clothing and other objects. From a Nehiyaw perspective, the owner of the dress may be a member of a certain clan or society and wants to honour the strength of the deer's life essence as part of their ceremonial duties. They may want to acquire the deer's energetic power to do their work in the world. They may need some deer medicine to strengthen or cure them from an affliction or imbalance. Whatever the reason, the dressmaker is aware of the central importance of life essence and how that energy circulates within us, around us, and between us. A red line on the back of the dress at the bottom traces the connection between an individual's life essence and the energy that flows down to the earth.

From a Nehiyaw perspective, good health is dependent on social relations, personal responsibility, a healthy spirit, and the health of the land just as much as it is on physiology. However, despite ample evidence that colonization has negatively affected Indigenous peoples and communities — as evidenced by higher rates of infant mortality, infectious diseases, respiratory diseases, digestive issues, metabolic issues, accidental death, and a lower life

Niisitapiikwan Siksika kidney dress, c. 1900–1940

(ACC1000 | Dress © McCord Museum)

expectancy — government policies and practices continue to support the Western biomedical model through expanded budgets and wider delivery of services that do little to address dis-ease or reduce the everyday impacts of intergenerational trauma.

One example of this is the government's willingness to fund on-reserve kidney dialysis services.

When Indigenous peoples on the Prairies signed treaties and were forced to settle on reserves, their active lifestyle and reliance on whole foods changed to a sedentary lifestyle and a diet based on simple carbohydrates, which has resulted in high rates of diabetes and kidney disease. The fear that is a daily ever-present reality for Indigenous peoples living within colonial society also contributes to both diabetes and kidney disease by creating a chronic stress response. To address these issues, governments (both federal and provincial) have spent millions of dollars building and staffing dialysis centres in remote on-reserve communities. Receiving dialysis will keep someone alive, but it will not deal with the unresolved emotions associated with the everyday impacts of trauma, the colonial control relationship, or the effects of CPTSD. It will not deal with the chronic stress that creates higher rates of diabetes and kidney disease. Meanwhile, in many places the Northern Store is still the only game in town, and it gets government subsidies that enable it to continue selling overpriced processed foods to a captive community where residents are diagnosed with diabetes at 25 years of age and sign up for dialysis by 28 years of age. In Indigenous communities such as Garden Hill First Nation, Manitoba, health care is the biggest industry. Dialysis is big business, benefitting everyone from the makers of the machines to the owners of the helicopters that bring patients to and from their appointments. But dialysis does not heal the dis-ease.

According to a CBC News piece written by Alika Lafontaine, an Oji-Cree MD, team leader with the Indigenous Health Alliance, and council member of the Royal College of Physicians and Surgeons of Canada, "Obedience to program design is strict and enforced through contract. To obtain funding for any health service, First Nations must . . . agree to government priorities set out in the packaged program, which often conflict with actual community priorities. The agreements have minimal flexibility and strongly penalize any deviation. . . . Decisions are made unilaterally by government at nearly every level of First Nations health care. While there is a recent emphasis on community engagement, it is . . . advisory. Spending and program design remains at the federal department's discretion. . . . The greatest barrier to change is government acknowledging its bureaucracy is designed to . . . minimize the role of community-centred priorities and solutions. The federal government has no strategy to transform the health system to produce something different."

Before colonization, Indigenous medicine people had knowledge that often gave them political power as well. They were respected for their ability to see things and for their knowledge about the workings of the world. Early settlers recognized their abilities and often sought care from Indigenous medicine people. In time, government agents and missionaries realized that these medicine people would be a huge barrier to assimilation, so they took deliberate action to weaken the position of medicine people within Indigenous societies. Missionaries began to take on a leading role as spiritual advisors and often took over the role of doctor, too. Medicine people were ostracized and criminalized, elders were unable to pass on their knowledge, and Indigenous science and medicine was lost or went underground.

Indigenous peoples went from proud, independent people with excellent health and strength of heart and mind to dependent people ravaged by the physical, mental, emotional, and spiritual consequences of colonization. The government policies and programs that seek to maintain the status quo are a continuation of the control relationship: by keeping Indigenous people sick, the government ensures that they are marginalized, unable to stand up and demand their rights.

The path to regaining health and wellness after colonization will look different for each Indigenous person and each Indigenous community, because each person and each community will have different goals, use different methods, and experience change at a different pace. But a crucial piece of the puzzle is recreating health-care models that reflect the holistic paradigms at the heart of Indigenous cultures. This will be difficult in the wake of the colonial destruction of Indigenous science and medicine and the breakdown in intergenerational knowledge transfer, but it is possible.

In 2007, the Native Women's Association of Canada (NWAC) published a list of 18 recommendations that clearly identify what is needed to re-establish pre-colonial healing practices in Indigenous communities and improve access to Indigenous science and medicine in the systems and institutions of the dominant society. The recommendations include calls to:

- recognize the diversity and value of traditional healing
- promote the revitalization of traditional healing
- provide support and recognition to traditional healers
- develop a deeper understanding of traditional healing through research and learning
- respect the intellectual property of traditional healers and their medicines
- research how traditional healing can be effectively combined with other health services
- research and publicize programs that work, whether these are traditional healing alone or a combination of traditional healing and Western medicine
- provide opportunities for Indigenous women to help develop traditional healing policies and programs
- encourage meaningful dialogue between Indigenous healers and non-Indigenous health-care providers

There are competent medicine people practising today in Indigenous communities across Canada. It wouldn't take much to set up apprentice training programs and institute the NWAC recommendations. However, the government has not yet chosen to do so.

Holistic medicine is key to the process of recovering from trauma because holistic approaches teach the survivor how to feel their bodies and how to describe what they're feeling. This is an important skill for survivors who are numb, dissociated, or disconnected from their bodies. Instead of covering up symptoms with pharmaceutical drugs, or removing painful or malfunctioning organs via surgery, holistic approaches help the survivor learn how to feel and understand their emotions via the organ-emotion link. This is a first step toward reflecting on where those emotions are coming from and why they are unresolved. In holistic medicine, patients also learn how to engage in self-care through diet, movement/exercise, and attending regular appointments that encourage them to focus on their needs. For many survivors of trauma, this self-care is a first step toward learning to love themselves and their bodies. Because holistic approaches such as TCM or Ayurveda are grounded in specific cultures, most holistic practitioners also understand and accept the world of dreams, visions, and other spirit-world phenomena. To the Indigenous survivor of trauma, heeding messages from spirit protectors, ancestors, and helpers is key to balancing mind, body, spirit, and emotion, and therefore key to healing.

Some Indigenous communities no longer have access to medicine people, because there are none left in the local area. In other places, the need is simply too great and there are not enough medicine people practising. So it is imperative that Indigenous peoples dealing with the physical manifestations of intergenerational trauma recognize that the holistic medical approaches of other cultures operate on the same knowledge base as Indigenous science and medicine and that these medical approaches can offer healing and relief.

Beyond government inaction and symptomology, the biggest barrier to achieving equity in Indigenous health care in Canada is epistemological racism: the belief that Indigenous science and medicine (or any other non-European knowledge) isn't valid unless Western science "proves" it. To achieve decolonization, Canada must stop engaging in everyday dialogue in media, government, and academia that denigrates Indigenous science and medicine, claims it is dangerous, and labels it as "pseudo-science" (or "unscientific") simply because it does not adhere to European ideas.

Indigenous science and medicine is a big picture "both and" approach to understanding the world through the lens of connectivity. European science and medicine based on Enlightenment ideas is a reductionist "either or" approach of looking at the world that assumes that all matter is discrete. In the short film *Okpik's Dream*, Inuk champion dog musher Harry Okpik talks about how the "current of the month" — a monthly cycle of very low and very high tides in the North — affects his father's Parkinson's disease. As he explains, "So whenever that happens, it affects his health, like, I have been noticing it on him." This way of seeing the world, and way of seeing *in* the world, is as valid as any European way of knowing. By rejecting Indigenous ways of knowing, colonial systems and structures control the nature of the debate and contain it within settler-colonial parameters. This creates yet another opportunity for the colonizer to effect control upon Indigenous peoples.

The severe headaches I experience throughout my life until I receive holistic care are created by stagnant manitow/qi in the gall bladder and kidney meridians that run across the top of the head and into the neck. I don't know this at the time, of course, so the spirit world engages in an intervention to try to tell me what I need to know. One night in my apartment in Parkdale, I dream of some fat little birdies at my kitchen window. They're green and yellow, unlike any local birds, and they're trying to get through the closed window and into my place, like they want to tell me something.

It's winter in the dream, so their green and yellow feathers are contrasted against pure white snow. The MD I go to never asks me about my dreams, so I don't ever tell her what I am shown, but if I had — and if Western medical schools educated MDs in Indigenous or other non-Western science or medicine — then we would have known from the colours in my dream exactly what organ systems were out of balance (Liver, Spleen, and Lung) and what the emotional connections were (Anger, Worry, and Grief). But because Western biomedicine does not have this knowledge, the MD does not ask and I do not tell. So instead of catching the imbalances before they are critical, I live in constant pain for years until I finally have a major health crash and seek holistic care.

One year after I begin my healing journey with the ND, I am given a distance healing treatment by an Indigenous medicine person from South America who now lives in Toronto. During his treatment, he connects with manitow and shifts the position of the green and yellow colours that are part of my energetic signature. I don't tell the South American about my bird dream, but he sees what's up and deals with it. I make the connection to the dream later.

If an Indigenous medicine person from South America conducting a healing when we aren't even in the same room sounds like hocus-pocus, then consider the work of University of Calgary physics professor Wolfgang Tittel, who worked with PhD students in 2016 to teleport a light particle to the university's downtown campus from a lab at the main campus six kilometres away. As Tittel told the CBC, "This information transfer happens in what we call a disembodied manner. Our transfer happens without any need for an object to move between these two particles." What Tittel and his students do is demonstrate the phenomenon of quantum entanglement, or what Albert Einstein once called "spooky action at a distance." Quantum entanglement describes the behaviours of particles that are linked to each other, so that actions affecting one particle have an immediate effect on the other, no matter how far apart the particles are. To complete the teleportation, Tittel uses advanced lasers, a dedicated fibre-optic line, and light-detecting sensors that have to be kept cold because they won't work at temperatures above −272 degrees Celsius. To connect with me, the South American just uses his mind, body, and spirit.

It's not just the principles of quantum mechanics that form the basis of Indigenous science and medicine. The balance contained within the medicine wheel and other culture-specific frameworks is also a guiding principle.

In order to maintain health and wellness, Indigenous nations across the Americas recognize the need to balance hot and cold inside the body, in keeping with the system of complementary opposites. Failure to do so results in illness. Hot and cold qualities apply to foods (meat is hot; most plants are cool), activities (such as touching cold ground), emotions (such as anger, which is hot), and physical states (diarrhea is cold, pregnancy is hot). Nehiyawak on the Prairies enact the hot-cold balance in practices such as the sweat lodge, after which they bathe in a cool river, lake, or snow. The Innu of Labrador use sweats to expel cold, and Tzotzil Mayan women in Chiapas, Mexico, take sweat baths after childbirth to ensure they do not become too cold after losing the heat of pregnancy. Pemmican is a healthful food for the Nehiyawak because it is the perfect combination of hot and cold foods (bison and berries). Inuit of the circumpolar region also recognize the hot-cold balance and say that country food strengthens their bodies by warming them from inside. When they eat other foods, they risk developing a cold condition.

None of this is reflected in Western biomedicine, which is why Indigenous science and medicine (and other non-European approaches) need to be part of Canada's health-care system.

Clara's liver dysfunction, constipation, and sore abdomen show that she has too much heat in her body. Clearing that heat will rebalance her and start the process of healing, because it will unblock the anger she is stuck in and enable her to become aware of the paralyzing fear and unresolved grief that lies below it. This is what will move her past symptomology and into true change, which is to say true healing.

Like Western biomedicine, there is an underlying philosophy to Indigenous science and medicine. This philosophy recognizes the fundamental processes of the universe. Where Western biomedicine operates from a place of disconnection from the natural world and separation of the body from the mind, spirit, and emotions, Indigenous medicine operates on the wholeness of the individual and connections among the human world, the natural world, and the spirit world. A Tzotzil Maya elder from the state of Chiapas, Mexico, once explained to me how her community conceptualizes this balance: the right side of the body is male/active and connected to the sky (up). The left side is female/receptive and connected to the earth (down). The limbs represent the four cardinal directions. In this way, the human body serves as a sacred reminder of the well-ordered whole of the universe and the fact that individuals are connected to that larger whole. This is why the physical body must be properly aligned and in balance. The individual can affect the whole, and the whole can affect the individual, as demonstrated by the phenomenon of intergenerational trauma.

When the late Oji-Cree politician Elijah Harper becomes drastically ill in 1994, the former NDP member of the Manitoba legislative assembly for Rupertsland and member of Parliament for the Churchill riding does not turn away from the story his body is trying to tell. The once-large man loses 100 pounds, and although he is only 46 years old, he begins to shuffle like an old man as his leg muscles atrophy. His long thick hair thins and turns white. He is unable to work, staying away from the House of Commons for months and cutting back appearances in his riding. Western MDs can find no reason for his illness, so Harper heads to the bush to find a cure to a sickness his elders say is spiritual in nature. In 1995, Harper tells the Canadian Press that he is experiencing grief, depression, and frequent tears. "I just want it to stop," he says. "I pray to God to take the agony away. Every day I am in constant agony. Not physically — it's worse than pain." After four years, Harper is well again, and when asked to explain what happened, he says that he took on and purged some of the pain of his people. He tells *Windspeaker* in 1998 that he took part in healing ceremonies and sweat lodges and also used holistic medicine, such as acupuncture, to heal. Harper says his healing happens after he had what he calls "an experience with the Creator." "I do not know how much more I can tell people," he said. "There is a Creator, a God. I'm well now. I'm healed."

The story of the Seven Fires, an ancient prophecy now told by Anishinabe storyteller Sally Gaikezheyongai and others, foretold the events that took place during the 1990s, after the resistance at Kanehsatake (Oka) and during the time that Harper is ill. The story says that the Seventh Fire — the seventh generation after colonization — will be a time of great healing and cultural renewal, after which the Eighth Fire will rise to ensure that Indigenous nations thrive once again. We are now in the time of the Eighth Fire. But if Indigenous nations are to thrive, then Indigenous peoples, especially Indigenous children and youth, will have to regain their health and heal from the events of colonization.

When I am teaching at a school with a large population of Indigenous students, I see that most of the children have health issues. Ginger, who is in grade 4, has a distended belly and is constantly bloated. Amanda, who is also in grade 4, often chokes during lunch, which tells me she is rushing and not chewing her food properly, and that her esophagus (and entire body) is tense and constricted. The anxiety and hypervigilance she often shows suggests that she is in a chronic stress response, and she has the telltale puffiness, flushed cheeks, and constant dry cough of a heat condition and chronic inflammation. Percy is always bouncing around the classroom, happy to tell anyone who asks that he has ADHD, while Matthew is always in a low mood, especially when his mother is unable to be emotionally available due to her experiences with what the Western mental-health system says is bipolar disorder, but what I see as periods of intense grief followed by periods of anxious, stress-response-related activity.

Statistics Canada says that 5 per cent of the school-age population in Canada is affected by ADHD. A 2006 study conducted in Canada with Indigenous children in grades 1 to 4 says that almost 23 per cent of Indigenous children — five times the rate of non-Indigenous children — exhibit the criteria for an ADHD diagnosis. Yet in France, only 0.5 per cent of children are diagnosed with ADHD. The reason for this discrepancy is simple: in Canada, ADHD is thought of as a biological disorder with biological causes, which means treatment is aimed at changing the chemical balance in the child's brain through the use of pharmaceutical medications. Health-care practitioners in France, however, view ADHD as a medical condition that has psycho-social causes, reflecting the tendency of many Western-trained practitioners in Europe to apply holistic approaches. Instead of treating a child's behaviour and focusing issues with drugs, French practitioners look for the underlying issue in the child's social environment that is creating the child's inability to focus and be present. Then, instead of masking symptoms or blaming the child — which causes the child to internalize the idea that they are bad or broken — they treat that social problem with psychotherapy or family therapy.

In an in-depth piece that appeared in *Indian Country Today* in 2016, exploring the connections among racism, phrenology — the idea that Indigenous and other non-European peoples have lesser intelligence and character than white Europeans — and the disproportionate numbers of Indigenous children diagnosed with ADHD in the United States, the Cherokee psychologist and writer David Edward Walker says that "the ADHD label may mask the effects of sexual and physical abuse. Children subjected to violence and traumatic loss are often anxious, bereaved, hyper-vigilant, demotivated, and preoccupied, and have trouble settling and focusing. Yet the entire approach toward diagnosing children with ADHD — the loose diagnostic criteria, reliance upon super ficial rating scales and classroom observations, and the many stigmatizing biases held against children who don't conform — make the traumatized child even less likely to disclose the factors behind their behaviour." Walker says it is "tragically ironic" that "epidemic child abuse in Indian country" is being "obscured by ADHD," thereby supporting or continuing the dominant society's portrayal of Indigenous peoples as less intelligent and less capable.

If Indigenous peoples are ever going to regain the health they once had, then the health-care system needs to stop separating the individual from their stories and looking at the body as if it has no context beyond its mechanical parts. If Percy and his mother had the opportunity to engage in family therapy, they could be supported in dealing with whatever is troubling Percy and making changes aimed at improving Percy's ability to connect with others and stay in the present moment. There's certainly nothing wrong with Percy's cognitive abilities: like all of my students, he is a very bright boy with his own special set of gifts and abilities. Unfortunately, the ADHD label reduces centuries of colonial trauma and the everyday impacts of intergenerational trauma to a biological issue that blames Percy and others like him.

But at least Percy has a label, which means he is getting the extra help he needs at school. Matthew, Ginger, and Amanda aren't getting any help for the ways that they experience colonization and the everyday impacts of trauma. When I look at them, I think *microbiome*.

The human microbiome is made up of micro-organisms that live in and on the body. Many of these micro-organisms live in the gut. The gut creates more than 70 per cent of the body's neurotransmitters — chemical messengers that nerve cells use to communicate in the body — including 95 per cent of all serotonin. Serotonin regulates appetite and digestion, mood, social behaviour, sleep, and memory, among other things. This means that the health of the gut plays a big role in feelings of well-being, including mental health.

In 2017, a research paper published in the journal *Nature* compared the bacteria found in the guts of a Hadza hunter-gatherer community in Tanzania with the microbiome of people from 17 other cultures around the world. The results show that the farther away a person is from the standard North American diet — which is typically low in plant fibre and high in nutrient-poor, high-calorie, and highly processed foods — the healthier their microbiome. Multiple studies have revealed the link between a healthy diet and lower rates of depression, anxiety, bipolar disorder, and suicide in adults. Other studies have shown that a higher intake of nutrient-rich foods such as vegetables, greens, fruits, and fish correspond to lower rates of depression, anxiety, and other emotional problems in young people. Research also shows that an unhealthy diet during pregnancy and early childhood, including processed foods, refined cereals, and sugar-filled drinks and desserts, increases the risk of attention deficit issues, aggressive behaviour, and symptoms of anxiety and depression in children.

The children at Matthew, Ginger, and Amanda's school live in a neighbourhood filled with strip malls, high-rises, and assisted housing. There are no grocery stores, and it is impossible to find affordable, fresh, good-quality food, so families rely on expensive takeout food or expensive processed food available at corner stores (when they have the money, which isn't often). Students often come to school hungry. One day, one of my students tells me that the other kids have been teasing her because she had hot-dog buns with margarine for lunch. Many of the physical and mental health issues these children are experiencing are a direct result of poverty and marginalization. Creating change in their lives — and in their heath — is a simple matter of political will.

Many Indigenous scholars have pointed out that in Indigenous cultures, there is no distinction between food and medicine. Pre-colonial teachings surrounding food highlight the human connection to the natural world and the reciprocal relationships that mediate survival. Certain foods are valued for their healing power. These foods are not powerful simply because of the vitamins and minerals they contain. They are also powerful because of the energy they contain: the sun, moon, rain, soil microbes, and other components of the universe. Because human beings are part of the energy of the universe, what we eat either supports or disrupts that energy. Creating harmony and balance means cultivating good energy and seeking out good energy to bring into our bodies. Many Indigenous peoples have addressed the poor health outcomes related to colonization and unresolved feelings of terror, anger, fear, and grief by returning to a pre-colonial diet made up of foods that are indigenous to the Americas. In so doing, they reclaim Indigenous science and medicine and create (or restore) a connection between themselves and the natural world.

Gabor Maté says in his book *When the Body Says No: The Cost of Hidden Stress* that illness "not only has a history but also tells a history. It is a culmination of a lifelong history of struggle for self." On the first night I take the sulphur remedy that the naturopath prescribes, I sleep deeply and wake up happy to meet the day. When I look in the bathroom mirror that first morning, I look at my face, and without thinking, I say, "I don't look like my mother anymore." It's a very strange thing to say. All I know is that something has shifted, moved, changed. And my face literally looks different. When I think about what the sulphur has done, my first thought is fire and brimstone, the sulphur of biblical story, the hell of tormented existence. Then I think about the rotten-egg smell of sulphur, which brings me to volcanoes and ocean vents. Nasty stuff, poisonous, hard to live in and with. But the oceans are also the birthplace for all life on Earth. I realize in that moment that my otherworldly anger at my mother presents me with the possibility for radical rebirth. If I can release that anger, I take the first step toward becoming myself and living my own story. I may be marked by my life experiences, but they do not define me. In that moment, I recast myself from silent victim to grateful survivor. This energetic shift is a part of — and perhaps even facilitates the actual business of — physical healing.

From a Nehiyaw perspective, dis-ease is a teacher. Experiencing dis-ease helps the individual learn deep lessons about the world and their existence in it. When those lessons are obscured by a health-care system that deals only in symptomology and ignores the underlying spiritual significance of the physical event, the individual is deprived of those lessons. Holistic medicine helps the individual reflect on their experience from a standpoint that helps them create a healing narrative: Why was I born into this body? What story has my body told so far in my life? What story is my body telling me now? Curing an individual from dis-ease is about curing their reality. It's about making peace among body, mind, and spirit and rebalancing the relationship among the individual, the natural world, and the universe. It's about creating a new sense of self.

CHAPTER 8

SACRED BEING

Peace River, Alberta, is known as Sagitawa ("where the rivers meet") in the language of the Nehiyawak. It's a major stop on an ancient Indigenous river highway that connects northern British Columbia and northern Alberta to the Prairies. Before European settlement, Sagitawa was a gathering place for Indigenous peoples from Alberta, Saskatchewan, northern BC, and the Northwest Territories. Sagitawa is the place where the Smoky River, which begins in the Rocky Mountains near Jasper National Park, meets the Peace River, which begins in the Rockies in northeastern BC. At Sagitawa, the Heart River also empties into the Peace. All this mixing — of rivers, of peoples, of Indigenous cultures — extends to the land, which is not prairie, not north, but both and more.

Peace Country is evergreen forest, muskeg, and slough; river valley and hillside; poplar groves, aspen parkland, and prairie. Before European settlers arrive, there are bison grazing above the river valley, and elk and woodland caribou in the boreal forest. There are still bears in the bush and moose on the lakes. It is a rich mixture that reflects prairie, woodland, and north.

The Peace Country is shared territory, used historically by the Dane-zaa, the Muskotew Sakahikan Enowuk, the As'in'i'wa'chi Ni'yaw, and the Aseniwuche Winewak. When European explorers arrive, they are led by Kanienkehaka guides from the Great Lakes area. The Haudenosaunee are joined by French-Canadian voyageurs and Orkney boatmen, who do the hard work of paddling and portaging while explorers Mackenzie, Fraser, Thompson, and Finlay pencil together maps based on the knowledge of their Indigenous guides. Highland Scots from the Northwest Company also have a strong presence in Sagitawa, joining the voyageurs and the boatmen in a mutual hatred of their English rivals in the Hudson's Bay Company. Sagitawa is where the rivers meet and where the people meet. It is a place for trade, for governance councils, for dispute resolution, for stopping and resting, and for ceremony. It is a powerful place, because it is a place of connection.

Alexander Mackenzie sets up the first European trading post at Sagitawa in 1792. The fur trading posts turn into settlements, the gold miners come, settlers arrive to stay, and Sagitawa turns into the town of Peace River, named after the peace treaty signed between the Dane-zaa and the Nehiyawak at Sagitawa in 1781. Nehiyawak, Kanienkehaka, Scots, English, French-Canadian, newcomer Ukrainians and Poles, and the Mennonites and Hutterites who arrive in the early 20th century: we live side by side, mixing in daily life, often mixing in ancestry, and yet in complete solitude from one another. An Indigenous person's identity is fixed, but there are boundaries and codes that determine who goes where and who gets to overcome the unfortunate circumstances of their birth.

If you live in town, you're more acceptable than the Indigenous people who live in the bush. If you're mixed or Métis and lucky enough to be light-skinned, then you don't talk about your background except when it comes time to check the appropriate box on the scholarship application. If you have athletic ability, then no one mentions "the Indian thing," because you're almost as good as they are (and useful). If you're being raised by a white parent and you don't hang out with other Indigenous people, then you pass. If your parents are Indigenous but they're non-drinking Christians and you go to the Catholic school, then everyone can see you're doing your best to overcome the Indian thing, so they don't mention it except in private conversation (*Indian, but*). If you live in a foster home or you're bussed into school from an Indigenous community outside town, you're invisible, so you stick with your own kind. If you're female, you are a squaw: fuckable but dirty.

My mother is able to transgress certain boundaries because her mixed ancestry means she is light-skinned. She's not from a local community, either, which makes her less knowable in some ways and less of a target. She is also useful, because my father's electronics retail and repair business is the only game in town. In other ways, however, she is bound by her Otherness. Because she is "dark," as my friend Whitney says, that means she is fair game for white men like the postmaster, Mr. Watley, who asks her one afternoon as she stands in the service window if she would like to rent a room with him sometime. Not all is well in the households of the white town fathers — one of the postmaster's sons will soon hang himself in the family garage — so Indigenous women are used as a convenient outlet for white men to enact their rage. Growing up in Sagitawa, I am surrounded by Indigenous stories inscribed in the land as visual and sacred text, but the superimposed settler town forces me into a different daily reality. Instead of learning about the mighty river that connects me to 100 million years of history — illustrated through the dinosaur tracks we find down at the riverbank and knowable through the oral tradition of Indigenous peoples in the area, who trace their existence through human ancestors to a life-giving connection to earth and sky, all the way back to emergence and creation — I learn about Alberta's 75th anniversary as a province, and the school hands out a medallion to each student. Outside of school, I learn the settler version of Indigenous-focused curriculum: I learn to fear the world around me. I learn that I am nothing and no one.

When my father repairs the television at my elementary school, I point proudly to the sticker he puts on the wheeled cart, and I tell the teacher, "That's my daddy." The teacher scoffs and rolls her eyes at a colleague: "She says that's her dad's business." The other teacher, who knows me, shakes her head and says, "It is." The other teacher looks surprised.

When I am given the band award for outstanding achievement in grade 9, I feel like I could be good enough. I only started playing electric bass in grade 8, and I'm already as good as the other players in the band. But I also know that I'm getting special attention from the teacher because I am Sexy Suzi. I am a commodity, not an individual with a real existence.

One sunny day in spring 1984, after my mother and I move again, away from the Prairies and to another province, when I'm smiling and I feel good in the minidress I'm wearing, one of my grade 10 classmates decides she doesn't like all that happiness. Nadine follows me to my locker, waits until I put in my books and lock up, then knocks me to the ground and proceeds to beat the living shit out of me. She kicks me repeatedly in the head and face and throws me around by my hair, which she rips out by the fistful. I don't ever try to get up or fight back, crying out instead,

"Help me! Help me!" as the students in the hallway stop laughing and fall silent. This isn't just a hallway slap-fest: it's a brutal display of Nadine's aggression and rage. And I am used to being compliant, used to thinking that I deserve what happens to me, so I let her take me down.

Nadine doesn't show up in court. At some point during the process, one of the court workers tells me, "She beat you up because you're white." And all of a sudden — bing! — I have a new identity. The city we move to is deeply racist, so since Nadine is Black and I am the victim and Not Black, then according to the standard narrative — and given the settler-colonial invisibilization of Indigenous peoples in the city — I must be white. However, my new white identity solves nothing, because the deep-seated sense of worthlessness that I carry (*Suck this, squaw! Why can't you be normal? I'm going to give you to a foster home*) still defines any identity I could possibly assume.

When we move I sign up for music class at high school and join the choir, where the Black girls are all altos, and the white girls are all sopranos. Choir members are encouraged to try out for the annual school musical. This year, it's *Guys and Dolls*. As I walk down the hallway toward the music room on an open practice day before auditorium tryouts, I don't see any of my Black friends. Instead, there is a sea of blond hair, alligator sweaters, and deck shoes crowded around the piano singing "Climb Ev'ry Mountain" — a song I have never heard before from a movie I've never seen, but a song I will remember from this day forward — so I veer away from the music room doors, turn right into the stairwell, and head out into the parking lot without even breaking my stride. I don't show up for tryouts. Weeks later, when I forget I'm not alone and start singing "White Christmas" at a family member's apartment, they look at me in shock and say, "What a beautiful voice." But it doesn't matter what anyone says, or that I hear the same thing 10 years later when I'm living in Toronto and I think no one will hear me when I sing along with a women's hand-drum group. I think I'm a worthless piece of shit who can't do anything right.

As a consolation prize, I decide that I will hide backstage: I join the makeup crew. On opening night, I am assigned one of the principal male cast members. He's a redhead from a very privileged neighbourhood, a descendant of old money and entrenched status. I stand in front of him and my hands shake as I apply his foundation and eyeliner. I don't say anything — not one word — as I work on his face. I feel different, wrong. I want to be part of the world I see around me, but I don't know how. I have never been this close to another human being by choice before, and I'm sure I'm doing this all wrong. Later, I see him with a cast mate, touching up his face, and I know it's all my fault. I don't go back for the second night's performance, and I know deep in my being that they're happy I'm gone.

Exactly 24 years later, I am sitting on the steps of the Art Gallery of Ontario on Dundas Street West in Toronto, early for my interview in the Education Department. It doesn't matter that they picked my résumé out of the hundreds that they received. I watch people walk by and I have the same feeling: I don't belong here. I am nothing and no one.

A year after I'm hired at the AGO, I attend a conference hosted by the Indigenous Studies department at Trent University in Peterborough, Ontario. I haven't seen it on the calendar, and I don't plan to attend, but I stumble across a sign announcing that there will be a women's *haka* workshop from 1 to 4 p.m. It's 12:50, so I enter the room. The woman who is facilitating the workshop — Mihirangi, a Maori singer-songwriter who will be a finalist (and judges' favourite) in the 2012 season of *New Zealand's Got Talent* — comes from a long line of women who are keepers of Maori spiritual knowledge and healing. We begin the workshop with the *hongi*, a Maori greeting that is done by pressing one's nose and forehead against another person. The hongi is the exchange and intermingling of the breath of life and the sharing of both people's souls. When Mihirangi circles around the room to do the hongi with each participant, she gets to me, we do the touch — then she steps back and says, "Huh." It's not a derisive sound, or an amused sound, just a contemplative pause. Although I don't know it at the time, what she is noticing is how walled off I am. I lean my forehead and nose toward her, but I do not in any way join with her. I am separate, and in my trauma-related belief system, that means I am safe.

The Maori haka is known as a war dance performed only by men, a tool to challenge and intimidate an opponent, a way to show defiance and resistance. But as Mihirangi teaches us, the haka is also about honouring one's opponent and creating a sacred space. It raises the vibrations of the person doing it and the person receiving it. Like all Indigenous music, whether singing or drumming, the aim is to create entrainment, whereby the individual's inner rhythms synch up with the external environment and the other people around them. And the haka is not only done by men. Mihirangi tells us that women have always had their own haka, which they use to invoke and express their ancestral spiritual power, or *whakapapa*. When we wave our open hands, we gather and spread our energy and the energy of the universe. As Mihirangi explains it, our downward movements gather energy from the Earth Mother, while upward movements gather energy from Father Sky. The waving movements we perform on the lower torso speak to receptive energy and the power that comes with it; the action of our fists on other places on the lower torso speak to active energy and the power that comes with it. When we extend our arms and close one fist around the other arm, we are gathering energy around ourselves. The haka is about joining the human physical body to the energy of the universe to create balance, strength, and connection.

At the end of their haka, men make terrifying faces to frighten the enemy. At the end of their haka, women jut out their chins to display their genealogy tattoos and bulge out their eyes, which allows the ancestors to enter the room through their bodies.

As we work together for those three hours on a Saturday afternoon in Peterborough, I feel the energy shift in the room. I feel myself open and connect to the manitow we embody and the manitow we create. Learning Mihirangi's haka helps me inhabit my body. It also helps me learn how to connect myself to a larger external reality. When we debrief at the end of the workshop, I thank Mihirangi for her wisdom and teachings. She hugs me and says, "This is exactly why I do what I do. I just saw you transform before my eyes." Then she gives us permission to use her haka for our own purposes: as our own ceremony, or shared with others.

Three years later, I'm working with Celina, and we're talking about the problems I always have with my sacrum. It keeps popping out of alignment, giving me back pain. The sacrum forms the base of the spine, intersecting with the hip bones to form the pelvis. It supports the weight of the upper body as it is spread across the pelvis and into the legs. Celina tells me that fear causes our qi to drop down to the sacrum, toward the centre of the body, which causes the body to contract in self-protection. She also tells me that my weak spleen energy is a result of unresolved emotions and my tendency to be overly empathetic to the suffering of others while ignoring my own. This echoes what an Indigenous medicine person tells me 15 years earlier when I attend a one-on-one session at the Indigenous health centre. After we smudge and I'm finished talking, the medicine person says, "You think too much."

In traditional Chinese medicine, the spleen carries the qi of the earth. Celina says I need to get out of my head and spend more time connecting to the natural world. So I start doing Mihirangi's haka outside, on the grass in my bare feet. After I finish, I lie down on the earth with my arms spread out wide. One day, as Celina is treating yet another sacrum alignment issue, she gets to the heart of the matter. She takes her fingers away from my wrist, where she has been feeling my pulses, looks at me, and says, "You have a right to be here, you know." Celina's words help me understand my worth. I am part of creation, connected to the wind that whips up from Skanadariio (the "handsome lake" in the language of the Haudenosaunee, also known as Lake Ontario), the trees outside my window, the hawks that hunt pigeon in the parking lot up the street, and the water that flows underground, feeding the Humber River watershed. I am part of a web of creation. If the natural world is sacred, then that makes me sacred. I'm not nothing and no one. I have a right to be here.

Eight years after that first haka workshop, Mihirangi plays Toronto as part of a Canadian tour. After her set, I go to the side of the stage where she's talking to fans and selling CDs. We exchange a hug, and I say, "Thank you. Thank you for the work that you do." The next day, after a one-hour haka session, Mihirangi and the two young women who are touring with her go around the circle to exchange the hongi with participants. When Mihirangi gets to me, we touch foreheads. I breathe in and out and connect to her life force. She breathes slowly and deeply and says, "Thank you, Suzanne. Thank you." We give each other the gift of connection and relationship. This is the foundation that makes us human. This is what makes us whole.

Prior to colonization, Indigenous societies were structured by systems that emphasized connection. Communities were structured so that individuals had to be part of something larger than themselves. Ceremonial lodges, teaching societies, clans, and council fires assisted the individual in learning how to create a balance between the internal environment (an individual's own active and receptive energy) and the external environment connecting the self to other people, the natural world, and the spirit world. However, colonization has disrupted the connection between Indigenous individuals, their communities, and the wider world around them. Today, the Aboriginal Healing Foundation includes "the breakdown of the social glue that holds families and communities together," "disconnection from the natural world," and "spiritual confusion involving alienation from one's own spiritual life and growth process" as three of the everyday impacts of intergenerational trauma.

In the Nehiyawak worldview, an individual's spirit surrounds and holds within it everything that exists in the natural world: rocks, soil, trees, plants, air, water, wind, minerals, and animals. Even things that are made through human innovation — tools, technology, housing, and clothing (which themselves all contain aspects of the natural world) — become part of the world around us and therefore part of our spirit. These entities hold the basic mysterious energy of the universe; the manitow that drives and connects all existence. How an individual connects to these forces accounts for their ability to live well in the world.

In contemporary Indigenous communities, people often speak about things being done "in a good way." This means that people approve of an action and the way a person goes about that action. It also means that a person chooses to live the right way and do the right thing — according to the principles of respect, responsibility, reciprocity, and relationship — because it serves the health of their spirit to do so. To do something "in a good way" is to create beneficial energy in thought and action. In the Indigenous universe, the spirit is affected by everything and affects everything, in accordance with the principles of frequency, resonance, and similarity. A person's body, health, and mood are all created by the spirit, by the power within each individual and by the power that surrounds each individual. Elders and knowledge carriers say it is important to speak softly and thoughtfully, because words have power. When telling or listening to a story, the task for teller and listeners in the Indigenous universe is not just to perceive meaning but to create a field of energy within the circle and within the world. This energy can, of course, be used for good or for evil purposes, to support or to derail. This is why it is important to be disciplined and kind in one's thinking and one's words — because what an individual puts out into the world not only affects the world but also affects the shape, frequency, and resonance of their own being. We are what we do, think, and say.

In the Nehiyawak universe, what we do, think, and say is a reciprocal process mediated by interaction with the spirit world, the natural world, the animal world, and other human beings. The aim of life is to create health, wellness, and power by cultivating awareness of and exchanges with those worlds. True power does not come from having *power over* other things — it comes from creating *power with*.

Innu elder-activist Elizabeth Penashue once told me that she worries about the caribou antlers she sees Innu hunters throwing out into the yard in her homeland of Nitassinan (Labrador). She feels that the influence of the Hudson's Bay Company, the Christian church, and the colonial government have changed the way that some of the hunters interact with the caribou spirits. In the old days, antlers would be placed together in a special holding spot, before being taken back out to the bush and disposed of properly, with ceremony and respect. Penashue says that today, many hunters just throw the antlers down on the ground and fail to take them back out to the bush. She is concerned about the negative energy these actions are creating in Innu communities — and what effects this is having on the human and natural world.

Abe Stewart, an elder in Fort McPherson, Northwest Territories, tells the CBC in 2015 that he is happy that the community has "come to life" since caribou have returned to the area. But he also says that young hunters are not respecting the animals or the land. Conservation officers have found caribou left dead or injured off the Dempster Highway. Stewart says that most older hunters are taking caribou to feed themselves and their families, but that younger hunters are often killing for sport, "to have fun and to shoot at something. From what I see, there was no respect at all." Stewart says that parents should go hunting with their children so that they learn how to demonstrate that respect. The problem is colonial policy and practice has interrupted the ability of many families to pass on this knowledge. Residential schools, land dispossession, Christianization, the demonization of Indigenous knowledge, and changes in migration patterns and the number of animals in an area due to resource extraction, highways, and other interferences means that young people are not learning what they need to know. So if young people are disconnected, it isn't their fault. It is the duty of elders, parents, and knowledge keepers to tell the younger generation what they need to know. And those in the dominant society have a duty to ensure that colonial structures and systems do not interfere with this way of life or this knowledge transfer.

Joe Karetak, an Inuk hunter and director of the Arviat Wellness Centre in Arviat, Nunavut, is addressing this need by running a Young Hunter program in his community. Karetak says that the program gives young people the opportunity to take part in activities that allow them to learn about the land, including survival and harvesting techniques. But that's just the surface. As Karetak tells me in 2016, "It's not only about learning how to harvest animals — it's about learning your identity. You can see how happy the young people are, because they're doing something that feels natural to them, and for a long time, they've not felt like they are a part of this, or could feel natural about the way they've been living, because there's no cultural content in their lives."

Karetak believes that forced settlement into communities has had negative effects on Inuit youth in terms of their connection to the natural world. "Back in the 1960s," he says, "here in this community, the community used to provide instruction, especially to youth that didn't have someone to take them out [on the land]. To this day, they are able to provide for their families. But the way things changed so fast , , , they were discouraged from teaching their kids their own culture for quite a while. And when they got moved to the community, they immediately changed their nomadic lifestyle to being stationary. So it took awhile to get used to living in this one place. Once people started doing that, they started passing on some of the skills and knowledge again."

Empathy is the ability to understand the experience of another being. Reconnecting to the natural world — recognizing that everything around you has a life force that is equal to your own — helps people develop empathy. Understanding another being's experience involves identifying with that being and seeing yourself as that other being: taking their experience into yourself, feeling or thinking about that experience, and then withdrawing from the other being in order to regain your own individual perspective. This process of identifying with the other requires the individual to have a sense of self. If an individual is never treated as a sacred being, or their needs are never met, then they don't learn to see themselves as individuals, let alone sacred beings. If individuals don't see themselves as sacred, then they cannot possibly know or understand the sacredness present in anyone else.

In 2016, a young person from Easterville, Manitoba, is arrested by the RCMP after he posts a video on Facebook that shows him raising his arms and throwing a German shepherd puppy to the pavement. The friend who is recording the video says off-camera, "That's fucked up," but doesn't stop it. Some people might think the story has a happy ending because the dog — who is initially thought to be paralyzed — not only lives but regains the ability to walk. But that's a misapprehension of the story. If he is convicted, the young person might be fined, sent to jail, or put on probation. But going to jail, paying a fine, or reporting to a probation officer is not going to address the story that this young person is carrying.

Easterville was created by the federal and provincial governments in 1962 after the hydroelectric dam project at Grand Rapids, Manitoba, flooded Indigenous communities in the area. The relocation of these communities to Easterville resulted in the loss of pre-colonial Indigenous economies, broken kinship structures, unstable leadership within a colonial governance system, a breakdown in family cohesion, increased use of alcohol, interpersonal violence, child neglect, and incidents of crime and vandalism committed by young people. According to researcher Michael Landa, the relocation disrupted "the continuity of their social relationships, economic base, worldview, and ecological setting." When trapping, gardening, and harvesting seneca root became impossible — because the new community lacked soil and vegetation — people became disconnected from the natural world. Young people saw no hope for the future, and, as University of Saskatchewan professor James Waldram says, they began to "view the traditional occupations of their parents with disdain," which led them to "no longer respect the authority of their elders." Without connection to the natural world, young people miss an opportunity to learn how to create a sacred self. Without that sense, they cannot recognize the sacredness in others. And here's why that matters: the young person who throws the puppy to the pavement is also charged with injuring a different animal a few months before the incident that is caught on camera. That kind of pattern — a need for power and control, with no ability to comprehend or care about the distress they are causing — will have profound implications for the wider community as this young person grows into adulthood.

In 2017, a 19-month-old toddler is found dead outside a church in Edmonton, Alberta, where his body has been dumped. Police say the bruises all over his body show he lived a "horrible life of violence and abuse" before finally dying of head trauma. In 2014, a two year old boy from the Tsuut'ina First Nation near Calgary, Alberta, is admitted to hospital with injuries and dies a week later. His mother is charged with his murder. At the Peguis First Nation in Manitoba in 2014, a 21-month-old girl dies of blunt force trauma to the abdomen and internal bleeding after suffering prolonged physical abuse at the hands of her mother, who hit, kicked, and dragged her. She has a dislocated shoulder, several broken bones, bruises, scars, five missing teeth, and is so malnourished that she is anemic and stunted in height and weight. In 2017, the body of a 19-year-old girl is found at Manitoba's Sagkeeng First Nation after a video is posted to Facebook showing two other girls — one 16 years old, the other 17 — beating the victim and stomping on her head with a heavy boot. In Duncan, BC, an 18-year-old girl from the Cowichan First Nation is strangled and beaten to death in 2011 by another member of the community, and, according to the *Toronto Star*, one of the items returned to the victim's mother by police is "four teeth knocked out from their roots, braces still attached."

The horror in the above paragraph is not included for shock value or to arm any right-wing "news" organizations with more material to pathologize Indigenous peoples and communities. It is included to underscore the disproportionate presence of interpersonal violence within Indigenous communities — and just how *personal* that interpersonal violence is. When Nadine knocks me down and kicks me in the head and face, she is attempting to erase me and the smile I have that day in a moment of hard-won, minidress-related confidence. My happiness triggers in her a visceral rage, which she directs toward me simply for the crime of existing. This kind of rage is created by disconnection and invalidation.

The human relationship with the natural world is one of our earliest reciprocal relationships. Discovering our connection to the land — what ecopsychologists call "embeddedness" and Indigenous people call interrelatedness — and our moral obligation to care for a specific place not only results in inclusion within community but also teaches us purpose. The lessons we receive from the natural world are vital to our development, teaching us awareness and giving us a sense of place — both of which help balance the internal and external worlds. When an individual is in a state of disconnection, it deprives them of a sense of security and responsibility, altering their feelings about themself and negatively affecting their ability to connect with others.

In the Florentine Codex — a series of 12 books on Aztec culture created from interviews with Aztec elders conducted by the Spanish friar Bernardino de Sahagún in the 16th century — elders recount the following proverb: "On earth we live, we travel along a mountain peak. Over here there is an abyss, over there is an abyss. If you go over here, or if you go over there, you will fall in. You should go only in the middle, you should live only in the middle." Balance is integral to health and wellness, and this balance is defined and illustrated partly by our relationship with the Earth. The Aztec proverb mirrors the Nehiyawak concept of *pêyâhtakêyimowin*, or "peace within yourself." Pêyâhtakêyimowin is the state of being wherein an individual takes things slowly, which means being careful, being quiet, and not getting riled up. The natural world teaches the individual how to create peace within themselves by teaching them about balance and caution. A hunter will only be successful if they are careful and quiet. A medicine person trying to locate a certain healing plant will only be given the gift of finding that plant if they are deliberate and slow. Indigenous ways of seeing the world, and ways of seeing *in* the world, are based on connection and a balance between being and doing.

This idea of balance, or the middle way, is reflected in Indigenous cultures across the Americas. In the Inuit universe, there is a world above and a world below, and certain Inuit traditions are about maintaining the distinction between complementary opposites such as land and sea or men and women. Maintaining balance ensures order, much as the maintenance of the internal and external worlds of the individual also ensures order. In the universe of the Eeyou, there are wind people who mediate the realms of space and time to ensure order in the everyday world. The wind people also connect the human world and the natural world with the spirit world. They live in the upper world, but they affect the lower world on Earth. Again, the lesson is one of balance and order and connection.

Métis doctoral student Jesse Thistle has created a 12-part definition of Indigenous homelessness in Canada that covers a range of historical and contemporary contexts, including something Thistle calls "spiritual disconnection homelessness." Thistle defines spiritual disconnection homelessness as an "Indigenous individual's or community's separation from Indigenous worldviews or connection to the Creator or equivalent deity." For Indigenous peoples, the concept of home is rooted in a web of relationships and responsibilities that involve "connections to human kinship networks; relationships with animals, plants, spirits, and elements; relationships with the Earth, lands, waters, and territories; and connection to traditional stories, songs, teachings, names, and ancestors." Without these circles of connection, Indigenous peoples are "rootless, unanchored, or homeless," deprived of the healthy social, cultural, spiritual, emotional, and physical relationships that once led to what Thistle describes as a "holistic metaphysical understanding of emplacement." For people who have experienced trauma, or who are dealing with the everyday impacts of trauma, this lack of emplacement results in a sense of homelessness within themselves, which results in an inability to navigate into and out of the external world as well.

Complex post-traumatic stress disorder leads to alterations in self-perception. According to Judith Lewis Herman, survivors of trauma often develop a feeling of separateness or difference from others. This phenomenon is connected to a lack of trust, a general sense that they are unsafe in the world, and a belief that they must rely solely upon themselves in order to ensure their survival. These beliefs prevent survivors from feeling connected to anyone or anything.

I learn how powerful connection really is when I am asked to facilitate a talking circle for a neighbourhood group in Toronto. We spend three hours together, eating a meal to start, co-creating the principles that will guide our work, and then passing the stone around the circle as we each take a turn to talk. The stone is a gift from a friend. It was painted by an artisan co-operative in the Philippines, and it's the perfect size for holding in one hand. After we close the circle, I place the stone and some other items off to the side of my chair while I collect the flip charts and individual pieces of paper we used to create our principles of engagement. The mood in the room is good, so people want to talk. It takes me 15 minutes to get back to my chair. When I return to my chair and pick up the stone, it is warm to the touch. The room we are in is a tiny north-facing storefront, and at this time of the evening, the sun is behind us, and we get no direct light. There is no lamp nearby, and we did not use a candle or other flame. The overhead lights are a cool, flickering fluorescent. It's summer, so the heat isn't on — and it's not a particularly hot day, which means the room is comfortable. No one has touched the stone since we ended the circle. As I sit there and think about what I am being shown, the heat stays constant: not hot but a nice, constant warmth that does not change even when I put the stone down and pick it up again. Somehow, the stone has stored all the energy of the people in the circle. Who we are, what we think, and what we said is here inside the stone. The stone — our link to the natural world — is mediating and linking our world to the spirit world, guiding the group as they seek to make change in their community.

If we did not have the stone to mediate for us in the spirit world, we would have to rely solely on talking. The European focus on talking as a form of therapy has its roots in the writing of René Descartes and reflects his belief that "I think, therefore I am." The resulting Cartesian dualism — wherein the mind is separated from the physical and spiritual aspects of the individual, and the individual is separated from the natural world — does not reflect Indigenous ideas on healing or wellness. And in the context of healing from trauma, talk therapy has its limits.

Therapy is good at helping individuals explore their thoughts and feelings, and it provides survivors with a chance to focus on their past and create a coherent narrative of their traumatic memories. Connecting with a therapist in the safety of a therapeutic relationship can also help the survivor understand any issues they may have with lack of trust and the dissociation they use as a survival instinct. However, even in a supportive environment framed by a practice relationship with the therapist, talk is limited in dealing with the physical and spiritual issues caused by the experience of trauma. In order to heal, Indigenous survivors need to undertake a physical or somatic journey, undergo a spiritual awakening, and dislodge the traumatic story on an energetic level. Words alone cannot integrate disorganized sensory knowledge that is buried deep within the survivor's body. Talking can also be an avoidance technique, where survivors use the time with the therapist as a way of avoiding distressing sensations and traumatic memories. This is why pre-colonial Indigenous healing methodologies included art, ceremony, activities on the land, somatic approaches, herbal medicine, storytelling, and talk. To resolve the disconnection created by a traumatic experience, the survivor needs to engage in activities that rearrange their relationship with their physical body and renew their connection to the spirit world.

Many on-reserve communities and urban Indigenous communities have advocated for youth recreation centres as a major platform for dealing with the everyday impacts of trauma. It is definitely a good idea to create a space where young people can gather, somewhere where they are not turned away if they are under the influence of drugs or alcohol, somewhere where they can engage in physical activity or games that allow them to exist as children for a while, free of the adult responsibilities they often face in dysfunctional families and communities. Here they can engage with staff and learn valuable life skills by working through the usual problems that arise out of everyday relationships and challenges. But a recreation centre is not a complete recipe for healing from chronic or intergenerational trauma, because young people need more than just unstructured fun time. They need to engage in activities that dismantle their trauma-related coping mechanisms and dislodge their internalized feelings of shame and self-blame.

A Calgary non-profit agency is using an innovative approach to engage Indigenous youth in activities that require thinking, feeling, and doing. The Urban Society for Aboriginal Youth (USAY) set up three interconnected escape rooms in the city library as part of a free program called Unlocking Homelessness. Teams of young people volunteer to enter the rooms, where they have to solve a series of interactive puzzles in order to escape. Each room has a different theme: the party room contains props related to drug and alcohol abuse; the alley room — which is entered by climbing through a cabinet — deals with death and grief; and the nice house represents success and happiness. As USAY executive director LeeAnne Ireland tells the CBC in 2017, "We've built in all these metaphors — follow the light, follow the positivity. . . . We have this whole theme about layers, so it's all about unlocking different layers in your life and overcoming one step, then the next step, and the next step." This is exactly the kind of learning that ongoing land-based activities offered Indigenous peoples in pre-colonial times.

Developing a connection to the natural world is possible anywhere. When we see a tree growing out of concrete, we learn that it's possible to thrive in less than ideal conditions. When we see a city bird making a nest on top of a business sign on a busy commercial street, we know that it's possible to create a home anywhere, as long as we live in balance with everything around us. When we look to the natural world, we take that strength into ourselves — and we can give back what we don't want to carry anymore. The natural world provides a chance for connection when survivors can't (or don't want to) connect with other people.

Lakota scholar Maria Yellow Horse Brave Heart has written about the concept of "disenfranchised grief," which she defines as "the sense that you cannot grieve; that no one hears or is listening to your grief." Disenfranchised grief is created "when a loss cannot be openly acknowledged or publicly mourned." Yellow Horse Brave Heart says the absence of rituals to facilitate the mourning process — a situation created by colonization and cultural genocide — can severely limit the resolution of grief, leading to sadness that becomes deeply buried, eventually turning into malignant anger, depression, or a sense of shame. According to Yellow Horse Brave Heart, "Grief covered by shame negatively impacts relationships with self and others and one's realization of the sacredness within oneself and one's community." With that, Yellow Horse Brave Heart identifies exactly what is behind the youth suicide crises in so many Indigenous communities.

Complex trauma affects an individual's sense of self and their ability to form relationships. Survivors of chronic trauma or people dealing with the everyday impacts of trauma often develop negative beliefs about themselves, their worth in relationships, and the motivations of others. These beliefs are reinforced when survivors enter into adult relationships only to find that they replay the dissatisfactions, abandonment, and abuses of the survivor's past. That's why land-based activities and recreation centre programming must be intentional and trauma-informed. Relationships with peers and elders can become a testing ground for the development of skills relating to relationships — creating and experiencing connection, trusting others, developing a sense of self-worth, setting boundaries, learning to feel and to trust their physical and emotional states — but only if those peers and elders are not re-enacting trauma-related behaviours themselves. Given the impact of colonization on Indigenous communities, and the everyday impacts of trauma, this is a tall order — but it is certainly not impossible.

The Eeyou community of Chisasibi, in northern Quebec, has developed a land-based healing program that addresses colonization, land dispossession, forced relocation, and the everyday impacts of intergenerational trauma through the renewal of relationships and the reclamation of Eeyou identity. Elder Eddie Pashagumkum came up with the vision for the program in 2012, which he describes as aiming to "improve the mental health of individuals so that they can effectively participate in the life of their family and community and make positive contributions to the collective development of their nation." The program is structured around Pashagumkum's knowledge about Eeyou personhood and the Eeyou belief in creating harmony through relationships, using a "healing pedagogy" that employs storytelling, detoxification, physical activity, and the science of connection to create change in the realms of mind, body, spirit, and emotion, with effects in both the internal and external realms. It takes place on his family's hunting territory 500 kilometres east of Chisasibi over a period of two to three weeks. Although the program is culture-based, it is also intentionally educational in design and delivery, using bush lectures and instruction in bush skills as the central curriculum. A typical day includes morning lectures given by Pashagumkum, an afternoon bush activity (hunting, fishing, trapping, picking berries, building shelter), and an evening lecture or group discussion to ensure reciprocity. One-on one counselling with Pashagumkum or another elder takes place as needed throughout the day at the request of the participant or as part of the bush activity. All participants are expected to contribute to the health and success of the camp by cleaning, cooking, chopping wood, fetching water, and helping other people. On occasion, Pashagumkum sends participants into the bush alone, to give them the chance to reflect on the information presented in the lectures and to think about how that information might relate to their own lives. Lecture topics include Forgiveness, Impacts of Hydro Development (Loss and Grief), What Has Hunting Got to Do With Abuse?, and Jealousy (Within You and Toward Others).

The Chisasibi program pursues a path of decolonization and personal transformation so that participants can understand the reasons for their past actions and behaviour and begin to make changes, creating an "ordered and productive self" that lives in harmony with others, including the natural world. According to a research paper on the Chisasibi program, "The constant interaction with the land, by knowing it with all five senses, guides individuals and provides what is needed to live in harmony with the environment, with each other, and with oneself. The reciprocal and dialogic relationship with nature provides not only the material needs but also the ethical, moral, and spiritual underpinnings of living a good life." In Pashagumkum's words, "If I sit down in the middle of the woods with all this pain, what am I going to do? If I look up I see all the trees. If I look at the tree that is alive and well, beautiful . . . how did he become like that? He didn't get mad at anybody to be like this. Ask nature to take care of you. Don't be afraid to talk to nature."

In a 2014 study published in the journal *Science*, researchers at the Hebrew University of Jerusalem sequenced the genome of a Neanderthal bone and a Denisovan bone — human species that interbred with today's *Homo sapiens* before going extinct. When the researchers compared the ancient epigenetic maps to those of contemporary humans, they discovered that 99 per cent of the ancient and contemporary maps were the same — except in the regions associated with psychological and neurological disease. This suggests that genes in the human brain have changed recently and that disorders and diseases such as autism, schizophrenia, and Alzheimer's are the result of these changes. The researchers believe that the changes — and the increase in psychological and neurological disease — are related to the cognitive abilities of contemporary humans. This proves what Indigenous peoples already know: that the shift to a purely intellectual existence is creating imbalance and dis-ease.

The good news is manitow is always ready to change. Manitow exists to provide the energy necessary for the transformation of everything in the universe, including the human body, mind, and spirit (and human relationships). When an individual is out of balance, they can always use manitow to rebalance themselves. They can use the medicine wheel to circle back around and revisit what they've missed in order to grow and change. It is never too late to change, because manitow is always waiting for human beings to enter into the harmonious relationships that will connect us to the natural world and to each other.

Pueblo scholar Gregory Cajete says that healthy societies can only be created from healthy communities made up of self-determining individuals taking responsibility for their actions and respecting all other beings in the universe. Prior to colonization, Indigenous communities were often created around something in the natural world, such as salmon runs or bison trails, that required ceremony to sustain. This ceremony mediates the space between human beings and the natural world, teaching balance and reciprocity. It helps reinforce community by enabling individuals to *practise* community. Ceremony also helps maintain and extend community.

Connecting to the natural world is a transformative force, one that is key to healing and change.

CHAPTER 9

RECREATING THE STRUCTURES OF BELONGING

Every week, we sit together. Sometimes it only takes three hours. Sometimes it takes six. We start at 6 p.m., and we sit in the circle until we are done. No one needs to get a drink of water. No one needs to pee. No one gets tired. The circle keeps us strong and connected. We are the circle, and the circle is everything. Afterward, we go around the corner to the Groaning Board on Jarvis Street for a sandwich or a tea.

The Monday Night Healing Circle happens at the Indigenous health centre in Toronto. We're a mixed group, Indigenous and non-Indigenous, and that's a good thing. We are learning about one another: what it means to have a voice, what it means to listen. We're learning that everyone has pain.

It is 1993. Some of us are returning to our roots, reclaiming our Indigenous identities. We protested in the streets in 1990 over the government's response to the land-rights issue in Kanehsatake (Oka). We marched to the legislature at Queen's Park to provide a counter-narrative to the 1992 Columbus quincentenary. We gather now to look inward, to create something personal out of our political (re)awakening.

If we are white, we come from a range of backgrounds — we are academics, health-care workers, students, and filmmakers — but we are all people who want a different world than the one we have inherited. If we are Indigenous, we are also from a wide range of backgrounds, but we have one important commonality: we are alone. We are foster kids or adopted out. We live far away from home territories. We come from families who deny their Indigenous heritage. We are residential school survivors and descendants of survivors. We are formerly incarcerated people with no ties to community other than the ones we know on the street. We are from broken families. We are in our 20s and in our 50s, and we want to belong.

It isn't pretty sometimes. Once, when the eagle feather comes to me, I say, "We need to treat each other better," and Nancy gets up from her seat and walks around the inner circle to put some tobacco in the bowl of burning sage. She says, "Ahow," to let everyone know she supports my statement, but she is clearly disturbed. We are all bothered by the way some people in the circle have been talking about other people, and tonight's circle has been heavy and weird. Another time, I get a phone call at 2 a.m. from Hilda, who says that Patrick just called her from a phone booth on Sherbourne. He's drunk and in crisis, so she's going to ride her bike over, and she wants to know if I can go with her. One night, Levi — the pipe carrier who facilitates the circle — shows up at my door with bloody knuckles and a jumbled story about his friend Fran and a fight on her street. We are imperfect, but we are trying. We are learning how to love ourselves. We are learning how to love other people.

One Monday, without warning, Levi hands me the eagle feather and tells me to do the opening prayer. My heart is racing and I have no idea what to say, but I start with what I know: it's raining outside, so I thank the rain. Halfway through, I catch Levi looking at me out of the corner of his eye, and I realize he's had this planned all along. The circle teaches me what it means to take responsibility for the well-being of my community.

The next year, the health centre decides that the circle should be for Indigenous people only. They bring in an outside facilitator and a box of cookies, and they tell us one night without Levi there. I say, "This circle has taught me so much. My first night, as soon as I walked in and heard Levi sing, I knew I was home." Someone, a man, sobs. The health centre is breaking up our family. When we take a break, the facilitator disappears and we all know that she has refused to continue. A staff member steps in to continue the dirty work.

We are wounded, but we learn. We learn that community is about possibility. What do we want to build now? How should we build it? Who will be our leaders? We become powerful when we decide to act in the world, instead of allowing ourselves to be acted upon.

I use this power to connect our communities, so we can work together on the things that matter. I work with non-Indigenous people to organize a benefit concert for the Muskotew Sakahikan Enowuk women's circle, bringing two Lubicon women from northern Alberta to Toronto, where a group of Quechua musicians from the Andes and some Haudenosaunee social dance singers donate their time to appear at the event. I borrow a kitchen at a local Indigenous organization and organize a feast for elder-activist

Elizabeth Penashue and the Innu people of Sheshatshiu, to let them know that they have support in their fight against military low-level flight testing in Nitassinan (Labrador). I volunteer to help with an online conference at Ryerson University that includes members of the Zapatista National Liberation Army, Mayan farmers, and a media co-op in Chiapas, Mexico, after NAFTA passes in 1994 and before the internet becomes a reliable thing. I learn that community is what we make it. I learn that being a citizen of a community is not about delegating: it's about being accountable.

We are the circle, and the circle is everything.

Kanienkehaka scholar Gerald Taiaiake Alfred describes colonization in Canada as having three components: ongoing multi-generational processes of dispossession and oppression, violent and systematic marginalization and assimilation, and accultura-tion via forced conversion to Christianity and forced integration to market capitalism. The connection between colonization and chronic trauma is clear. Market capitalism — from the fur trade to resource extraction to agribusiness to the provision of food and building materials to isolated northern communities — is a key part of colonization, tied to the appropriation of Indigenous lands and the marginalization of Indigenous peoples. So it is fundamen-tal that Indigenous peoples actively resist market capitalism and reinvent Indigenous economies as a function of decolonization and healing.

Prior to colonization, Indigenous economies were dynamic and highly evolved. Archaeologists have found copper from Lake Superior as far south as the Gulf of Mexico, and *American Anthropologist* magazine has published research showing that inter-locking trade routes criss-crossed the Americas, with asphaltum (tar) and obsidian traded from California to as far east as Oklahoma and the Mississippi, and textiles and pottery flowing back west. Inca traders made regular voyages up and down the coast of South America from Peru to Panama in ocean-going boats, according to cultural historian Ronald Wright in his book *An Illustrated Short History of Progress*. The Incan boats had crews of up to 20 men and carried tonnes of freight. These trade routes and relationships were based on negotiating ongoing shifts in the political, cultural, and environmental landscape. Indigenous economic systems supported small bands that travelled with the season, sedentary farming communities, hierarchical societies such as the Inca and those on the Northwest Coast, and vast political alliances such as the Haudenosaunee Confederacy.

Indigenous peoples lived sustainably, and they expected leaders and others with wealth to share that wealth so that everyone enjoyed a basic standard of living, no matter what their role, age, or health status. This is not a romanticized version of pre-colonial Indigenous societies. We know this to be true because it is embedded in the systems of Indigenous societies at the time of contact: the potlatch ceremony on the Northwest Coast, in which leaders distribute their wealth to the community; the seasonal shifts of the northern Nehiyawak, who knew not to overfish lakes; and the giveaway ceremony that redistributes the possessions of someone who has died. The market capitalist system introduced by the colonizer, however, has disrupted Indigenous relationships to the land and to each other. As Unangax educator Eve Tuck and educator and community organizer K. Wayne Yang have written, in market capitalism, "land is remade into property and human relationships to land are restricted to the relationship of the owner to his property." In this system, Indigenous economic frameworks — and the complex holistic philosophies that define them — are considered primitive and irrelevant. In this system, the natural world is used to create wealth and privilege for those in power. In this system, shared rights and responsibilities are not important, and ownership is used to exclude others. In this system, inequality in economic power translates into inequality in political power. Market capitalism is, therefore, inconsistent with decolonization and healing.

The work of geographer Jared Diamond — author of the Pulitzer Prize–winning *Guns, Germs, and Steel* — has advanced the now-popular idea that disease and differing material cultures were the sole reasons that Indigenous populations were decimated after contact and colonization. This portrays colonization as a collection of unfortunate happenstance, downplaying the fact that colonization was a deliberate and directed campaign aimed at dispossessing Indigenous peoples of their land so that settlers could profit from it instead. In the guns, germs, and steel scenario, Indigenous slavery is also never discussed. But the truth is Indigenous slavery predated African slavery, was more widespread, and continued into the 20th century, long after African slavery was abolished and despite laws in the United States and Mexico that were supposed to end the practice. The Americas were built on market capitalism that functions through the subjugation of Indigenous peoples and the appropriation of Indigenous lands.

As Andrés Reséndez puts forth in his book *The Other Slavery: The Uncovered Story of Indian Enslavement in America*, entire Indigenous populations on several Caribbean islands were annihilated in the years after contact, as Indigenous peoples were forced to work in gold and silver mines. The Spanish mission system in California, Mexico, and the U.S. Southwest removed Indigenous peoples from their lands and forced them into slavery. Spanish explorer Hernán Cortés, territorial governors in New Mexico, and U.S. officials all owned Indigenous slaves, and for many years, white Southern colonists exported more Indigenous people from the southeastern U.S. than they imported Black slaves. Reséndez says that conflicts such as the 1680 Pueblo Revolt were spurred in large part by the ongoing capture and enslavement of Indigenous peoples from various regions of New Mexico, who were put to work in the silver mines in Mexico. According to Reséndez, tens of thousands of Indigenous people were worked to death even after the monarchy in Spain outlawed slavery.

After the removal of the Choctaw, Seminole, Creek, Chickasaw, and Cherokee nations from their traditional territories in the southeast United States in the early 19th century, 25 million acres of land were opened for colonial resettlement. After the numbered treaties were signed on the Canadian prairies, the government of Canada gained all the land from Lake of the Woods to the Rocky Mountains to the Beaufort Sea for industrial development and white settlement. Indigenous lands are the economy of Canada, from resource extraction to conventional farming, and this economy has had drastic negative effects on Indigenous cultures and societies.

Nehiyaw medicine person Russell Willier of the Sucker Creek First Nation in northern Alberta shared his knowledge with University of Alberta researchers David Young and Lise Swartz and Grant Ingram, a graduate student at SUNY Buffalo, in the 1980s. He was concerned that the plants he used for his prescriptions were disappearing, and that this would lead to the eventual loss of Nehiyawak science and medicine. Back then, Willier said, "The ones that are really doing the worst damage are the farmers. . . . We often have to travel long distances to get certain kinds of herbs because they're either ploughed under or they've drained the water right out. Where the marshes go dry, the plants quit growing . . . A lot of the plants are disappearing. If a farmer clears out four sections of land, or four quarters like they do in my area, they just wipe out the whole works. . . . Perhaps it could be arranged by the government that so many acres could be put aside . . . and just left there so the herbs will slowly keep growing in their natural habitat." In the

Indigenous universe, balance is key, and humans are part of the natural world. In conventional farming practice, this would be seen as "wasted" or "unproductive" land, because export markets are more important than ducks and geese, and Nehiyawak medicine belongs to the past.

As the geographer Cole Harris has written, the imposition of private property rights is part of the colonial government's system for surveillance of Indigenous peoples. After the relocation of First Nations peoples to reserves, Indian Agents were given the responsibility for monitoring the movement of people and goods. Now that there are no more Indian Agents, the work of monitoring Indigenous activity has been taken up by farmers, who own the land as private property under colonial law. This makes Indigenous peoples trespassers on their own land. In the words of Gerald Taiaiake Alfred, this involves "private citizens and the public at large in the process of colonization. The private property regime displaces Indigenous land uses, cutting off access to traditional food sources, timber, water, and other necessary resources." This displacement is central to the control relationship, and it robs Indigenous peoples of their agency, contributing to complex post-traumatic stress disorder.

Indigenous peoples who disrupt market capitalism suffer dire consequences, especially those who fight for the natural world. Environmental organizers and activists across the Americas are being murdered at alarming rates, with 2015 the worst year on record. During that year alone, the non-governmental organization Global Witness says that 122 people were killed for their efforts to protect the natural world from environmentally destructive mega-projects. The worst industries to campaign against are agribusiness and mining, with poaching, hydroelectric dams, logging, and tourist resorts following closely behind. Indigenous communities are always the hardest hit, with many killings occurring in remote villages inside rainforests and isolated mountain ranges. In Peru, José Napoleón Tarrillo Astonitas is tortured and killed for opposing the clearing of land and the planting of cash crops in the Chaparri ecological reserve. In Brazil, park ranger Edilson Aparecido dos Santos is killed by poachers inside the Capivara National Park (a UNESCO world heritage site and home to 25,000-year-old rock paintings). In Guatemala, Q'eqchi' Mayan environmental activist Adolfo Ich Chamán is murdered near the village of Lote Ocho, where security forces working for a mining company set fire to dozens of homes in an attempt to force the Q'eqchi' off their ancestral lands. In Mexico, Gabriel Ramos Olivera, a ranger working in the Chacahua National Park in the state of Oaxaca, is murdered by poachers for defending endangered leatherback turtles and crocodiles. In Mexico, subsistence farmer Isidro Baldenegro López, a leader of the Indigenous Tarahumara community in the Sierra Madre mountain region who had recently returned from exile — he had been illegally detained by the state government in 2004 and was released only after pressure from Amnesty International — is shot after working to protect ancient forests from deforestation. (Baldenegro's father had been assassinated for the same work when Baldenegro was a child.) In Honduras, Indigenous leader Berta Cáceres is murdered in her home after enduring years of death threats and intimidation for her work against a hydroelectric dam project on the Gualcarque River, which is sacred to the Lenca people. Eight men have been charged in her murder, three with links to the Honduran military and two who worked at the company leading the construction work. The next year, Cáceres's daughter, Bertha Zúñiga, survives an attack by three men with machetes after being forced off the road after a community meeting about water shortages caused by the Zazagua hydroelectric dam.

No one is killed at the Dakota Access Pipeline protests in

North Dakota in 2016, but hundreds are injured by attack dogs, tear gas, pepper spray, high-pitched sound cannons, rubber bullets, concussion grenades, and water cannons. Cultural genocide is also an ever-present threat. During the protests, LaDonna Brave Bull Allard, who lives on the Standing Rock Reservation, tells Iowa Public Radio, "Of the 380 archeological sites that face desecration along the entire pipeline route, from North Dakota to Illinois, 26 of them are right here at the confluence of these two rivers [where the protests are taking place]. It is a historic trading ground, a place held sacred not only by the Sioux Nation but also the Arikara, the Mandan, and the Northern Cheyenne. . . . The U.S. government is wiping out our most important cultural and spiritual areas. And it erases our footprint from the world; it erases us as a people. These sites must be protected, or our world will end — it is that simple. Our young people have a right to know who they are. They have a right to language, to culture, to tradition. The way they learn these things is through connection to our lands and our history. If we allow an oil company to dig through and destroy our histories, our ancestors, our hearts and souls as a people, is that not genocide?"

In Canada, Indigenous people are also subjected to state surveillance when they question market capitalism and resource extraction. According to media reports, Maskekowiyiniwak environmental activist Clayton Thomas-Müller is surveilled on a trip to a We'suwet'en action camp set up to oppose the Northern Gateway pipeline in 2011. Grand chief Ron Tremblay of the Wolastoq Grand Council and Mi'kmaw environmental activist Barbara Low are surveilled during anti-fracking protests in Rexton, New Brunswick, in 2013. Tremblay is followed by the RCMP to and from his home in Fredericton, New Brunswick, and a white van is parked outside his house for three months afterward. Low's garbage and recycling go missing. In 1994 and 1995, I am surveilled by the Toronto Police

Service and other unknown parties for co-organizing a consumer boycott of paper products manufactured by Japanese multinational Daishowa-Marubeni, which is clearcutting on unceded Lubicon territory in northern Alberta and for organizing fundraising and public information events in support of Mayan people in Chiapas, Mexico, after the Zapatista resistance to NAFTA. Events are infiltrated, friends tell me they can hear clicks on the telephone line, and police cars are often sitting in the alleyway outside my door. On one occasion, I return home to find my front door unlocked, a pile of white dust on the floor, and a small hole in the acoustic ceiling. My landlord has not accessed the unit, so I assume that someone has removed the listening device they had previously installed, leaving my door unlocked as a calling card or tool of intimidation.

This kind of surveillance infringes on the Charter rights of Canadian citizens, including freedom of expression, freedom of assembly, and freedom from unreasonable search and seizure. It also contravenes several sections of the United Nations Declaration on the Rights of Indigenous Peoples. What concerns many Indigenous people is the fact that the RCMP regularly reports on the activities of Indigenous peoples working in their communities when there is no evidence of criminal activity and then provides this information to so-called industry partners in the oil and gas sector and the private sector. When the Anti-Terrorism Act is passed by the federal government in 2015 to allow government departments to share information on people and organizations the government deems a "threat" to Canada, Nehiyaw environmental activist Melina Laboucan-Massimo tells openDemocracy, "It is legislation like this that makes it difficult for people not to be scared into silence, and for people like me who believe that we need a just transition to renewable energy . . . but this history is not new for us as Indigenous peoples in Canada. It is the continuation of neo-colonialism seen now in the form of resource extraction and environmental and cultural genocide." As Shiri Pasternak, a professor at Trent University, tells the *National Observer* in 2017, "It's a vast network — a surveillance system of ministries and departments within the government that are all holding close hands with corporations." The federal government has, in effect, become the security arm of the oil and gas sector.

Not every Indigenous person believes that market capitalism is a bad thing. Colonial interference in Indigenous communities has led to internal divisions that have further weakened many communities, and government-mandated band councils are now often at odds with pre-colonial governance systems. Those working in some band councils and in pro-development lobby groups such as the Indian Resource Council are in favour of working with oil companies and those building pipelines. Some of these politicians and lobbyists claim that non-Indigenous environmental activists are "impoverishing" Indigenous communities, but in truth the contemporary anti-pipeline movement is being led by Indigenous peoples, including members of the Tsleil-Waututh, Musqueam, and Squamish First Nations, Kanahus Manuel of the Secwepemc Women's Warrior Society, the Wet'suwet'en hereditary chiefs, Kaneksatake grand chief Serge Simon and the Indigenous Treaty Alliance, and the 20-member Assembly of First Nations (AFN) Youth Council, which submitted a letter to chiefs attending the AFN's 2018 annual general assembly. And Indigenous culture-based definitions of wealth and poverty do not conform to market capitalism.

The Youth Council's letter asks the chiefs to "refocus efforts on the sacred duties of protecting our lands and waters, ensuring a future for our young ones, and respecting our teachings; prioritize the safety and health of our young peoples, and those yet unborn, over the supposed monetary gain; and support the young peoples and the direction they want to take when looking for alternative solutions." In light of this stance — which calls for a return to pre-colonial Indigenous values and economies — it's no surprise that the AFN, which represents Status Indians in Canada, and is composed of band council chiefs, blocked the Youth Council from speaking at the assembly. As Kiana Cardinal, an executive member of the Youth Council from the Alexander First Nation, later tells the CBC, "We are calling on our leaders . . . to remember, to look ahead and think of those seven generations to come and how this will affect them."

It would be a mistake to think that this debate, and these disagreements, are simply examples of the range of opinions usually found in any community. These issues are about decolonization and the relationship with the control figure. The Indigenous environmental movement is being led by young people, elders, women, and artists. It is a resurgence of Indigenous values in the realms of economics and governance and a rejection of patriarchy in all its forms.

According to former AFN national chief Noel Starblanket, who spoke to the CBC in 2018, the AFN is out of touch with Indigenous peoples at the community level. In the same article, former AFN senior official Rolland Pangowish says that the AFN has become "a prisoner of the federal government's funding and policy priorities." According to Pangowish, "It is very skewed in the government's favour. They manage the negotiations and set the rules." Pangowish believes the AFN is no longer an advocacy organization but is instead functioning as a "policy consultation mechanism" for the colonial government.

The Wet'suwet'en hereditary chiefs in northwestern BC say the same thing about government-mandated band councils. Although the 1997 Delgamuukw decision at the Supreme Court of Canada recognized the Wet'suwet'en hereditary system — including chiefs and matriarchs — the hereditary chiefs say that the federal government chooses to deal only with the elected council, bypassing the hereditary system and often passing on the responsibility for consultation with Indigenous peoples to corporations that are seeking to undertake development projects on Indigenous lands. The 2014 Tsilhqot'in decision upheld a central pillar of the Delgamuukw decision, saying that Indigenous title includes the right to exclusive use and occupation of land and the right to decide its use. In reality, however, land appropriation and the imposition of market capitalism continue to erode Indigenous lands and communities. The colonial government uses a divide and conquer strategy to, as the Wet'suwet'en hereditary chiefs say, "shove pipelines down our throat."

When members of the Yaakswiis Warriors from the Ahousaht First Nation in BC are arrested in 2016 by RCMP officers after protesting a fish farm in an effort to "protect the Ahousaht from unnecessary economic development and harmful practices" (as the warriors say on their Facebook page), the group calls out the connection they see between the forces of market capitalism and the systems of the colonial government. In a written statement after the arrest, the group says, "We will continue our defence of our food sources, our lands and waters, and our future generations. The RCMP should not be interfering in these matters. By doing so, it is clear that they have overstepped their role by acting as enforcers for corporations against and in violation of the clear rights we have to our territories as members of the Ahousaht Nation." But the Yaakswiis Warriors are operating in opposition to the direction taken by the chief and council elected under the colonial governance model. The chief and council of the Ahousaht First Nation — which administrates federal funding and policies at the community level in a system devised and enforced by the colonial government — supports the fish farms.

Indigenous cultures are not frozen in time or resistant to change. In fact, Indigenous peoples have proven themselves to be flexible and adaptable, especially when confronted with technological change brought about by contact with other societies. Indigenous societies across the Americas responded decisively to population changes created by the fur trade — as when the Haudenosaunee around the Great Lakes offered surviving Wendat full citizenship after both groups were decimated by war and European disease — as well as to the ongoing redistribution of power created by conflict among colonial forces. During the fur trade, Indigenous societies responded with intelligence and creativity to maintain their cultures in the face of changes to the ecosystem and the extirpation of some animal populations. And customs and norms have changed across centuries as Indigenous communities have migrated, split apart, and come together as allies. Resistance to market capitalism is not about resisting change. Resistance to market capitalism is about resisting cultural genocide and colonial control, and prioritizing Indigenous philosophies that centre on long-term — rather than short-term — thinking.

In 2012, Cameron Alexis, then grand chief of the Confederacy of Treaty Six First Nations in Alberta, speaks at a community consultation on food security that eventually becomes part of a United Nations report. "As First Nations people, our lives have been altered because of industry," Alexis tells the *Edmonton Journal*. "[Lac Ste. Anne] is contaminated . . . so much so that the fish and wildlife officers have told our elders that we can only eat one fish a week from the lake." Hunters living near the lake discover deformed livers and lungs in moose, as well as cancerous "bubbles" in rabbits. These types of issues are identified by other Indigenous peoples living in different areas of the province as well, including Nehiyawak in Lubicon Lake, Alberta, who report cancerous organs in moose in the 1980s and 1990s, after the oil and gas industry moves into the area.

The issue is summed up by Percy Potts, who attends the community consultation as a 61-year-old man with knowledge of how things were before oil and gas. "People have been doing things to us, taking things from us, trying to turn us into things we're not. We were very healthy. We didn't go outside for food; my dad got it for us. All these things that were central to life were held together through prayer and hard work."

That prayer and hard work created a great deal of social capital within Indigenous communities. Today, however, social capital has been eroded or destroyed as Indigenous peoples have become dependent on government-controlled systems. This is particularly evident in contemporary self-government agreements. Not only do self-government agreements fail to address the root causes of intergenerational trauma, they are, in many cases, the force behind chronic trauma.

After the James Bay and Northern Quebec Agreement was signed in 1975, the Eeyou on the Quebec side of James Bay went from a subsistence society, where food was hunted and gathered on the basis of need and homes were free, to a society that required money to pay for suburban-style houses, electricity, and water. With paid work available in various Eeyou communities, the Eeyou had to choose between paid work and going hunting — and there was really only one choice if people were going to be able to pay their bills. Even hunting was monetized: when young people returned from a goose hunt, they often sold their catch to other people in town instead of distributing it throughout the community for free, as they had in the past. Eeyou society changed from a sharing society to a society in which people work for the companies who "develop" their land.

If we look at the James Bay Agreement through a systemic and structural lens, and with an eye toward the ways in which market capitalism supports colonization, we see that the real winners in the agreement are governments, banks, and corporations such as Hydro-Quebec. In the early days after the agreement was signed, Eeyou hunters who had been vital contributors to the community began to, in the words of an Eeyou teacher who was interviewed by the *Toronto Star* in 1991, "wither away." Today, Eeyou communities still schedule an annual Goose Break, and children still take part in Walking Out ceremonies to be welcomed into the natural world as a hunter, but these events happen alongside the negative health and social effects of colonization, settlement, and the large-scale destruction of huge portions of what the community calls *Eeyou istchee*, or "the people's land."

Davey Bobbish, chief of the Eeyou community at Chisasibi, tells the Canadian Press in 2018 that children used to do Walking Out ceremonies right outside their front doors, but that today community members have to travel far to the south, because the eelgrass is gone and the geese no longer come to Chisasibi. Bobbish says that Hydro-Quebec dams and reservoirs along the La Grande and Eastmain rivers have destroyed the eelgrass beds for hundreds of miles around. As a result, the wild geese that once made up half of the meat eaten by residents of Chisasibi have been replaced by processed, store-bought food. Bobbish says this has also changed Eeyou culture: "It was excitement, a tradition. Ever since the disappearance of the eelgrass, we've lost a lot of it. The way we teach our children how to handle themselves out on the bay, even the names of the islands, Cree terminology. . . . This is what we're losing."

Part of the reason why market capitalism is a negative force for Indigenous peoples is because it sees land as a commodity. When land is seen as a product that can be exploited, then the people who are indigenous to that land are also seen as merchandise. Market capitalism also leads to the exploitation of Indigenous women and girls.

In 2014, the U.S-based Women's Earth Alliance and the Toronto-based Native Youth Sexual Health Network created a toolkit entitled Violence on the Land, Violence on Our Bodies, which identifies the links between Indigenous land and bodies and the effect on both when resource extraction companies enter Indigenous territories to drill, mine, frack, and otherwise interfere with the land and water. As the toolkit says, "Although the economic gains have been a boom to transnational corporations and the economies of the U.S. and Canada, they come at a significant cost to Indigenous communities, particularly women and young people." The "environmental violence" that results from chemical manufacturing and waste dumping, along with the "man camps" created by the oil and gas industry, result in what the toolkit identifies as "sexual and domestic violence, drugs and alcohol, murders and disappearances, reproductive illnesses and toxic exposure, threats to culture and Indigenous lifeways, crime, and other social stressors." The visible effects of resource extraction prove that colonization is not confined to the past. It is happening now, and it is contributing to the chronic trauma experienced by Indigenous peoples and communities.

There is a strong correlation between social and environmental conditions and the prevalence of mental illness. Although those with economic inequality are more at risk of developing certain types of health outcomes (such as diabetes) due to food insecurity and the chronic stress of economic uncertainty, those with economic privilege also suffer under the weight of their entitlement. Environmental pollution, the competition and aggressiveness that underline corporate deal-making and individual wealth creation, and the lack of meaningful spiritual practice all have a negative effect on health. Consumerism and materialism have been associated with higher rates of addiction, depression, and anxiety. As Nehiyaw writer Billy-Ray Belcourt writes in the January 2018 edition of *Canadian Art*, "If we are to adequately tell a story about the care of the self in a settler state like Canada, we must begin with the invention of the so-called New World, that brutalizing project of globalization that eroded, with vicious precision, the social worlds of Indigenous peoples from coast to coast to coast. That is to say, built into the thorny mechanics of settler colonialism was the racialized production of bad feeling as of a piece with everyday life."

The tiny community of Fort Chipewyan, in northeastern Alberta, is made up of Dene, Nehiyawak, and Métis people. Decades ago, hunters used to dip a cup over the sides of their canoes on hunting trips and drink directly from the clean, clear waters of Lake Athabasca. After the oil and gas industry moved in, however, cancer started to show up everywhere: cervical cancer, testicular cancer, uterine cancer, leukemia, lymphoma, and a rare form of bile duct cancer. The cancers — like all cancers, a disease of the immune system — have also been joined by cases of lupus (an autoimmune disease) and Graves' disease (also an immune-system ailment). In one recent year, six people in the community of 1,200 people died of colon cancer, the youngest just 33 years old. Although a non-Indigenous fly-in doctor, John O'Connor, notifies officials of the situation in Fort Chip as soon as he has the data, it takes more than three years for provincial and federal governments to launch a formal investigation. O'Connor believes that the delay was caused by one simple fact: that the oil and gas industry is the prime economic driver in the province. As former Fort Chip resident Ivy Simpson tells the *Globe and Mail* in 2006, the oil and gas industry means "there's going to be a bunch of rich people and a bunch of sick people." Which is a pretty good description of market capitalism.

If Indigenous peoples are ever going to escape the control relationship with the colonizer — and the colonizer's systems and institutions, which are the means and methods of control — they will have to take a good, hard look at the effects of market capitalism on Indigenous communities and begin the work of changing the model into something that better reflects Indigenous ways of knowing and being. There is an incredible bank of traditional knowledge and other expertise within Indigenous communities who can work in partnership with the private sector, the public sector, and government to develop and implement projects in Indigenous communities using the Sustainable Development Goals (SDGs) identified by the United Nations. The SDGs acknowledge that the planet is in crisis and that we need to change the global economic system to make it fairer for margin alized peoples and the natural world. The SDGs include but are not limited to:

- no poverty
- zero hunger
- good health and well-being
- quality education
- gender equality
- clean water and sanitation
- affordable and clean energy
- decent work and economic growth
- industry, innovation, and infrastructure
- reduced inequalities
- sustainable communities
- responsible consumption and production
- climate action
- care for life below water
- care for life on land
- peace, justice, and strong institutions

Indigenous communities across Canada, in almost every province and territory, are taking up their responsibility to the next seven generations by engaging in sustainable development projects on their traditional territories. The Indigenous Clean Energy (ICE) social enterprise says there are 152 renewable energy projects across Canada with Indigenous participation, including solar panels, wind turbines, and biomass. According to ICE, the projects have created more than 15,000 person-years of work and generated $842 million in employment income in Indigenous communities. This eliminates dependence on colonial systems and balances economic concerns with an Indigenous focus on stewardship. In many Indigenous communities, both on-reserve and urban, these projects are using co-operative or community-led structures as a way of ensuring that decision-making power stays at the local level and out of corporate hands.

Many Indigenous communities are also creating food sovereignty projects as a way to reclaim or preserve Indigenous knowledge, improve health outcomes in Indigenous communities, and create economic opportunities that are in accordance with Indigenous concepts of sustainability. Some projects highlight pre-colonial foods such as berries, fish, and wild game, while others focus on whole foods created through organic farm projects — and still others combine the two. Other projects, such as the one at Esquimalt High School near Saanich, BC, and the Tr'ondëk Hwëch'in First Nation's new farm school in the Yukon Territory, bring Indigenous students together with local farms or farm projects to offer land-based learning, nutrition studies, and carpentry skills instruction. Some of these projects provide food to local food box programs, regional processing operations (such as fish canneries), and local businesses that provide meals to people working in the bush. The aim is to address colonial control over Indigenous communities, foster community cohesion, and create the conditions for cross-generational knowledge transfer between elders and young people.

The Sqilxw people of current-day British Columbia and Washington state have a cultural concept called *en'owkin*. En'owkin is a constructivist model that uses the knowledge of everyone in the community to create self-sufficiency where people are responsible for taking care of one another and of everything in the natural world, beyond what is necessary for survival. This philosophy of voluntary co-operation emphasizes wholeness and teamwork, and when used as a deliberate and intentional organizational process, it cultivates co-operation as a basis for sustainability at the levels of individual, land, family, and community. It also employs cross-generational collaboration, which teaches compassion and consideration. En'owkin is a reciprocal process that requires each person in the community to, first, take responsibility for including the whole community within their thinking and, second, to expand their understanding to accommodate the whole of the community. It creates solidarity and innovation through collaborative thinking and doing, and it ensures that community building supports each person's physical, emotional, intellectual, and spiritual well-being. Since en'owkin includes the natural world, development guided by en'owkin — or any other similar pre-colonial Indigenous framework — would also ensure the well-being of the natural world.

When the Supreme Court of Canada dismisses an appeal by the Ktunaxa Nation Council to stop the development of the Jumbo Glacier ski resort in the Kootenays region of BC in 2017, it misses a chance to create a Canada where Indigenous ideas on land use and development are considered equal to settler-colonial ideas. The Ktunaxa Nation Council opposes the development of the resort because it will be built in an area the Ktunaxa call Qat'muk, which is home to the Grizzly Bear Spirit. But although two judges on the court agree that the resort would do "irreparable damage" to

Ktunaxa spiritual beliefs, the court still rules against them, saying that the province has the right to administer Crown land and dispose of it "in the public interest." In 2018, the Supreme Court also denies the 'Namgis First Nation's attempt to prevent the restocking of the Swanson Island fish farm, which is operating without the 'Namgis First Nation's consent in their traditional territory off the northern coast of Vancouver Island. Under Canadian law, corporations have the same rights as people. But Canadian law also denies Indigenous peoples and the natural world those same rights. This illustrates how the systems of colonialism support market capitalism and also demonstrates how settler-colonial thinking is routinely forced upon sovereign Indigenous nations.

If Canada is ever going to change its relationship with Indigenous peoples, it will have to problematize colonial systems that position the natural world as a commodity. To do that, Canada can take a page from New Zealand's system of law, which has now granted personhood status to three sacred places of the Maori belief system. Under this status, Maori groups and the government of New Zealand agree to share guardianship of a geographic feature, so that the land is managed sustainably. After the most recent legal understanding is signed — a decision that makes Mount Taranaki a legal person — Andre Little, the non-Indigenous minister of treaty negotiations, says, "Today's agreements are a major milestone in acknowledging the grievances and hurt from the past." That's what reconciliation looks like.

If Indigenous communities — both urban and on-reserve — are to address the everyday impacts of trauma and complex post-traumatic stress disorder, they need to recreate communities where each citizen knows what it feels like to be connected to the people around them, where each person feels useful and has a sense of accomplishment based on their knowledge and effort, and where their safety and wellness are dependent on the success of others. Community-led planning that leads to community-led projects create opportunities for people to work together in exactly these ways. This work creates a connectedness that leads to transformation on both the individual and collective levels. However, it will require the dominant society to recognize new forms of wealth. Social capital is a form of wealth — but instead of stockpiling an abundance of material possessions, social capital prioritizes *people*.

Being connected to community is about being related to and a part of something. This relatedness creates the experience of belonging. Belonging leads to a sense of ownership. Ownership translates into a feeling of responsibility. And responsibility creates reciprocity — which creates safety. To create social change within Indigenous communities, Indigenous peoples must create social capital where there currently is none and capitalize on the social capital that does exist. This will require factions in the community to come together, and it will also require new patterns of communication between the colonial government and Indigenous communities. It might also require the wholesale rejection of colonial systems and structures, from the Indian Act to band councils to outside models for education, health, and child protection. It will certainly require strong leadership, as well as a realization on the part of individual community members that leaders don't create communities. In fact, communities create leaders. If the government-mandated band council or the national band-council chiefs organization isn't listening to the people or following the lead of communities, then they're not the rightful leaders.

Colonialism brought riches to Europe. It created the first global markets for cotton, tobacco, and sugar, and it was the reason Europe could embark on an Industrial Revolution. Now, two U.K. scientists, Simon Lewis and Mark Maslin, say that the colonization of the Americas was also the dawn of a new geological epoch called the Anthropocene, in which human activity dominates the planet. In their book *The Human Planet: How We Created the Anthropocene*, Lewis and Maslin argue that colonization allowed manufactured goods from Europe to be sold to Africa in exchange for people who could be enslaved and transported to the Americas to grow cotton and tobacco for Europe. For the first time, the world was functioning as a global economic system. Globalization had begun. The impact on the planet has been unprecedented, pushing the rate of plant and animal extinction, increasing CO_2 in the atmosphere, and creating a crisis of plastic pollution in the world's oceans. More and more land has been converted to large-scale conventional monoculture, and animal habitats have been destroyed. As Lewis and Maslin told *The Guardian* in 2018, "The Anthropocene began with widespread colonialism and slavery. It is a story of how people treat the environment and how people treat each other."

During the 2014 protests against fracking operations near Rexton, New Brunswick, and the Mi'kmaq community of Elsipogtog, non-Indigenous people stand alongside Indigenous peoples to protect the ability of all Canadians to control what goes on in their communities. After non-Indigenous protestor Dallas McQuarrie and his wife, Susan McQuarrie, who are both senior citizens, are arrested on Highway 126 near Rexton as they pray in the middle of the highway, Dallas writes in a New Brunswick–based blog that the anti-fracking protest "united English, French, and First Nations peoples around a single issue, something rarely seen here. The Catholic church . . . the New Brunswick College of Family Physicians . . . the province's Chief Medical Officer of Health. . . . The opposition to shale gas is homegrown. The protestors are the folks one sees at farmers' markets every summer. Demonstrations seem like family reunions with parents, grandparents, and children much in evidence, along with teachers from nearby schools, local business people, doctors, clergy, and even elected officials." The issues in Rexton/Elsipogtog — of corporate versus citizen control, and of the effect that government legislation and industry has on communities and the environment — underpin colonialism in Canada. If we work together and include Indigenous ideas, knowledges, and structures at the core of our systems, we can change how we treat the natural world — and we can change how we treat each other.

In European society, people are deemed powerful when they have privilege and influence. Power is synonymous with supremacy, dominance, and rule, usually over something or someone else. Power is understood in a much different way in Indigenous societies, however. In the Indigenous world, power is constructed through connection: connection with manitow, connection with other people, connection with the natural world, connection with the spirit world, and connection with oneself in the form of self-awareness of one's deepest thoughts and feelings and ways of being and doing.

Human suffering (illness, sadness) is part of life. Political suffering (poverty, hunger, homelessness, marginalization) is avoidable and unnecessary. When Indigenous peoples dispense with colonial systems and structures that create and entrench inequality, they act as owners of their own communities, they build the social capital necessary for individual and community transformation, and they create a new vision for life beyond the parameters imposed by the colonial control figure. When non-Indigenous peoples make room for Indigenous systems, they create the foundation for reconciliation. Both are central to ending intergenerational trauma.

CHAPTER 10

KILLING THE WITTIGO

A husband and wife head out one autumn to find a winter camp-
site and stockpile game for the long winter ahead. One day, the
woman is tying snares near the wigwam when she hears rustling
in the bush. When she turns, she comes face to face with a horrify-
ing figure: a giant, hairy man in tattered clothes whose shoulders
and lips are gnawed away. It's like this giant man has gone insane
with hunger and eaten his own flesh. The giant is grinning at
her, his teeth too large for his mouth. The woman knows this is
Chenoo, the terrible cannibal creature. She knows she is in trouble,
so she decides to be kind to this creature, in the hope that Chenoo
might spare her life. She says, "My dear father! My heart is glad
to see you again. Where have you been so long?" Chenoo, who

always hears screams of horror and fear from the humans he encounters, is so amazed at her reaction that he cannot speak. In the silence, the woman reaches out and takes his hand. Chenoo allows himself to be brought into the family's wigwam.

"Dear father," the woman says, "I am sorry to see you in such a state, dirty and with worn clothes. Please make yourself comfortable." She brings Chenoo a birchbark basket filled with warm water and also brings him some of her husband's clothes. This kindness is new to Chenoo, so he stays quiet. He bathes himself and changes his clothes. Then he sits by the fire. He is sullen and sad but quiet.

When the woman goes outside to chop wood for the fire, Chenoo follows her. She thinks, *This is it. He's going to kill me now and devour my flesh.* Chenoo says gruffly, "Give me the axe!" The woman hands the axe over quietly, expecting to die at any moment. But instead of attacking her, Chenoo begins to split the wood. The woman watches as great logs of pine are split in an instant. She has never seen such chopping! Wood is tossed everywhere on the ground, and it looks as if the family's winter camp has been visited by a hurricane. "Father, we have enough now!" the woman cries. Chenoo puts down the axe and walks back into the wigwam, taking his place by the fire, silent once again.

As she is making the woodpile, the woman hears her husband return from the bush. She runs to greet him and tells him about Chenoo. She tells him of her plan, and her husband agrees that her strategy is wise. So he agrees to do the same. He, too, will be kind to Chenoo.

"Dear father-in-law!" says the man when he enters the wigwam. "Where have you been for so long? Many things have happened. It is good to see you return." Chenoo stares in amazement, but as he listens to the man talk about hunting and family and events in the community, Chenoo's fierce gaze changes into a gentler, more human look.

The man and his wife eat and offer Chenoo food. He hardly touches his meal, though, and lies down to sleep instead. The man and his wife lie awake in terror all night, sure that Chenoo will devour them in their sleep. But the only thing Chenoo does is move his bedding away from the fire and toward the door. "The fire is hot," he says. The man and his wife know that Chenoo's heart is made of ice, so they understand why he needs the cool air to shield him from the heat of the fire.

For three days, Chenoo stays in the wigwam. He is sullen and grim and does not eat. Then on the fourth day, something changes. He says to the woman, "Do you have any tallow?" She says, "Of course. How much would you like?" Chenoo fills a large kettle with many gallons of tallow, puts it on the fire until it is scalding hot, then drinks it all at once. Chenoo then becomes very sick. He goes pale and vomits up all the horrors and atrocities of the world, things unspeakable and horrendous. When it is all over, he is changed. He lies down to sleep.

When Chenoo awakes, he asks for food. He eats a lot, and afterward, he stares at the fire as usual. But he is no longer sullen and surly. Instead, he is kind and good. The woman and her husband can see that they do not need to be afraid of him anymore.

Chenoo lives with them throughout the winter. During one intense blizzard, when the snow keeps them inside and all they have is the dried meat from the snares, Chenoo says, "I am tired of this small meat. Tomorrow, we will go hunting." After the sun rises, Chenoo, who used to be so withdrawn and sad, flies fast over the new snow. He uses his medicine power to catch a small shark, which he makes grow to many times its size. Chenoo and the man come back with enough meat to feed the three of them until the spring. The wife does not want to touch this strange meat, but the husband tastes it and finds it good. He and Chenoo feed on it, and they all live together as friends.

One day, Chenoo warns the man and his wife that another chenoo is coming to kill them. This chenoo is coming fast, on the wind from the north. This chenoo, he says, will be far more angry and far more cruel than even he had once been — so they must fight. Chenoo does not know how the battle will end, but he knows he must try to keep the woman and her husband safe. So Chenoo asks the woman to bring him his bundle, which has been hanging from a tree since he arrived at their wigwam. He tells the woman, "If you find something inside my bundle that offends you, throw it away. But make sure to bring me the smaller bundle inside." The woman goes to the tree, opens the bundle, and finds a pair of human legs and feet, from one of Chenoo's earlier frightful and revolting meals. She throws the flesh far away into the forest and brings Chenoo the smaller bundle. Chenoo removes two dragon horns from this bundle, keeping one for himself and giving one to the husband and his wife. He tells them that these are magical weapons, the only ones that will work in this fight.

"Stay back until after the chenoo screams," Chenoo says. "If you hear this scream, it will kill you. But if you hear me scream, then the danger has passed. If I ask for you, come running. Bring the dragon horn. You may save my life."

The husband and wife do exactly as their friend says, hiding deep in the bush. When they hear the evil chenoo arrive, they hear a sound like screaming thunder. They cover their ears and writhe in pain, almost dead from the sound. Then they hear their friend scream in response, and they know they are no longer in danger of dying from the other chenoo's sound.

The battle begins, and the fight is fearsome and forbidding. The chenoos, in their rage, grow to the size of mountains. Trees are torn from the ground, and the ground trembles as if there is an earthquake. The conflict goes on until Chenoo says, "My son-in-law! Please come and help me!"

The man runs to the fight, and when he arrives, he sees two giants, taller than the highest clouds, struggling on the ground. The evil chenoo is on top of Chenoo, trying to force the dragon's horn into his friend's ears and eyes. His friend is rolling his head from side to side, trying to escape the evil chenoo. This evil chenoo mocks his friend. It says, "You have no son-in-law to help you. I will take your cursed life and eat your liver."

The man is so small in comparison to the giants that the evil chenoo does not notice him. He creeps up to the evil chenoo. Chenoo says, "Now! Use the dragon horn!" and the husband pushes the horn into the evil chenoo's ear. When the dragon horn touches the evil chenoo, it grows in length. It pushes through the evil chenoo's head and out the other ear, and when it senses ground on the other side, it changes direction, pushes downward, and pins the evil chenoo to the earth, taking firm root. Chenoo says, "Now, take the other end of the dragon horn and place it against a nearby tree." As soon as the dragon horn touches the tree, it wraps itself around the trunk like a snake. In this way, the evil chenoo is held tightly and unable to escape. To avenge the evil chenoo's threat, Chenoo takes out the chenoo's liver and eats it right there, in front of him, before he is even dead.

Then Chenoo and the man begin their long and weary work. There is only one way to kill an evil chenoo: they must be cut into tiny pieces and all the flesh and bones put into the fire. Everything must be consumed by the flame. If even a small fragment of flesh or bone is left unburned, that small fragment will sprout again into an evil chenoo, as large as the original one, and with all the evil force of the first creature. The hardest task is melting the evil chenoo's heart, because it is much colder and much harder than regular ice. When they put the heart into the fire, it almost extinguishes the flame. But they watch over it, stoke the fire, and eventually the ice heart breaks into small pieces. Then Chenoo and the man take these small pieces and break them up using a hatchet, to make sure they melt completely away. Then they return to the camp.

When the weather warms, the snow changes to water and flows with the rivers to the sea. The man and his wife also move toward the sea, and Chenoo, with his softened soul, goes with them. The husband and wife build Chenoo his own canoe. After many days on the river, passing through fast-flowing rapids and gliding under forest canopy, they arrive in sunshine on a beautiful lake. Suddenly, Chenoo lies down flat in his canoe. He says, "I have just seen another chenoo, standing there on top of the mountain. He cannot see me right now, but if he does see me, he will become very angry and will attack. I do not know who will win that fight. I want peace."

The husband and wife tow Chenoo's canoe for a while, but when they finish crossing the lake, Chenoo says that he can no longer travel by water. So they tell him where they plan to camp that night. Then the husband and wife paddle easily down the river, following the flow. Chenoo walks over mountains and through woods in a very long, roundabout route. The husband and wife think he will never reach them that way, but when they arrive at the place where they plan to spend the night, Chenoo is waiting for them by the fire, which he built for them.

As they travel farther toward the village, great changes come over Chenoo. Chenoo's fierce and formidable face is now that of a normal man, and his teeth are of normal size. He no longer grins wildly or stares at others all the time. His flesh has healed, and he is no longer hairy or a giant. He becomes so weak that the husband must carry him like a little child.

When they arrive at the village, the wife sends for her mother. When the mother sees Chenoo, she knows that he has travelled far and that he is very tired. She tells her daughter, "He must be cared for like a child for a few days. Then he will have to go on a fast, so that his spirit helpers will reveal themselves to him. Once he does this, he will be strong and we will introduce him to the others." When Chenoo hears this, he feels grateful, and his heart is at peace.

European anthropologists have long been fascinated with what they call "wittigo psychosis." To them, the Indigenous fear of wittigo possession is a culture-bound mental illness, and killing a wittigo is a way for Indigenous societies to get rid of people who are experiencing mental health challenges.

Not only is this conclusion ethnocentric — with "culture-bound" serving as a label to group together and marginalize all non-European beliefs, and European values about the supposed "worth" of people who are experiencing the symptoms of mental illness superimposed onto Indigenous cultural practice — but it is also incorrect.

Disconnection and a lack of self-control are dangerous threats to collective societies. Historically, the wittigo represented the balance between the individual and the collective and illustrated the dangers of selfishness and over-consumption. When Indigenous people claimed they were possessed by the wittigo, it was a way of stating that they felt disconnected from other people and unable to control their feelings or desires. As a symbol, the wittigo represents core ideas within Indigenous belief systems, illustrating what happens when individuals turn away from the values of respect, responsibility, reciprocity, and relationships that are central to Indigenous cultures. The well-being of the individual depends on staying in balance in both the internal and external worlds, and the well-being of the community depends on the individual's ability to regulate greed and excess. The consequences for endangering community well-being were severe. Children were warned never to let the wittigo near, and adults were told that wittigos had to be killed.

Although the wittigo's place as a symbol for greed and selfishness persists in today's world — neo-liberal capitalism and the environmental destruction that accompanies it can definitely be seen as wittigo possession and/or cannibalism — the wittigo has taken on many other forms in the contemporary Indigenous world. Today, it represents the lateral violence that fuels the intergenerational cycle of trauma within Indigenous communities, as the possessed person engages in predatory behaviours that are a threat to the collective. The wittigo also represents the distress of an Indigenous person who has experienced trauma, whose daily life is impacted by unresolved emotions that are eating them away from the inside. Today, the idea behind killing the wittigo has been distorted, describing the tendency for Indigenous people with unresolved anger and fear to gang up and condemn in others what they most fear within their selves, to the point where their victims — those they bully, harass, and act aggressively toward — are redefined as the perpetrator in order to justify a witch hunt. This has happened to countless Indigenous people who have been targeted within dysfunctional communities and workplaces, in situations ranging from whisper campaigns to harassment to wrongful dismissal.

The wittigo also represents the colonial control figure: the systems, institutions, and ways of thinking that enacted historical cruelties; the contemporary government policies and practices that continue to oppress and marginalize Indigenous peoples and communities; and the willful neglect that underpins the failure to adequately address issues of poverty, poor housing, and lack of infrastructure within Indigenous communities.

The wittigo's craving for human flesh is about predation: not actually cannibalism, but something like it. Today's wittigo cannibalizes other people's souls through sexual abuse, and it eats away at another person's identity by inflicting emotional abuse. It cannibalizes the strength of communities by engaging in toxic communication patterns: the "backbiting, gossip, criticism, putdowns, personal attacks, sarcasm, and secrets" identified by the Aboriginal Healing Foundation as an everyday impact of the intergenerational cycle of trauma. Today, the wittigo craves alcohol and empty sex to numb the pain and fill the gap created by a lack of love and belonging. The wittigo destroys connection: to others, and to oneself.

The wittigo story at the beginning of this chapter is told by the Peskotomuhkati people in present-day Maine and New Brunswick, who call their wittigo figure the chenoo. It is an ancient story, and it illustrates Indigenous concepts of health and healing. Despite the incorrect assumptions of European anthropologists, killing a wittigo isn't about murdering someone who is mentally ill. Killing a wittigo is about destroying the negative energy that makes an individual feel disconnected, angry, fearful, or sad. It is about destroying the terror that characterizes the everyday life of someone who has survived trauma. It is about destroying the cannibal: the selfish, greedy behaviours of individuals, systems, and institutions that destabilize communities and prioritize individual gain over collective well-being. In the context of intergenerational trauma, killing the wittigo also means unpacking the traumatic story that keeps Indigenous peoples tied to the past and creating a new story of our own choosing. The Peskotomuhkati story illustrates exactly how health and well-being can be restored to the individual and to the community.

In the story, the wife chooses to be kind. Kindness is the only way to bring an individual back into the community and the only way to heal a community. It's very simple: people must demonstrate kindness if they want to experience kindness. When kindness becomes a mainstay of daily interpersonal relationships and part of everyday life in a community, then the community becomes a safe place to be.

The story also tells us what to expect when we are interacting with people who have experienced trauma. When Chenoo moves his bedding to the door, he is backing away from the symbol of the fire: the centre of the home, which represents the warmth provided by the husband and wife. He is just not ready to accept their kindness and inclusion right away, because he feels vulnerable. This speaks to the idea that healing cannot be accomplished overnight or on any but the survivor's own schedule. The woman and her husband are ready to show kindness and to include him, but to Chenoo, kindness and inclusion are unfamiliar and therefore threatening. His choice to move farther away from the fire is respected by the husband and wife. When Chenoo makes an attempt to contribute to the life of the community by chopping wood, he makes a mess, retreating afterward to stare at the fire. Chenoo needs time and space to make mistakes and then spend time thinking about those mistakes — and about the way he will do things in the future.

For Indigenous peoples, healing describes processes that relate to mind, body, spirit, and emotion. When Chenoo cannibalizes others, he is taking something that does not belong to him. When he drinks the tallow, he is taking something that has been offered to him. In Indigenous philosophies, animals offer themselves to humans because humans need them to survive. That is why humans must be thankful and humble and strive toward regulating greed and over-consumption: because the natural world is a gift, a gift that helps us live without having to assume power over others. After he accepts the gift of tallow, Chenoo "vomits up all the horrors and atrocities of the earth." He is letting go of the unresolved emotions that turn him into a predator, letting go of the traumatic inheritance that fuels the negativity he carries within him. This letting go is a necessary step toward rebuilding his sense of self and his sense of connection to others. Purging is considered part of healing because it changes the makeup of the physical body, restoring the energetic signature (or spirit) of the sick person.

After they talk and Chenoo requests his bundle, the wife follows Chenoo's suggestion and throws away the human legs and feet that are inside. This section of the story is about setting boundaries. When the community sets standards for behaviour, it does so in consultation with its citizens, rather than imposing rules and regulations. Because his autonomy is honoured, Chenoo does not adopt an inflexible position. Instead, he shows a willingness to understand the needs and values of others. When she retrieves the bundle, the wife does not judge Chenoo's prior actions — there is no disgust or contempt. She cleans up the bundle while also giving Chenoo the things he needs. This shows how we balance kindness with the boundaries that ensure collective safety.

When Chenoo warns his friends that the evil chenoo's scream will kill them, he speaks about the power of traumatized people to negatively affect the lives of the people around them. In some cases, people might choose to set a boundary of non-engagement to protect their own well-being (as the wife does, when she refuses to eat the meat that Chenoo and her husband bring back from their hunt). In other cases, the community must come running — as the husband does to Chenoo, when Chenoo asks — to assist their fellow citizens in their battle to become whole. Healing is a social process that involves everyone. Part of that process is learning how to assist others and at the same time protect yourself.

The story makes reference to the "long and weary work" of killing the evil chenoo because healing is not a straight line from there to here. It is filled with small successes and large failures, with huge gains and a reduction in (but sometimes not elimination of) the behaviours and beliefs that bind the survivor to the traumatic past. When Chenoo lies down in the canoe after seeing the second evil chenoo, he is succumbing to his old fear, even while experiencing the beauty of the lake and the company and assistance of friends. When he eats the evil chenoo's liver, he forgets the lessons in kindness that the husband and wife are teaching him and slides backward into vengeance and anger. He forgets the lessons he has been shown — such as the husband's small size leading to victory over the evil chenoo — and relies on the familiar tools of vengeance and anger to try to increase his power through artificial means. Eating the evil chenoo's liver does not bring Chenoo back to his self or increase his medicine power. He regains his sense of self through the journey he takes to become whole.

Chenoo is tired at the end of the story because healing is hard work. His mind, body, and spirit have transformed because he has accepted love and can now show love. But now he is like a little child: he has to revisit the stages of development that his past experiences of trauma have prevented him from achieving. When the wife's mother tells him he must fast, this is the final step in rebuilding the self that he should have been at this point in his life. When he fasts, he will meet his spirit helpers and discover who he is and what he has to offer to the community.

So, why kill one wittigo (the evil chenoo) and treat the other wittigo (Chenoo) with kindness? Because the evil chenoo is a metaphor for Chenoo's disconnected self, the self that is out of balance. Chenoo must rid himself of that creature in order to regain his well-being, aided by the kindness and assistance of others. Once he regains that well-being, he will become part of the foundation for community wellness.

The story describes Chenoo's journey to become human again as a gradual process that involves several different activities and some inadvertent steps backward. This is another teaching provided by the story: that healing is only accomplished by transformation over the long term. Unfortunately, short-term approaches and one-off programs that fit easily into election cycles and funding calendars are the most common method of addressing current challenges within Indigenous communities.

After the government of Pierre Trudeau released its 1969 White Paper — a federal policy document that proposed to do away with the Indian Act and treaties and assimilate Indigenous peoples into the Canadian state — Indigenous peoples began to exert political pressure on various levels of government, asking for Indigenous culture–based social and educational programs that would help them reclaim and recreate their identity and self-determination. In the decades since, many of these programs have evolved into shining examples of successful Indigenous-controlled service delivery models, doing important work to improve the lives of a great many individuals.

So how then is it possible that Indigenous communities are in worse shape today than they were in the 1970s, especially as regards individual health outcomes, rates of suicide, levels of violence, and child welfare issues? The reason is twofold. First, as Murray Sinclair pointed out in his speech quoted earlier, the effects of cultural genocide get worse over time as the older generations die out. So the effects of that trauma manifest as intergenerational trauma up to seven generations later. Second, healing from chronic trauma and complex post-traumatic stress disorder (CPTSD) requires a multi-step approach that cannot be achieved through a weeks- or months-long program in basic literacy skills, addictions recovery, or cultural programs in fishing, beadwork, sled-making, or dance. As the Chenoo story says, killing the wittigo is "long and weary work."

CPTSD emerges from a history of chronic, repeated trauma that is relational or interpersonal in nature, often involving attachment figures and happening early in life within a framework of control. Healing from CPTSD, therefore, requires a multi-step approach that addresses the wide-ranging consequences of complex trauma: healing attachment-related dysfunction, reacquainting the individual with developmental stages they missed during childhood, addressing ongoing emotional reactivity and the lack of emotional self-regulation (which often damages the survivor's adult relationships), changing maladaptive patterns relating to interpersonal relationships, and reframing negative perceptions about self and world.

A short-term culture-based program or one-off immersive cultural experience may assist some individuals with one or some of the steps in the above list. But the effects of CPTSD are multi-layered, hidden beneath maladaptive coping strategies and multiple layers of unresolved emotion. This means that the healing process must be characterized by a spiral-like series of gradual steps that include building a sense of safety, restoring control, creating a narrative that restores the survivor's connection with the past, mourning loss, and rebuilding a connection to self, world, and others that will allow the survivor to begin living in the present moment. A short-term or one-off program cannot possibly address all of this in an individual, let alone the long-term, cyclical intergenerational transmission of trauma within families and communities.

Long-term programs require long-term funding. Yet despite repeated pleas from Indigenous organizations for multi-year funding models, the government of Canada still provides financial support to such programs with short-term transfer payments. This rigid and unchanging government approach illustrates exactly what is meant by the term "control relationship." The federal government extracts billions of dollars from unceded, contested, and treaty Indigenous lands in the form of timber, energy, mineral, and hydroelectric benefits that prop up the Canadian economy, yet refuses to change its funding model or Indigenize its way of working with Indigenous peoples and communities. This is no accident. By controlling the funding models and program approaches, the government seeks to control the well-being of Indigenous peoples and communities, thereby preventing them from having any real power in Canadian society. (In December 2017, the federal government proposed a new 10-year funding agreement for First Nations, which would be approved by a third-party body called the First Nations Financial Management Board. The exact details of the proposal are still not clear, but if it moves forward, the federal government says that 100 First Nations could receive funding under the new model by 2019. There are more than 600 reserve communities in Canada, so this means that just 17 per cent of all First Nations communities will have multi-year funding. Perhaps the biggest issue, however, is that the new plan does not address funding issues for urban and off-reserve Indigenous organizations and agencies. The 2010 Environics Urban Aboriginal Peoples Study and the 2011 Canadian census show that 60 per cent of all Indigenous people live in urban areas, and these numbers keep increasing. This is a huge issue for Indigenous people and a huge failure in planning on the part of Canada's political leadership at the municipal, provincial, and federal levels.)

Indigenous peoples certainly experienced traumatic episodes before the current era of chronic trauma resulting from colonization. When warriors came back from battle, when a community emerged from famine, or when a group was displaced after war or other conflict — all of these things would have required a community response to the traumatic episode. Healing a person or a community after such an experience would have combined art in the form of sacred stories created and/or delivered by a shaman-storyteller, using masks or animal dress; ceremony such as sweat lodges, the shaking tent, and doctoring; individual talk therapy in the form of consultation with an elder, knowledge keeper, or dream interpreter; and group therapy in the form of feasts, circles, and community art activities such as totem-pole raising or the creation of a wampum belt. These activities would have taken place over the course of months and years, leading a person, and a community, toward wellness. The process was an holistic one that addressed mind, body, spirit, and emotion: the purging of negative energy to get the individual "unstuck" and back into the present day; the rebalancing of the person's organ systems and energetic signature; the use of stories to awaken awareness and plant new ways of seeing (both of which are necessary in the process of transformation); and making meaning through art, story, and the creation of a narrative that could be passed down and used as a tool for learning in future generations. In addition, each individual had a responsibility for personal reflection, which would have been accomplished through psycho-spiritual-somatic means such as prayer, fasting, or ceremony. These ceremonies required the individual to reconnect to their ancestors, spirit helpers, or the land (water, mountains, earth) and, eventually, to other community members.

Because survivors of trauma are dealing with issues of identity, emotional self-regulation, and an inability to relate to other people, it takes longer for them to establish trust and create relationships. Although a short-term or one-off program might provide a survivor of chronic trauma with the opportunity to begin working on trust issues and relational skills, a short-term program will not afford the survivor the opportunity to practise these skills within the context of a real-life relationship or the real-time challenges that come with any long-term relationship (even a helping one). And although some cultural programs might give survivors an opportunity to narrate their life experiences and explore their emotional state, these programs never address family dynamics or physical symptoms or provide an opportunity to consider how the survivor's life experiences have created physical, emotional, and cognitive patterns and behaviours. To do that, programs must be long enough — and intentional enough — to provide the survivor with opportunities to question, explore, and practise a different way of doing things.

The words "culture" and "healing" are often used as synonyms, as if one leads directly to the other. They do not. In order to be effective, culture-based programming must directly address participants' trauma-related beliefs — the voice inside the survivor's head or the feeling they carry within themselves; the things that tell them "The world is unsafe" or "I am bad" — and intentionally disrupt the acceptance and normalization of the perceptions, beliefs, and behaviours identified in the Aboriginal Healing Foundation's list of intergenerational impacts of trauma.

Prior to colonization, cultural activities such as canoe-making, dancing, and beadwork were part of everyday life, undertaken within the context of a healthy community where the Indigenous 4Rs — respect, responsibility, reciprocity, and relationships — were embedded in every endeavour. Given the effect of colonial policy, conversion to Christianity, chronic trauma, and intergenerational trauma, however, this is no longer the case. Sometimes, the people who run the programs have their own trust issues, lack of relational skills, and inability to self-regulate their emotions.

In order to interrupt the cycle of intergenerational trauma and create change within Indigenous communities, culture-based programs must have the right people to lead them. Organizations shouldn't ask the only Indigenous staff member to take on the culture file simply because they are Indigenous. Institutions shouldn't hire people just because they're Indigenous, or because they know the material aspects of Indigenous culture. You might be a great singer, or make awesome moccasins, but that doesn't mean you know how to embed the 4Rs in your program, de-escalate conflict, or model relational skills. People who facilitate culture-based programs must be able to integrate cultural values and the corresponding behaviours into their daily work and interactions — and they must be able to explain how those values will disrupt the cycle of intergenerational trauma and support personal and collective healing.

Greater political self-determination is also not a synonym for — or a surefire pathway toward — healing from the trauma of colonization or stopping the cycle of intergenerational trauma. Consider, for instance, the James Bay and Northern Quebec Agreement. That agreement, which was signed in 1975 after the first phase of the James Bay hydroelectric project, guaranteed the Eeyou in Quebec and Inuit of northern Quebec the ability to manage local and regional governments, create their own health and school boards, and work with provincial and federal governments on issues related to economic and community development, policing, justice, and environmental protection. In 2016, however, the Inuit Tapiriit Kanatami (ITK) revealed that suicide rates in northern Quebec were 10 times the national average: 113 suicides per 100,000 people, as compared to the national average of 11 suicides per 100,000 people. And a 2010 report from the Cree Board of Health indicates that the suicide rate in Quebec's nine Eeyou communities is eight times higher than the suicide rate in the rest of the province. Meanwhile, data from the Cree School Board show that only one out of every 10 students graduates high school. And according to a 2013 report from the Cree Board of Health, the rate of diabetes in Eeyou Istchee is more than three times higher than in the rest of Quebec — and it's a recent phenomenon. Only 2.4 per cent of the Eeyou population had diabetes in 1983, but by 2011 — 35 years after the James Bay and Northern Quebec Agreement was signed — the rate was 22 per cent.

Given that CPTSD relates to a relationship with a control figure — in this context, the colonial government — it might be assumed that having more say in local systems might lead to a decrease in chronic trauma or a disruption in the cycle of intergenerational trauma. But where the economic system in an agreement is based on a colonial model, and the community development programs within that model are funded according to government-funding goals instead of the needs of the Indigenous community — meaning that organizations write grant applications to match a particular year's funding envelope, as opposed to filling the actual needs of the community — then community development remains tied to colonial values and the annual whims of the colonial control figure. When Indigenous peoples are given a "say" in operating foreign policing and justice systems on their lands, then Indigenous peoples and communities remain unable to exercise their agency or live in accordance with their own cultural values. When the education system that Indigenous peoples are invited to "create" is based on colonial frameworks and methodologies, then Indigenous peoples (and their children) continue to be subject to the control relationship.

American psychiatrist and trauma specialist Judith Lewis Herman has identified three stages in healing from CPTSD: safety, remembrance and mourning, and reconnection. Survivors of trauma feel unsafe in their own bodies, unsafe feeling the emotions associated with traumatic memory, and unsafe with other people. Safety is largely about the survivor gaining control so they can reduce maladaptive coping mechanisms and engage in self-care: control in relationships, where they are equal partners and able to make their own decisions, and control over their environment (finding a safe place). Remembrance and mourning allow survivors to reconstruct their stories in order to transform traumatic memory and release themselves from the past in order to live in the present. Once they reconstruct the story, they can mourn what happened to them and grieve what they have lost.

During reconnection, the survivor learns to face their fears and fight for themselves. Through this work, they become comfortable with the idea of being vulnerable, because they learn how to set boundaries.

Is it possible to create safety, connection, a sense of identity, and reconstruct a personal and community narrative for marginalized peoples within the systems of colonial control? Yes, but only when Indigenous values and systems are afforded equal merit and allowed to change the underlying principles of the colonial framework. This is what we mean when we talk about "Indigenization." Having a say in economic and community development does not automatically confer connection to self, others, or creation — unless community development is conceptualized around Indigenous values. Creating an education system does not automatically confer a sense of safety — unless the 4Rs are embedded in that system, educators are aware of the personal issues they bring into the classroom, and the methodologies are based on Indigenous frameworks relevant to the local population.

When the ITK released its 2016 *National Inuit Suicide Prevention Strategy* to address suicide rates in northern Quebec, northern Labrador, Nunavut, and the Northwest Territories, it identified six core areas of action: the creation of social equity, the creation of cultural continuity, nurturing healthy Inuit children from birth, access to mental-health care, healing unresolved trauma and grief, and using Inuit knowledge to build strength and increase protective factors against suicide. In other words, the ITK's comprehensive approach doesn't just recommend a sled-making workshop as a way to heal the community. The ITK's strategy specifically identifies the negative impact of historical oppression by the Canadian state, including colonialism, residential schools, relocation, and the slaughter of Inuit sled dogs by RCMP officers and government officials in the 1950s and 1960s; the everyday impacts of intergenerational trauma, such as family violence and a family history of suicide; and the effect of current social inequities, such as overcrowded housing, food insecurity, and lack of access to services. It then responds to these negative forces by prescribing an equity-based strategy involving economic and education resources and a culture-specific strategy that builds Inuit identity. Both the equity strategy and the cultural strategy address families, healthy homes, and mental wellness along the way. The overall strategy is holistic and intentional, with culture-based strategies embedded into the framework for improving Inuit society through a social justice lens. The ITK also specifically identifies the need for an Inuit-specific approach to trauma-informed care, which it says is needed in health, education, social services, and policing.

Numerous research studies in both the United States and Canada indicate that Indigenous language– and culture–based approaches to healing have positive effects on the health and wellness of Indigenous people. Many studies have shown a connection between land-based activities and the reformation of Indigenous identity, for example. Program reports have highlighted the role that traditional foods, drumming and dancing, and cultural ceremonies, such as healing circles, have in improving and sustaining physical, emotional, intellectual, and spiritual health. A U.S. study found that increased knowledge of Indigenous spiritual practices reduced the suicide rate for young people in one community. So it's not that culture-based programs aren't useful. The problem is that such programs can be limited in their ability to address the full range of feelings, ideas, and behaviours that arise as a result of chronic trauma or CPTSD.

The BC community of Esk'etemc (formerly known as Alkali Lake) illustrates the dangers of approaching healing as a one-step process that does not address the anger, fear, grief, and disconnection that results from chronic trauma.

In the 1970s and 1980s, Esk'etemc was considered a success story by media, academics, and government officials for its approach to dealing with alcoholism in the community. Bootleggers were arrested, and no liquor sales were permitted on the reserve. Weekly alcohol awareness meetings were set up. Instead of receiving welfare payments in the form of cash, community members were given vouchers that they could use to buy food and other necessities at off-reserve stores. People who were found guilty of committing crimes related to their alcohol addiction — anything from drunk driving to assault — were given a choice: either go to jail or go to treatment. When someone went away for treatment, their children were taken care of and their house was cleaned up and repaired. The community elected a new chief and council, who spearheaded an economic plan for on-reserve employment, including a pig farm, a chicken and egg facility, a greenhouse, a laundromat, a grocery store, and a logging operation. A community newspaper was launched, allowing people to speak openly and honestly about issues in the community. Youth meetings were held once a month. Non-Indigenous people who opposed these changes (such as the Catholic priest) were asked to leave the reserve. By 1980, more than 90 per cent of the community was sober. By 1985, employment was at 80 per cent. Pipe ceremonies, drum dancing, singing, smudging, and sweat-lodge ceremonies were reintroduced to the community, and they helped many people achieve and maintain sobriety.

But there is one major problem with this utopian vision of community wellness: according to research conducted in 2011, up to 90 per cent of children and youth report being sexually abused and up to 30 per cent of youth now abuse alcohol.

The community of Esk'etemc accomplished something extraordinary: they drew on existing social capital to make drastic positive changes in the lives of both individuals and the wider community.

However, they turned their attention to one impact of intergenerational trauma — alcohol addiction — at the cost of other deeper and even more scarring ones, such as the continuation of patterns of sexual abuse, shame, and lack of identity and agency. Addiction is merely a symptom of the underlying issues that characterize the human response to chronic trauma. It is not the root cause. Decades of chronic trauma in Esk'etemc — or in any Indigenous community — do not simply disappear in a handful of years as a result of a limited suite of programs, no matter how well structured. The journey to health and well-being — for people and for communities — is going to be a generational journey of transformation, where there are multiple opportunities to learn and practise new habits of thinking, feeling, and acting.

The community of Hollow Water, Manitoba, was aware of the work taking place at Esk'etemc. So in the mid-1980s, Hollow Water created a resource team made up of political leaders, community volunteers, and service providers from various local agencies — such as Manitoba Public Health, the school division, the RCMP, and child and family services — to develop strategies to address community healing and individual well-being. At the outset, and like the people of Esk'etemc, they believed their own work would centre on alcoholism. Then they began to think that the real issue was suicide. As the work continued, however, they saw that child neglect was a huge contributing factor to both the suicide crisis and to alcohol addiction. That's when members of the community began disclosing their experiences of sexual abuse — and the resource team realized that all of the offenders had themselves been victimized in some way. At that point, the team realized that they couldn't continue dealing with single issues, because all the issues were interrelated.

Eventually, the resource team at Hollow Water evolved into the Community Holistic Circle Healing (CHCH) program, which uses Indigenous knowledge and justice approaches to address the issue of sexual abuse in a more effective way than the police and courts ever have. Instead of putting offenders in jail — where they can avoid being accountable to the community for their crimes — the 13-step CHCH process employs a series of healing circles, a cleansing ceremony, a healing contract, and probation requirements that require offenders to attend individual therapy, addictions counselling, and healing circles on an ongoing basis. Family counselling is undertaken once the children involved are returned to the family.

The process is intended to bring lasting personal change to offenders, while also holding them accountable. Supporting victims and their families is also part of the process, starting with the decision not to require survivors to testify in court. The aim is to return everyone — survivor, offender, and the wider community — to a state of balance by nurturing "right relationships" with the spirit world, the earth, and with those who are in pain. Although the CHCH program is based on Anishinabe cultural beliefs, these beliefs mirror Judith Lewis Herman's three steps in healing from complex trauma: creating safety for everyone involved, creating space for remembrance and mourning, and reconnection.

The holistic, long-term, multi-step approach taken at Hollow Water goes beyond treating symptoms to create real results: of the 107 offenders involved in the CHCH program at the time of a 2004 report, only two reoffended. That's a 2 per cent recidivism rate, in comparison to the usual 13 per cent recidivism rate for sexual offenders in the wider population. By 2004, approximately 500 people had been helped. And according to a cost-benefit analysis conducted by Ed Buller, a Nehiyaw community worker and former director of Aboriginal Corrections Policy for Public Safety Canada, the CHCH program has cost the federal Department of Justice *half* of what it would have cost to send the offenders to prison.

Long-term change and healing within Indigenous communities will only occur when Indigenous peoples unlearn the coping mechanisms they've used to survive colonization and the learned or compensatory behaviours that make up the bulk of the everyday impacts of intergenerational trauma. That process must include a re-examination of colonial systems and institutions of control and an unflinching examination of the ways that Indigenous peoples and communities have internalized the control figure's behaviours and now inflict those behaviours on one another. Some of those involved with the Hollow Water approach have referred to the process as "decolonization therapy." Today, the situation in Hollow Water is far from perfect, but that's to be expected, because healing is a long-term, multi-generational process.

Indigenous communities often frame the process of healing around the healing of children and youth. Leaders in these communities say they need youth centres, and many communities are actively including young people in culture-specific activities aimed at reviving Indigenous cultures and developing a sense of identity. In 2015, for example, the Mi'kmaq community of Eskasoni organized a march against drugs, led by young people. After the march, the community held its annual feast, where they served the four moose that were killed the month before during a Youth Moose Hunt. The feast was a way for the community to come together, and the hunt and feast contributed to a sense of accomplishment and self-worth for many of the young people involved.

But communities must be mindful of the daily reality of children and youth. What happens after the hunt, or after the feast, when young people are dropped back into the same situations they were in before they took part in these activities? If the aim is to reduce substance abuse among youth — or suicidal ideation, or any of the other challenges — then the culture-based activity must be intentionally designed to address the real issues that lie beneath the symptom: the family dysfunction, unresolved anger, layers of grief and loss, disunity and conflict in the community, voicelessness, toxic communication, and other everyday impacts of intergenerational trauma as identified by the AHF.

Tracee Smith is the founder and CEO of Outside Looking In, a non-profit organization that works with on-reserve schools and Indigenous friendship centres across Canada to deliver a dance program aimed at keeping Indigenous youth in school. When students complete the program, they earn a school credit and a chance to appear in a year-end performance at the Sony Centre for the Performing Arts in Toronto. When Smith spoke to the CBC in 2017, she identified the reasons for the program's success. "What's different about our program," she says, "is that a lot of programs go into communities for a week, or a weekend, or a day. And they light up the kids — but then the kids don't have anything to latch onto after the fact. There are multiple programs like that. What's different about us is that it's over the course of a whole academic year. Kids have a long-term goal . . . [and they] have to learn how to go up and down, ride the waves of life, in terms of persistence and hard work, and those life skills." Riding those "waves of life" is an essential factor in creating new patterns of thinking, feeling, and acting.

At Mother Teresa Middle School in Regina, Saskatchewan, drum carrier Evan Whitestar has created the Buffalo Boys drum group, a program that works with students over the course of several academic years. When the program began, students fleshed and tanned the buffalo hide in a workshop. Then Whitestar began teaching the boys how to sing, how to take care of the drum — and a lot of other things. As Whitestar tells the CBC, "It's teaching a young group of boys here to be respectable, to be teachable, to be honourable, to carry these ways as First Nations individuals, and it gives me that opportunity to come here and grow and learn with the students."

Whitestar's comment reveals his approach. Becoming "First Nations individuals" is about creating identity and embracing the constant transformation that keeps an individual well. When he talks about learning from the boys, he demonstrates both humility (from the Seven Sacred Teachings) and reciprocity (from the Indigenous 4Rs). "To carry these ways" is about responsibility. Being teachable and honourable is about creating relationships among themselves, with other people, and with the drum. And being respectable is the final R of the Indigenous 4Rs, with the adjectival form of the word serving to focus the idea of respect on the ways in which the boys are perceived by the community (again highlighting the reciprocal nature of an individual's way of being in the world).

Other aspects of the program directly address the voicelessness, low self-esteem, disunity, and fear of personal growth, transformation, and healing identified by the AHF. As one 12-year-old participant told the CBC, "I was quiet at first, but then I started speaking up." That student is now singing leads, prompting another student to say, "When [he] leads, I feel like I should do that, too. I want to be a leader when I grow up." The program creates and teaches safety and reconnection. "They don't have that fear in them no more," Whitestar says. "They've overcome it together." Culture and healing are not synonyms — but one can create the other if you know what you're doing.

Schools are able to offer long-term programs because they see students for 10 months of the year (11 counting summer school). This timeframe allows for longer-term development of the individual. But school programs aren't the only way to support long-term holistic change. Community hubs allow non-profit organizations and institutions of the public sector to work together under one roof to deliver integrated services to a target population over a sustained period of time. Community hubs can be small — offering space for a parent coffee club, a youth meet-up, or community events — or they can be big, with a drop-in centre, housing services, health services, mental-health supports, harm reduction services, and access to lodging and other basic needs on demand.

Imagine a place where Indigenous peoples and families could readily access family counselling, culture- and trauma-informed psychotherapy, naturopathic doctors, traditional healers, elders-in-residence, occupational therapists, and take part in weekly community kitchens that promote healthy eating, traditional foods, and co-operative meal preparation. Where there is a weekly healing circle and space for the planning and completion of community-led art projects. Where there are employment services, skills-training programs, yoga classes, allopathic doctors in a clinic setting, dental services, pre-natal and post-natal support for parents, culture-based counselling for substance abuse (including tobacco reduction), a library, and an early childhood education centre. Where youth have access to cultural programs, art classes, and sport leagues on an ongoing, long-term basis. Where parents have access to culture-informed play groups, early childhood literacy groups, speech and language support, and a daycare centre. Where there are festivals and community events that encourage engagement with members of the wider community and the wider world.

Indigenous peoples are consistently marginalized by many of the systems and institutions of the dominant society, and they have a deep mistrust of these institutions as a result. However, community hubs are designed with input from the community itself. Hubs are spaces where people can get their needs met, creating health equity, social justice, cultural reclamation, and a sense of community wellness and belonging. They are by far the best model for addressing intergenerational trauma within Indigenous communities.

The city of Regina, Saskatchewan, knows this. The Mâmawêyatitân Centre opened in 2017, offering services for youth and families in the North Central Regina neighbourhood. The idea is to improve health and social well-being in the neighbourhood through the combined services of a public high school, public library, 33-space child-care centre, meal program for children, city recreational complex, community policing centre, elders' ceremony room, outdoor basketball court and soccer pitch, green space for storytelling and cultural teachings, a food store focused on food security, and a community association that provides health promotion and youth employment services, a community garden, and a community newspaper. There's a reason why the Regina Police Service, the Regina Qu'Appelle Health Region, and the Ministry of Corrections, Public Safety, and Policing were behind the Mâmawêyatitân Centre from the beginning: because offering community-based services reduces crime, improves health outcomes, and creates a more engaged community. Addressing health and social well-being means that Indigenous peoples have a chance to overcome trauma-related feelings and beliefs that limit their vision of life, which will in turn enable them to dismantle the systemic barriers that continue to marginalize them.

The Mâmawêyatitân Centre operates according to principles the leadership describes as "learning across the community": recognizing that people learn differently, from everyday experiences and across a lifetime, from others, and from doing — especially when it is connected to culture and place. The centre also prioritizes the pre-colonial Indigenous focus on collectivity and reciprocity, and its operating principles reflect the principles of the medicine wheel. When individuals have access to integrated services and interdisciplinary learning programs, they re-enter the community eager to pass along what they've experienced. This makes them agents of change within the wider community.

But it's not just access to health care, learning, and community initiatives that will lead to better health and wellness for Indigenous peoples and communities. If Canada is going to take up its responsibility in the business of reconciliation, then the systems and institutions of policing and justice must become trauma-informed. As Robert Chrismas, a staff sergeant with the Winnipeg Police Service and author of *Canadian Policing in the 21st Century*, told the *Toronto Star*, "Just arresting gang members, throwing them in jail, oftentimes they come out worse. If we're just reacting and not reducing victimization and crime, then what are we doing? We're spinning our wheels. We need to be proactive and get at the root causes and bring in the other service sectors." If the police are going to keep people and communities safe, then they are going to have to start preventing anti-social activities, conflict, and violence before they happen. If the justice system is going to keep society safe and rehabilitate offenders, then they must understand the reasons why offenders break the law in the first place — and what they can do to prevent offenders from repeating those behaviours once they have served their time.

In 2012, a friend of mine whose son is from the Dene community at Fort Chipewyan, Alberta, sends me the following email after I ask about him: "Joe has been released from another stint in jail but says he has another case coming up. He has applied to go to a dual diagnosis clinic in Ponoka [Alberta] for assessment. He has been waiting for a while but can't go until he sorts out his criminal charges. He sounds depressed and frustrated. All I can do is encourage him to get help and to work things out. It is so frustrating, because the system treats people with addictions through the criminal justice system rather than through mental health. While he is in jail, he gets cleaned up but receives no other help. When he is done his sentence, they toss him back on the street with no supports. It is a vicious circle."

The reason why Joe keeps going to jail or prison is because he is addicted to heroin and other opiates. When he can't buy the street drugs that help him manage his emotional, physical, and spiritual pain, he steals the money he needs to buy them or breaks into a pharmacy to steal narcotics. Instead of punishing Joe for his pain, a trauma-informed policing and justice system would work in tandem with other agencies to ensure that Joe gets the help he needs. This would keep Joe safe and save public money, because it's a lot cheaper to help Joe than to lock him up all the time.

Preserving the peace is an essential aspect of preserving law and order within civil society. For that reason, the role of those working in policing and justice should not be to criminalize Indigenous people who engage in behaviours related to intergenerational trauma. Instead, their job should be to develop cultural competence in dealing with Indigenous peoples and communities, along with an understanding of complex trauma and its effects, so that they can provide trauma-informed services that prevent crime before it happens.

This is exactly what the police have accomplished in Prince Albert, Saskatchewan. Prince Albert — where 40 per cent of the population is Indigenous — has the highest crime severity index in the province. Indigenous households in Prince Albert struggle with food insecurity, low income levels, and epidemic levels of diabetes. Prince Albert struggles with high youth mortality across the population (15 per cent above the national average), lower rates of school completion and higher rates of absenteeism, and a lack of affordable housing. Studies also show that alcohol addiction plays a large role in community dysfunction, crime, violence, victimization, and a range of other negative health and social outcomes in the area. In 2011, police chief Dale McFee — who also served on the Prince Albert Parkland Regional Health Authority — recognized that these issues would not change with criminalization and law enforcement alone. So he began using a crime-risk reduction strategy to deal with these and other social issues. That included the creation of something called Community Mobilization Prince Albert, as well as an Indigenous Women's Commission.

The CMPA is a virtual hub, an ongoing conversation between the police and other agencies that focuses on identifying the risk patterns that lead to negative social outcomes. As McFee says, "If it's predictable, it's preventable." Instead of responding to social disorder by taking people into custody, police officers in Prince Albert connect people and families at risk to the services they need when they most need them. By addressing the hopelessness and lack of connection experienced by people who are in distress — many of whom carry a lifelong burden of chronic and complex trauma — the CMPA prevents crime, improves public safety, and creates community well-being for both victims and perpetrators. The hub takes a multi-disciplinary approach to its work, using research, knowledge, and practice from the health-care sector, education, child and family development, parenting, addictions, mental health, and criminology. Since the CMPA was created, violent crime in Prince Albert has been reduced by 37 per cent.

Other police services across Canada are taking a look at the CMPA model. In 2016, the Winnipeg Police Service began testing a Block by Block program in a 21-block area of that city's North End, which is home to many Indigenous peoples and families. The program aims to connect families with social services, health agencies, community groups, and schools so that issues such as substance abuse and domestic violence can be resolved before the police need to be involved. As now-retired Winnipeg police chief Devon Clunis said when the model was unveiled, the aim is "crime prevention through social development."

When a system or institution declares itself rooted in social development, it means it is approaching its work based on an understanding of how social structures and relationships shape and are shaped by the work that system or institution does. Looking at social structures and relationships yields an understanding of cause and effect, the implications and limitations of theory and practice, and the balance of power. Armed with that knowledge, the process of social development becomes one of reforming and enhancing the system or institution to support the work of improving the well-being of people in society. Well-functioning societies are characterized by well-functioning people. When people have the opportunity to grow their sense of self and develop skills, they contribute to society instead of operating at the margins of it.

In 2014, the Sault Ste. Marie Police Service partnered with 35 local agencies to create the Neighbourhood Resource Centre (NRC) in the city's Gore Street area, a marginalized neighbourhood that residents describe as "low income," with social issues including substandard housing, isolation, addictions, interpersonal conflict, and a sex trade involving marginalized and trafficked Indigenous women and girls from nearby reserves. The NRC offers increased access to a variety of services and has created a safe space for community members to have contact with other community members, as well as casual contact with agency staff. It provides events aimed at increasing social cohesion and opportunities for volunteers to engage in community projects and develop leadership skills. The NRC model has also improved the approach taken by workers at the centre. Indigenous residents who attend the NRC can no longer be shuffled off and ignored as they might be at other agencies. Even if the staff member dedicated to Indigenous community members isn't on site, the other workers know there are services that Indigenous residents can access. As a result, they are much more likely to engage with that resident.

According to a 2016 report, the police are "highly visible" at the NRC. Although some community members — particularly Indigenous residents — say they still don't trust the police and that they don't feel comfortable with the police presence, other community members say the police presence is "creating feelings of safety, physically and psychologically, for them and their children." The report says other positive outcomes include a feeling that people now know their neighbours, a decrease in "public displays of arguing and fighting," increased respect for public space, more people walking in the area, and "pride and purpose in the community." This has decreased crime and victimization rates.

Creating a one-stop service hub at the NRC has also improved service delivery to community members who need the most support but are also the most likely to be triggered or retraumatized — and therefore most likely to give up on engaging in a process of change. As one community member says in the report, "Most government offices you're treated like a fuckin' number, you've got to repeat your story 12 frickin' times before you get to the person who *might* help you, and a good 50 per cent of the time you don't get any help so you've wasted your whole day and your breath and your pain and your anguish repeating your story over and over." By housing multiple agencies under one roof — including policing — the NRC is building relationships with the most marginalized people in the city. When people live in safe communities and are able to build reciprocal relationships, they can invest in future-oriented thinking instead of living each day in short-term survival mode. That, in turn, creates space for them to build connection with the wider community. It also creates space for parents to nurture children, creating stronger families and a healthier, more prosperous society for everyone.

Educators often employ the principles of social development in their everyday work with children and youth in schools across Canada. Yet the graduation rate for Indigenous students in the Vancouver School Board was 32.1 per cent in 2011, compared to 82.5 per cent for non-Indigenous students. And in the Toronto District School Board (TDSB), the latest data show that Indigenous students have a graduation rate of 50 per cent, which is 20 per cent lower than the overall TDSB rate. The absenteeism rate for Indigenous students in the TDSB is also higher across all grade groupings, and Indigenous students are suspended from TDSB schools at a higher rate than any other student population. Attendance and graduation rates for Indigenous students attending school on-reserve or in urban centres offering secondary education to on-reserve Indigenous students is similarly bleak across the country, from Labrador to Nunavut to the Prairies. Clearly, the education system as a whole is simply not working for Indigenous students, despite the best efforts of individual educators. The solution is simple: first, Indigenize the school system and create programs and approaches that honour Indigenous ways of knowing, teaching, and learning (for all students). Second, employ cross-sectoral approaches, holistic models, and school-community hubs to give Indigenous students and their families access to trauma-informed programs and services.

Half of Indigenous students in the TDSB live in a one-parent household, which is associated with lower income levels. Only 26 per cent of Indigenous students in the TDSB apply to university, compared to 50 per cent of the general student population. Report after report has shown that school-community hubs promote better attendance rates, less isolation, increased social skills, and a change in how communities see themselves — which in turn leads to greater engagement in the wider community, greater social cohesion, and better outcomes later in life.

The ultimate goal of the healing journey is to move from hauntedness and disconnection to being present in the here and now, where an individual can respond to daily experiences without resorting to maladaptive or learned behaviours. To do this, an individual must learn the skills that they did not learn in childhood: the ability to tolerate and regulate emotional experiences, modulate their hypervigilance and other physiological responses to stressors, express what they think and feel, and establish caring relationships with other people. This requires the individual to construct identity, develop a sense of agency, build a coherent narrative, and develop the ability to ask for help from others. Building healthier communities means repairing the structures of the dominant society and the cultural dislocation within Indigenous communities, so that individuals can get to a place where they can imagine other possibilities and new options in life.

My father benefits from the programs offered at the Oakalla Prison Farm in the 1950s and early 1960s. He learns a trade, and he learns to read and write in English, which enable him to create a successful business with my mother. But his spirit isn't brought back into balance. His heart is not healed. The wounds created by his experience growing up in a Duplessis orphanage in Quebec — abandonment, anger, lack of attachment, low self-esteem, spiritual confusion, and disconnection from the natural world — create a range of unresolved feelings, negative thoughts, and maladaptive behaviours. His personality development is interrupted and his sense of self, safety, and connection is destroyed. The prison courses do not address these personality and development issues, and they do not address the thoughts, feelings, and behaviours created by his childhood trauma. Throughout his life, he projects the fear, anger, lack of identity, and internalized shame and inferiority that he feels onto others in patterns of violence and victimization that recreate his childhood trauma. The everyday impacts of this trauma are then felt by the people around him, including his wives, his children, and his stepchildren, negatively affecting their own sense of self, safety, and connection.

To break the cycle of trauma, an individual must acknowledge negative thoughts and maladaptive behaviours, make a connection between those thoughts and behaviours and their life experiences, and develop new behaviours and a new way of looking at themselves and the world. To support this work, the systems and institutions of Canada must become trauma-informed. The various levels of government in Canada will also have to consult with Indigenous communities to fix the current disconnect in services. Under the current model, federal funding flows to on-reserve communities, yet more than 60 per cent of Indigenous peoples in Canada live off-reserve. And in 2016, the Supreme Court of Canada ruled that the federal government has a responsibility to Métis and non-status Indigenous peoples, which means providing services to all Indigenous peoples — not just those recorded in treaty agreements and government rolls. To ensure that the work of healing can proceed, the government of Canada will need to pass legislation that supports the creation of trauma-informed systems and institutions. This should be a fast and easy step, because the U.S. has already set a precedent.

In March 2017, three Democratic senators in the United States Senate introduced the Trauma-Informed Care for Children and Families Act, a bill that promotes trauma-informed services across the country. The aim of the bill is to create opportunities for law enforcement, education, health care, and other service providers to learn how to address and reduce the impacts of trauma on children, with a particular focus on Indigenous children. It also aims to promote collaboration between federal and state agencies and the creation of culturally relevant, trauma-informed programs. The legislation would:

- create a task force to identify best practices that improve capacity and coordination for the identification, referral, and support of children and families who have experienced trauma
- increase funding to the National Traumatic Stress Initiative to evaluate new models for improving trauma-informed care
- create federal grant programs that will make trauma-informed training accessible to service providers
- create a coordinating centre for law enforcement that will share information, improve awareness of childhood trauma, and train officers on the impact of trauma
- require the federal Centers for Disease Control and Prevention to improve data collection on the prevalence of trauma and identify barriers to and opportunities for information sharing and service delivery
- expand treatment capacity by ensuring that health-care coverage includes a comprehensive set of trauma-informed screening and treatment services
- promote trauma-informed service delivery by expanding student loan repayment programs for clinicians who work in high-need communities
- develop licensing guidelines at the state level to ensure that non-clinical providers can receive credentials in trauma-informed care
- improve pre-service and professional development training for teachers and health-care providers in trauma-informed best practices
- create a grant program to support coordinating bodies that bring together stakeholders to identify needs, collect data, build skills, and leverage resources at the community level

Such legislation, if introduced in Canada, would bridge the gap between the federal government's talk of creating a "renewed relationship" with Indigenous peoples to actually creating systemic and institutional change.

Trauma-informed care in this context is not a set of specific treatment and healing interventions. It is about recognizing the pervasiveness of trauma within Indigenous communities, meeting people's needs without retraumatizing them, and understanding the connection between an individual's life experiences and the impacts of trauma that they may experience. Attempting to reassure a terrified child or a terrified adult with words — or using threats to get them to comply with commands — will not help the individual or lead to compliance. The traumatized brain — especially when activated by a stressful experience — has a difficult time processing words and remembering what has been said. Trauma-informed care and trauma-informed service delivery is about assisting the individual in replacing their trauma-related logic — their belief that "You are not to be trusted," "I am not safe," "I must fight any person I feel is a threat to me," or "I must resist control, because if I do not, I will be hurt again" — with a different logic based on new experiences. These new experiences must be safe, empowering, and focused on altering the way that individuals view themselves and the world around them. Being trauma-informed is about supporting survivors of trauma in regaining a sense of control over their daily lives and actively involving them in the planning and evaluation of their healing journey. This means institutions must involve community members in the design and evaluation of programs. Being trauma-informed means understanding the necessity of relationship building as a means of promoting healing and wellness.

Over the course of her marriage to my father, my mother is repeatedly failed by the systems and institutions that are supposed to protect and assist her. Whenever she calls the RCMP in Peace River about an assault, they say the issue is a "private family matter" and decline to press charges, which is standard police conduct in the 1970s when it comes to domestic violence. When my father racks up half a million dollars in debt, my mother is forced to declare bankruptcy — which forces her and her three children into poverty — because she is considered a subset of her husband's credit file, and the bank holds her liable for my father's activities. Because of previous negative experiences in the health-care system with her pregnancies and deliveries, my mother seeks medical care only when it is unavoidable. One time, my father stomps on her foot in the middle of Main Street, putting my mother on crutches for weeks. But no one at the Peace River Hospital calls the police. No charges are laid and my mother is not directed toward any counselling or support services whatsoever. She does receive a prescription for Seconal, however, a tranquilizer that makes her lethargic and turns her into an amnesiac robot. The lack of response from the systems and institutions of the state means that my mother never receives the support she requires to change her situation or make a connection between her life choices and her childhood experiences. This systemic and institutional failure also means that I become a target for my mother's rage against my father, creating the conditions for my mother's traumatic experiences to become intergenerational.

These kinds of systemic and institutional failures continue today, more than 40 years later.

Across Canada, provincial advocates for children and youth are shedding light on what former BC representative for children and youth Mary Ellen Turpel-Lafond calls a "brutal and cruel approach" toward handling Indigenous case files. Turpel-Lafond is speaking about the case of a 19-year-old Indigenous woman named Paige who died of a drug overdose on Vancouver's Downtown

Eastside in 2013 after experiencing constant violence and neglect during her childhood. The Office of the BC Representative on Children and Youth puts it in very plain terms: "Professional indifference to [Paige's] life circumstances continually left her — and at times even actively placed her — in harm's way." Although Paige dies from an overdose, the Office of the BC Representative says, "it was actually years of abuse and neglect, persistent inaction from frontline professionals, and an indifferent social care system that led to this young woman's demise."

The Truth and Reconciliation Commission's final report makes specific mention of the need for culturally appropriate programs created by all levels of government — municipal, provincial, and federal — aimed at Indigenous peoples who are dealing with intergenerational trauma. The TRC report also asks the federal government to fund healing centres that will address the effects of residential schools. According to the TRC, parenting programs are most urgently needed, because, as the Office of the BC Representative points out, in Paige's case — and in so many others — abuse and neglect by traumatized parents and other caregivers is one of the biggest internal forces behind chronic trauma.

In 1993, Canada was shamed on an international scale when video surfaced of six Innu children between the ages of 11 and 14 huffing gasoline in the community of Davis Inlet, Labrador, shouting that they wanted to die. In 2002, at a cost of $150 million, the federal government agreed to move the Mushuau Innu to a new community, Natuashish. The new community has sewage and water systems, an airstrip, a telecommunications system, a fire hall and recreation centre, and a school the federal government calls "the most modern in the country," with a large gym, stage, drama room, "life sciences kitchen," daycare centre, and playground. Natuashish was supposed to restore cultural identity, pride, and a sense of purpose in the Mushuau Innu, and as such, it was considered a major component in addressing the social challenges in the community. And there have been changes: the local RCMP detachment says the crime rate has gone down by half over the last 10 years, and the suicide rate has decreased from four or five a year to just one between 2009 and 2015. These changes are significant and point toward a renewed sense of agency and a renewed sense of connection to the land. (The new site is a pre-colonial site used by the Mushuau Innu. The Davis Inlet site was chosen by the government.) But vandalism is common in the new community, and gas sniffing has followed the Mushuau Innu to their new home. By 2012, children as young as seven were once again being shipped out of province to receive treatment for solvent abuse. And in 2015 — in a situation almost identical to 1993 — an Innu Nation official found a group of young people sniffing gas inside an abandoned house.

And that shouldn't be a surprise. Although relocating the Mushuau Innu to a new community has relieved some of the most pressing quality of life issues, it doesn't address the fact that many Innu children are still living in environments where the everyday impacts of trauma are a normalized part of life. According to Innu Nation chief Gregory Rich, "The kids are depressed at home when there's a lot of drinking, and that's one way the kids show it, through gas sniffing." As Rich tells the CBC, "We need to target the families, we need to target the parents."

As one Inuk father from Labrador tells the CBC in 2017, his children "are in very good care with the [foster] family they are with. Of course they miss me . . . and the house in Nain." But he is clear about the reason that child protection workers removed his children: "I was passed out, sleeping, intoxicated." An Inuk woman in Nain, whose daughter is also in foster care, added, "It would be good for the parents to see how they're being taken care of and for them to realize they need to take care of their children like that, too."

Many Indigenous communities are now addressing the connection between the impacts of intergenerational trauma and the reasons why so many children are not safe in their homes. These communities are making changes to the child welfare system in an effort to address the needs of both children and parents.

The Nisichawayasihk First Nation in Nelson House, Manitoba, has developed an innovative way to help adults in the community acknowledge negative behaviours and the effect those behaviours have on others, including children. Whenever they receive a report that a child is in danger, workers attend the home, assess the situation, and if the child is deemed to be in need of protection, the *parent* is removed. The parent is taken elsewhere on the reserve — usually to the home of friends or family — where they sit down with workers the next business day to discuss the incident. Then a determination is made as to whether, and when, they will be returned home. Some parents are away from home for as long as three months, receiving counselling or treatment. (A respite worker moves to the home on the first day to care for the children, but extended family eventually take over.) According to Felix Walker, the CEO of the Family and Community Centre at Nisichawayasihk, "This reduces trauma on the children and creates an awareness of the behaviours a parent or caregiver needs to start addressing in order to start having a fully functioning family again." Nisichawayasihk has been using this procedure since 2002, and it's lowered apprehension rates in the community by 85 per cent. Initially, Walker says, the parents were "quite irritated, quite irate" at being removed from their home, but the system is working because it forces parents to take responsibility for their actions. It also gives the parent a sense of what it's like for a child to be removed from their family. This often leads to a life-changing decision to begin their healing work, for the sake of themselves and their family. A similar approach is being used in the Misipawistik Cree Nation (formerly known as Grand Rapids), also in Manitoba.

Removing the parent from the home puts the emphasis — and consequences — on the perpetrator, instead of punishing or retraumatizing the child (who, after all, has done nothing wrong). By framing family reunification around the parent's plan for healing, the Nisichawayasihk and Misipawistik approach also shifts the standard binary understanding of victim and perpetrator. When the parent is removed from the home and offered assistance, they are not pathologized. Rather, it is understood that the parent is also a victim/survivor, and that the trauma they have experienced has had negative effects on their ability to be a loving and competent parent. This approach to child welfare repairs relationships, in keeping with Indigenous cultural frameworks. It also uses another cultural approach: when the parent is removed, it calls to mind the Indigenous practice of banishment. Although parents are offered every form of assistance available, it is up to them to make the changes that will lead to family reunification. Until they do so, they are banished from the family home.

Other communities are using circles to reinvent child welfare. At the Sagkeeng First Nation in southern Manitoba, the Circle of Care program brings a family together with all of the agencies that would have worked with them separately in the past. Together, the agencies and the family create an action plan for identifying the steps that need to be taken to reunify the family. The community of Atikamekw, near Trois-Rivieres, Quebec, uses family conferencing circles conducted in the Atikamekw language to deal with child welfare cases. According to child welfare advocate Cindy Blackstock, writing in the *Toronto Star*, this approach has reduced the number of children sent into care outside the community by 80 per cent.

In Toronto, Aboriginal Legal Services has created the Giiwedin

Anang (North Star) program, which handles 50 to 60 child wel-fare cases every year through the Aboriginal Approach to Dispute Resolution process used in Canada's court system. Giiwedin Anang starts with a meeting between the parent(s) and elders from the community, where the issues are discussed. Then a circle is held to bring together all stakeholders, including the child welfare agency. A volunteer "auntie" works with the child to identify their needs and may also take part in the circle. If the child is old enough (in their teen years), they may also participate. After a series of circles, a plan is put in place, with an emphasis on mending relationships. Nishnawbe-Aski Legal Services in Thunder Bay, Ontario, uses a similar approach across northern Ontario. That program uses kin-ship co-parenting approaches in which the child is not removed from the home. These kinds of community-led approaches are not widespread, however, which means that non-Indigenous models continue to dominate the child welfare system.

If systemic change is key to addressing the needs of people and communities, then good governance is also a key factor in addressing intergenerational trauma. It takes visionary leaders to create visionary programs. However, Innu surgeon Stanley Vollant told *Windspeaker* in 2014 that he believes many Indigenous leaders "struggle to manage the complex and at times conflicting demands of elected office." And Nehiyaw political scientist and scholar Kiera Ladner says that many band councils "simply cannot cope" because "they do not exhibit the characteristics or knowl-edge of good leadership and good governance."

Brian Calliou, a lawyer and expert in Indigenous leadership and self-government, has written about the qualities leaders had in pre-colonial Indigenous communities. Calliou, who is Nehiyaw, says those selected by the elders for leadership positions would often be chosen at an early age and groomed for the role. Typically, elders would look for people who were industrious, courageous, generous, and had a great deal of self-control. Calliou says that chiefs were experts at consensus building and collaboration, because they had to gain the trust of community members and the support of other leaders in the community, such as spiritual leaders, elders, and leading hunters. In addition, Calliou says that pre-colonial governance models ensured that a chief's power was held in check by other centres of power within the nation, including policing, the young men's warrior society, the women's society, and community officials such as shamans, storytellers, messengers, elders in charge of seasonal migrations, and the war chief. (Other Indigenous cultures had/have the same checks and balances. In the Haudenosaunee longhouse, for example, the power of a chief is kept in check through the Clan Mothers, who can remove a chief and recommend their replacement.) In any Indigenous nation, part of a chief's job is to preserve group harmony and ensure that everyone in the community is taken care of and their needs met. Today, those checks and balances have been erased, leaders are not groomed for the role, and the band council model often operates in isolation from pre-colonial Indigenous governance models where they still exist.

Part of the reason that so many Indigenous leaders face challenges when they assume positions within the band council structure is because they have no one to teach them what it means to be a leader. As the cultural genocide described by the Truth and Reconciliation Commission has progressed through the generations and old people who knew the pre-colonial ways have died off, there are no true elders left in many communities to guide the young or advise the leadership. And in some communities, there might be true elders, but they are not given the chance to be involved in band council activities and Indian Affairs–mandated models of governance.

The late Nehiyaw elder Joseph Couture — who was the first

Indigenous person in Canada to achieve a PhD in psychology, an ordained priest who served his order for 12 years, and a hockey star scouted by the Chicago Blackhawks — defines a "true elder" as "capable of relations so that all others can equally flourish." Couture says that true elders are "familiar with energy on a vast scale, in multiple modes . . . energy as healing, creative, life-giving, sustaining." True elders know how to tap into, and share, that energy in their work and in their daily lives. According to Couture, they also carry and employ intuition, intellect, memory, imagination, emotion, humour, and a profound moral sense. If we look at Couture's biography, we see the mark of a true elder: someone who is comfortable in the intellectual, physical, and spiritual domains and who shares those gifts with the community.

Because the effects of trauma describe issues of disconnection and an inability to create relationships, being "capable of relations" is now a challenge in many contemporary Indigenous communities. So it is of crucial importance that true elders are involved in choosing, grooming, and advising the leaders of that community — no matter what the Indian Act says about band councils, elections, and meetings. In communities where true elders no longer exist, then steps must be taken to create a new generation of elders and to ensure that they are involved in activities undertaken by the band council. In off-reserve and urban communities, the same steps must be taken so that a new generation of elders can contribute leadership in a variety of situations, from provincial agencies and city councils, to law courts and school boards, to boards of directors and advisory circles.

Part of the problem with the band council model, according to Kiera Ladner, is that band councils are an "illusion of government." Band councils were created as a tool of colonial control to administer federal policies and programs at the local level. They were never set up with the proper jurisdictions, revenue streams, or systems of accountability to actually function as a government. And although band councils are elected by community members, they are actually accountable to the federal Department of Indian Affairs. They have legitimacy in Canadian law but not Indigenous law. Under the Indian Act, band councils must also have elections every two years, which makes it difficult to plan and implement long-term holistic programs. As such, Ladner says that band councils have no real capacity to address the "problems, needs, and aspirations of communities." That's why we so often hear about on-reserve communities that lurch from crisis to crisis.

In 2017, the Manitoba Keewatinowi Okimakanak — a non-profit political advocacy organization that represents 30 First Nations communities included in treaties 4, 5, 6, and 10 — created a mobile crisis team composed of seven mental-health workers. The crisis team is part of a three-year, $10-million plan that will deliver mental-health programs for the province's 63 First Nations. The mandate is to focus on people who experience traumatic incidents (such as a family member committing suicide). That same year, the Peter Ballantyne Cree Nation and the Lac La Ronge First Nation in Saskatchewan received federal funding to develop 10 mental wellness teams employing both Western clinical approaches and Indigenous culture–based approaches. And in 2016, teams of mental health workers travelled to Attawapiskat in northern Ontario to provide emergency aid to the community in the wake of an epidemic of youth suicides. This work is of critical importance. Eventually, however, the framework for the work being done within Indigenous communities is going to have to shift from short-term resiliency to long-term healing — which means switching from crisis management to dealing with the root causes of the distress that people feel. Averting crisis will require Indigenous peoples to work on rebalancing the individual and rebuilding and repairing the structures of family and community.

That work can only happen if it is supported by systemic change that prioritizes long-term, community-based interventions.

Treena Wynes, a social worker and member of the Lac La Ronge First Nation, told the CBC in 2017 that she is "grateful" for the additional federal funding offered to Indigenous communities in Saskatchewan. But she also knows how limited short-term, crisis-oriented responses are. As she tells the CBC, "There are some kids who have had traumatic incidents and experiences and live in unhealthy conditions, and we need to have something in place for those youth. There really is nothing. There is maybe a high-school counsellor."

Hilda Green, a psychotherapist from the Kamloops First Nation in BC who specializes in mental health and wellness in Indigenous communities, agrees. In a 2017 article on Indigenous youth suicide in *The Guardian*, Green said, "I have a client who has been through so much trauma. All five of my client's siblings committed suicide, leaving them as the only one left in their family. Yet I am expected to help them and so many others within a few hours and with little to no resources. That is not right. More needs to be done to prevent this from happening. When I fly into these isolated communities, all I do is contain the situation. I am temporarily putting out fires — but if the community does not have full time mental-health experts to help them after I leave, those fires will ignite again."

The distress felt within many Indigenous communities — the negative emotions, feeling unsafe and isolated, lack of connection and identity, lack of family support, and the feeling that individuals have no control over their own lives — will only be successfully addressed when communities are able to create and support true elders and leaders, all of them with visionary ideas. In communities without effective leadership, the needs of community members are not met, there is no one for children and young people to emulate, there is no trauma-informed planning, and there is little hope for change.

When Corey O'Soup, the advocate for children and youth for the province of Saskatchewan and a citizen of the Key First Nation, speaks to CBC Radio in 2018, he identifies the main issues that factor into Indigenous youth suicide. In a year-long project during which his office visited 12 First Nations across the northern part of the province, O'Soup says youth in those communities "talked about issues around bullying and cyberbullying, around substance misuse, drugs and alcohol. They talked about lack of emotional support. They talked about not feeling safe in their communities. They talked about not having enough diverse activities. And they talked about emotional and mental health and wellness, and the lack of those things in their communities. . . . [But] when they talk about bullying and cyberbullying, they're not talking just about youth bullying other youth. They're talking about adults in the community and professionals in the community bullying them as well. So when it comes to a topic like that we just can't put in programming for youth bullying youth. We need to put in programs for adults bullying youth."

It is unrealistic to expect that leaders in any Indigenous community are somehow immune to the impacts of trauma felt by the community members they serve. To kill the wittigo, Indigenous peoples and communities must take an intentional approach to dealing with the trauma-related beliefs and behaviours shown or tolerated by leaders and officials: the threats, personal attacks, blame, hostility, and retribution directed at community members by leadership in some communities; the climate of toxic communication, bullying, and harassment that exists in many Indigenous political and social service organizations; and the complete lack of empathy and compassion shown by some individuals in positions of authority.

When former Assembly of First Nations national chief Shawn Atleo takes a doctor-mandated sick leave in 2013 to recover from norovirus, other chiefs and political officials mock his decision, sending emails — published by the Aboriginal Peoples Television Network — accusing him of "seeking pity and endearment." When community members speak out about vote-buying and other corruption during band council elections — according to widely available media reports and third-party investigations conducted by the RCMP, this has happened most recently at a First Nation in Saskatchewan and two First Nations in Manitoba — they are evicted from their homes, lose their band jobs, have paycheques held back or left unsigned, are refused band benefits, and face other types of punishment.

The first time a community advisory committee meets at an agency with which I am associated, the so-called elder on the committee cuts other people off as they speak, finds fault with their thoughts and ideas, challenges everything that is said, and blocks any form of energetic connection or consensus among members of the group. The "elder" contributes absolutely no usable information during the meeting and no assistance in framing the issues under discussion. By the end of the meeting, everyone is looking down at the table, and the optimism that had characterized the beginning of the meeting has disappeared.

If healing from colonization and intergenerational trauma is going to be community-led — and it must — then the process must include finding the right people with the right skills for the right roles. That means dealing with issues of leadership in on-reserve and urban communities. It also means reinstating Indigenous governance models.

When five women are elected to the band council at the Saik'uz First Nation near Prince George, BC, in 2017, they decide to do things differently. The women, who range in age from 31 to

72, have jettisoned the standard portfolio system, opting instead to work together, by consensus, on four key areas: governance and finance, environmental stewardship, sociocultural issues, and education and employment. In media coverage of the election, one thing stands out: the way the members of the new council speak about each other. At a Women in Indigenous Leadership event at the University of Northern British Columbia in November 2017, chief Jackie Thomas says, "I really appreciate them," and each member of the new council speaks about how the other women on council inspire them. This is exactly the kind of generosity and emotion that Couture says characterizes effective leadership.

Effective leadership for on-reserve communities also means recruiting and electing people who have ideas about sustainable development, a systemic analysis of oppression, and are comfortable with the fact that more than 60 per cent of Indigenous peoples live off-reserve. At the Squamish Nation in BC's Lower Mainland, eight new councillors, all under the age of 36, are elected to the band council in 2017. According to 28-year-old Dustin Rivers — one of the new councillors, who also goes by his traditional name, Khelsilem — 40 per cent of the Squamish Nation's voting population is under the age of 36, and they want "some sort of change." That change seems to be young people with new ideas and ways of doing business. The eight new councillors run on a slate that focuses on greater band council transparency and consultation with members, changing the election rules to allow online voting or mail-in ballots for members living off-reserve, creating more on-reserve housing, opposing the Woodfibre LNG natural gas pipeline on Squamish territory (which the previous council had supported), pay equity for band employees, increased monthly allowance for post-secondary students, online streaming of council meetings, and online publication of band council motions and minutes.

Being a leader does not mean an individual has to be perfect.

In fact, many elders and leaders in contemporary Indigenous communities use their own experience of healing from chronic and intergenerational trauma to inform their work with people and with communities. Because their healing has, in many cases, been mediated by pre-colonial Indigenous values and ways of knowing, they are able to pass along these values and the insight they have achieved. Their imperfect and sometimes hardscrabble path toward personal change often creates leaders of extraordinary compassion who demonstrate deep insight into what Couture calls "the structure, functioning, and manifestation" of human societies and the natural world. One example is Natan Obed, president of the Inuit Tapiriit Kanatami (ITK).

In his election speech to the ITK membership in 2015, Obed says, "I would likely not be as emotionally strong, sympathetic, or driven to succeed if I had not experienced adversity as a child." This adversity included physical and emotional abuse at the hands of his father, Enoch Obed, who was addicted to alcohol. As Obed recounts in his speech, "He didn't speak to us in Inuktitut or teach us anything about the land. After many separations, he eventually disowned us and left my mother to raise us on her own with no financial support. I know what it is like to have nothing to eat and not know where my family is going to live." Despite his father's failures as a parent, however, Obed acknowledges that his father "overcame enormous obstacles to achieve success in his chosen fields," eventually becoming a Moravian minister, counsellor, director of land claims for the Labrador Inuit Association, and playing a role in the 1982 repatriation of the Canadian Constitution. Obed understands that his father's traumatic experiences — being forcibly relocated from one Inuit community to another in 1956, losing his parents to early deaths two years later, and being taken to an orphanage in Newfoundland, where he lost most of his Inuktitut language skills and experienced abuse — are the reasons why he self-medicated with alcohol and was unable to effectively parent Obed. Obed has moved past blame and judgment to arrive at a place where he sees the cause and consequence in his father's story, the complex layers of his father's public and private personas, the effect of his father's experiences on Obed's own childhood, and how those challenges have affected his choices in life. As a leader, he is able to apply this insight — this *seeing* — into a wide-ranging body of work with Inuit at the community level and at the policy level, from directing an Inuktitut-immersion daycare to developing the Nunavut Suicide Prevention Strategy to working on issues of poverty reduction and food security to serving as a trustee for the Nunatsiavut government's business ventures.

Developing strength of character after adversity is not a result of experiencing adversity — it's a result of the process of reflection and the insight gained into that adversity. Once insight is gained, then it can be used to assist others in their processes of transformation.

In Clyde River, Nunavut, a 10-year-old program called Our Life's Journey — *Ilisaqsivik* in Inuktitut — has been using Inuit knowledge and European techniques to train counsellors to work with Inuit throughout Nunavut. The training program is delivered in four parts over the course of two years, and it has a dual focus: training community counsellors to help others and helping counsellors-in-training learn how to understand and manage their own thoughts and feelings. Counsellor Aisa Piungituq told the CBC that the program has helped him become more in touch with his own emotional needs and more empathetic to the needs of others. "When you don't talk it out," Piungituq says, "you feel alone and ashamed, like you're the only person who feels that way." He now uses that insight to create a safe place for other Inuit to talk about their struggles, including poverty and overcrowded housing, the intergenerational effects of residential schools, and unhealthy relationships. The program has been so successful that a 2015 coroner's inquest into the suicide rate in Nunavut called upon the government of Nunavut to "pilot Clyde River's Ilisaqsivik model in other communities." To do so will take public funding and commitments from multiple levels of government — and that will depend on the type of political leadership elected by the non-Indigenous citizens of Canada. If the dominant society does not choose leaders with vision, then reconciliation will remain an abstract concept rather than a force for systemic and institutional change.

Killing the wittigo is not just work for Indigenous people. To truly heal from the traumatic history that has created this country, Canada must address the fear and mistrust settlers feel toward Indigenous peoples. This sense of unease — the assumptions and biases that are based not on actual experience or reliable information but on myths and stereotypes — must be interrogated and properly understood as both individual manifestations of, and the systemic forces behind, the oppressive model of colonial control. Non-Indigenous Canadians must also address the trauma that they carry as bystanders to the events of colonization and as descendants of the first wave of settlers. Non-Indigenous Canadians have witnessed, and still witness, the trauma visited upon Indigenous peoples and the natural world. They are also often affected by the everyday impacts of trauma as they manifest in Indigenous peoples.

After Catherine McKay kills four members of the Van de Vorst family on a highway near Saskatoon, Saskatchewan, while driving drunk in January 2016 — father Jordan, mother Chanda, five-year-old daughter Kamryn, and two-year-old son Miguire — she pleads guilty to four counts of impaired driving causing death and is sentenced to 10 years in prison. It is the most severe sentence for drunk driving ever handed down in Saskatchewan, and one of the most severe in Canada. But Jordan Van de Vorst's family is outraged when McKay is sent to a healing lodge for Indigenous women. "We're hurt. We're angry. We're upset," Jordan's father, Lou Van de Vorst, tells the CBC. "To me, the punishment does not fit the crime. Something's not right here."

Van de Vorst is understandably angry. He is traumatized by the sudden death of four members of his family, who were taken from him in a criminal act. What his anger may be preventing him from understanding is that incarcerated people will not be rehabilitated until they develop some awareness about their patterns of behaviour, accept responsibility for their actions, and understand the consequences that they have created for themselves, their victims, the victims' families, their own families, and the affected communities.

Healing lodges were created because prison programs do not work for Indigenous offenders. The programs available at healing lodges address intergenerational trauma and pay particular attention to the histories, experiences, and perspectives of Indigenous peoples. Healing lodges offer incarcerated people the chance to reclaim cultural identity, learn how to live independently, and build self-esteem — all things that have been negatively affected by colonization and the everyday impacts of trauma. Programs focus on parenting, spirituality, developing a connection to the natural world, relationships, loss and recovery, substance abuse, family violence, anger management, problem solving, and leadership. Some healing lodges allow the participation of families and offer victim–offender circles. Some provide training to Indigenous communities in prevention and intervention, so that chronic trauma is reduced and people can avoid involvement in the criminal justice system. Healing lodges offer incarcerated people the chance to make changes to their lives. Without these changes, incarcerated people will not be rehabilitated when they are released back into society, and the cycle of chronic trauma and criminalization will continue — and Van de Vorst will have to pay for it through his taxpayer contributions to public funds.

According to André Poilièvre, a member of the Order of Canada and Catholic priest who was the chaplain at the Saskatoon Correctional Centre for seven years and has now created the STR8 UP program for former gang members in Saskatchewan, "All [offenders] have been victims before becoming victimizers." Sentencing Indigenous people who engage in criminal acts as a result of chronic or intergenerational trauma to lengthy periods of incarceration will not achieve rehabilitation or a change in their patterns of behaviour. And putting survivors of trauma into prison without programs or supports is a further victimization. It is part of the continuing violence perpetuated by the colonial control figure and no solution to the colonization, marginalization, and oppression that creates chronic trauma in the first place.

A few months after 26-year-old police officer Thierry LeRoux is shot and killed while responding to a 911 call in the Anishinabe community of Lac-Simon, Quebec, in 2016, LeRoux's father, Michel, works with his son's colleagues to establish a foundation in Thierry's name. The Fondation Thierry LeRoux supports education for Indigenous youth. "It's a way to prevent this type of tragedy," LeRoux tells the CBC. "The funds will be distributed to youth between the ages of four and 25 in the community of Lac-Simon but also in other communities . . . to create a vision for these youngsters. That they can have a future without having to leave their own culture, their own ancestry. . . . It's part of the emotion we have to go through. To be able to talk about [Thierry's death]. To try to make sense of something that makes no sense."

This is how we kill the wittigo: we make sense of what has happened, we share our stories, we get to the root of the pain, and then we work together to create change.

AUTHOR'S NOTE

I've related my experiences of people, places, and organizations from my memories of them. In order to protect the privacy of others I have changed the names of living people referred to in the book, anonymized others, and omitted the identifying details of some locations and organizations.

Since the mid-1990s, grandfather/elder Michael Thrasher has graciously shared what he calls his "meagre learning" about the medicine circle. I am grateful for his generosity. However, what appears in this book is not the final word or the final truth on the medicine wheel. What is included here is what I am able to understand about the medicine circle at this moment in time, offered as a contribution to the collective development of awareness, understanding, knowledge, and wisdom on the subject of intergenerational trauma.

Grandfather Thrasher does not look for fame. He has agreed to be named in this book to point toward the source of the ideas contained in the text. I am grateful for his kindness.

ACKNOWLEDGEMENTS

This book took six years to research, write, and live. During that time, I have been supported by a caring community of people who gave hugs, took me out to dinner, loaned/gave me money, sent supportive texts and emails, listened to my ideas, challenged my thinking, and offered feedback and support. I would not be the person I am, or in the place I am in — and this book would not exist — without the fierce intelligence, unfailing patience, generosity, and love they have shown me. Thank you to my alphabetically ordered friends, who are also my chosen family: Bishakha Chowdhury, Helene Donnelly, Joanne Hill and John Holland, Marie Leduc (and Jim), Ingrid Mayrhofer (and Werner), Paula Messina, and Alex Stairs.

I am grateful to Wendy Ng and my colleagues at the Royal Ontario Museum for their commitment to systemic change. I am also grateful to Molly Falconer, Patrice Peterkin, and the team at Scholastic Education for (a) keeping me somewhat employed and

(b) working hard to bring young people the information they need to become agents of social change. The privilege is mine.

Angie Ortlieb, you are the best. Your dedication to changing the world one little person at a time inspires me on a daily basis. To Angie's crew at Avondale Alternative School, and to Tammy Hardwick and the team at the Halton District School Board Equity and Inclusive Education office: your work matters. Thank you for everything you do. Isabelle Mignault, where would I be without our talks. Nahúm Flores, your art inspires me and helps me see farther, both inward and outward. Doug Friesen, thanks for being an educator who takes risks. Stay weird.

Thanks to Rebecca McGowan at A Space Gallery for the hardware. In 2011, I was still using a Mac LC-575 (circa 1994), so you took pity on the writer and loaned me a G4 (circa 2003). This gift made instant and immeasurable changes in my working and writing life. I used that G4 until 2015 and remain eternally grateful for your kindness.

This book would not be what it is without the guidance of my agent, Stephanie Sinclair, at the Transatlantic Agency. Her astute reading, skillful telephone therapy sessions, and unwavering support made it all possible. To my editor, Susan Renouf, and the team at ECW: thank you for your patience with my writerly ways and for asking the questions that helped me tell this story better. I'm honoured to have been one of the lucky ones.

Thank you to Susanda Yee (R.TCMP, R.Ac.) at Six Degrees Health for offering feedback on Chapter 7 and to Monica Kendel (PCC) for helping me fix Chapter 4. A big hyi-hyi to Patricia Vickers for the beautiful cover artwork. Finally, thank you to grandfather/ elder Michael Thrasher (LLD) for reading the manuscript and speaking with me about my interpretation of the medicine wheel. Any mistakes are mine.

SOURCES

Media sources are cited in the text using date and name of publication. Some books and some research studies are spelled out in the text. The sources listed here include books, journal articles, conference presentations, videos, and webpages quoted in the text and used as background to inform the chapter. Although Judith Lewis Herman's work on complex post-traumatic stress disorder informs the entire book and her ideas are employed throughout, her work is listed below in the chapters that deal specifically with CPTSD.

Chapter 1: How Things Work, and Why Stories Matter

Aguiar, William, and Regine Halseth. "Aboriginal Peoples and Historic Trauma: The Processes of Intergenerational Transmission," National Collaborating Centre for Aboriginal Health, 2015.

Alexander, Jeffrey C. "Toward a Theory of Cultural Trauma," *Cultural*

Trauma and Collective Identity, Jeffrey C. Alexander, Ron Eyerman, Bernhard Giesen, Neil J. Smelser, and Piotr Sztompka, eds., 2004.

Bellamy, Sherry, and Cindy Hardy. "Understanding Depression in Aboriginal Communities and Families," National Collaborating Centre for Aboriginal Health, 2015.

Bombay, Amy, Kim Matheson, and Hymie Anisman. "Intergenerational Trauma: Convergence of Multiple Processes Among First Nations Peoples in Canada," *Journal of Aboriginal Health*, National Aboriginal Health Organization, November 2009.

Connors, Edward. "Intergenerational Trauma and Healing," address to the Association of Canadian Court Administrators Annual Conference, Winnipeg, Manitoba, 2007.

De Las Casas, Bartolomé. *The Devastation of the Indies: A Brief Account*, 1552. Available online.

Dziuban, Zuzanna. "Memory as Haunting," *HAGAR Studies in Culture, Polity, and Identities* 12, Winter 2014.

Kellermann, Natan P.F. "Transmission of Holocaust Trauma: An Integrative View," *Psychiatry* 64(3), Fall 2001.

Rice, Brian. *Seeing the World With Aboriginal Eyes: A Four Directional Perspective on Human and Non-Human Values, Cultures, and Relationships on Turtle Island*, Native Studies Press, 2005.

Sinclair, Murray. "The Historical Relationship Between the Canadian Justice System and Aboriginal People," presentation to the Aboriginal Justice Learning Network, Constituency Group Meeting, Aylmer, Quebec, April 16–18, 1997.

Sorscher, Nechama, and Lisa J. Cohen. "Parental Communication of Trauma Among Children of Holocaust Survivors," report to the Institute of Education Sciences, U.S. Department of Education, 1992.

Thrasher, Michael. Various sessions on understanding and applying the medicine wheel, Trent University Annual Elders and Traditional Peoples Gathering, 1994, 1995, 1996.

Wenger-Nabigon, Annie. "The Cree Medicine Wheel as an Organizing Paradigm of Theories of Human Development," *Native Social Work Journal* 7, 2010.

Yellow Horse Brave Heart, Maria. "From Intergenerational Trauma to Intergenerational Healing," keynote address at the Wellbreity Conference, Denver, Colorado, 2005.

Zinn, Howard. *A People's History of the United States*, Harper Perennial, 1980.

Zohar, Danah. *The Quantum Self: Human Nature and Consciousness Defined by the New Physics*, William Morrow, 1990.

Chapter 2: What It Means to Be Colonized

Bryant-Davis, Thema. "Healing Requires Recognition: The Case for Race-Based Traumatic Stress," *The Counselling Psychologist*, 2007.

Cardinal, Clifford. "An Explanation of High Cancer Morbidity and Mortality in a Cohort of Aboriginal People," thesis submitted to the Faculty of Graduate Studies and Research in partial fulfillment of the requirements for the degree of Master of Science, Faculty of Medical Sciences-Public Health Services, University of Alberta, 2000.

Erbes, Christopher. "Our Constructions of Trauma: A Dialectical Perspective," *Journal of Constructivist Psychology* 17(3), 2004.

Fonagy, Peter. "The Transgenerational Transmission of Holocaust Trauma," *Attachment & Human Development* 1(1), 1999.

Herman, Judith Lewis. "Complex PTSD: A Syndrome in Survivors of Prolonged and Repeated Trauma," *Journal of Traumatic Stress* 5(3), 1992.

Herman, Judith. *Trauma and Recovery: The Aftermath of Violence from Domestic Abuse to Political Terror*, Basic Books, 1997.

Hinton, Devon E., and Roberto Lewis-Fernández. "The Cross-Cultural

Validity of Post-Traumatic Stress Disorder: Implications for DSM-5," *Depression and Anxiety*, 2010.

Jenkins, Janis H. "Culture, Emotion, and PTSD," *Ethnocultural Aspects of Post-Traumatic Stress Disorder: Issues, Research, and Clinical Applications*, Anthony J. Marsella, Matthew J. Friedman, Ellen T. Gerrity, Raymond M. Scurfield, eds., 1996.

Jones, Edgar, and Simon Wessely. "A Paradigm Shift in the Conceptualization of Psychological Trauma in the 20th Century," *Journal of Anxiety Disorders* 21, 2007.

Marshall, S.G. "Canadian Drug Policy and the Reproduction of Indigenous Inequities," *The International Indigenous Policy Journal* 6(1), 2015.

McClelland, Mac. "Hearts and Minds: PTSD at Epidemic Levels Among Returning Vets," *Mother Jones*, January/February 2013.

Pole, Nnamdi, Joseph P. Gone, and Madhur Kulkarni. "Post-Traumatic Stress Disorder Among Ethnoracial Minorities in the United States," *Clinical Psychology: Science and Practice* 15(1), March 2008.

Robertson, Lloyd Hawkeye. "The Residential School Experience: Syndrome or Historic Trauma," *Pimatisiwin: A Journal of Aboriginal and Indigenous Community Health* 4(1), 2006.

Smelser, Neil J. "Psychological Trauma and Cultural Trauma," *Cultural Trauma and Collective Identity*, Jeffrey C. Alexander, Ron Eyerman, Bernhard Giesen, Neil J. Smelser, and Piotr Sztompka, eds., 2004.

Thrasher, Michael. "Winds of Change: The Medicine Wheel as Movement," presentation at the Celebrating Indigenous Knowledges: Peoples, Lands, and Cultures conference, Department of Indigenous Studies, Trent University, 2010.

Zinn, Howard. *A People's History of the United States*, Harper Perennial, 1980.

Chapter 3: Becoming Human

Ards, Sheila D., Samuel L. Myers Jr., Patricia Ray, Hyeon-Eui Kim, Kevin Monroe, Irma Arteaga. "Racialized Perceptions and Child Neglect," *Child Youth Services Review*, August 2012.

Arnold, Cheryl, and Ralph Fisch. *The Impact of Complex Trauma on Development*, Jason Aronson, 2011.

Bonanno, George A., and Anthony D. Mancini. "The Human Capacity to Thrive in the Face of Potential Trauma," *Pediatrics*, 2008.

Fonagy, Peter. "Transgenerational Consistencies of Attachment: A New Theory," paper to the Developmental and Psychoanalytic Discussion Group, American Psychoanalytic Association meeting, Washington, DC, May 13, 1999.

James, Angela. "The Exploration of Aboriginal Student Achievement through the Reflexive Analysis of a Dialogue Circle: A View of Aboriginal Education through the Eyes of Community," *Pimatisiwin: A Journal of Aboriginal and Indigenous Community Health* 10(2), 2012.

Van der Kolk, Bessel A. "Developmental Trauma Disorder: Towards a Rational Diagnosis for Children with Complex Trauma Histories," *Psychiatric Annals* 35(5), 2005.

Wiehe, Vernon R. *Working with Child Abuse and Neglect: A Primer*, Sage Publications, 1996.

Yehuda, Rachel, Sarah L. Halligan, and Robert Grossman. "Childhood Trauma and Risk for PTSD: Relationship to Intergenerational Effects of Trauma, Parental PTSD, and Cortisol Excretion," *Development and Psychopathology* 13, 2001.

Chapter 4: The Angry Indian and a Culture of Blame

Bar-Tal, Daniel, Lily Chernyak-Hai, Noa Schori, and Ayelet Gundar. "A Sense of Self-Perceived Collective Victimhood in Intractable Conflicts," *International Review of the Red Cross* 91(874), June 2009.

Bombay, Amy, with Kim Matheson and Hymie Anisman. "Origins of Lateral Violence in Aboriginal Communities: A Preliminary Study of Student-to-Student Abuse in Residential Schools," Aboriginal Healing Foundation, 2014.

Brenmer, J. Douglas. *Does Stress Damage the Brain? Understanding Trauma-Related Disorders from a Mind-Body Perspective*, W.W. Norton & Company, 2005.

Cloitre, Marylene, Bradley C. Stolbach, Judith L. Herman, Bessel van der Kolk, Robert Pynoos, Jing Wang, Eva Petkova, and Nathan S. Kline. "A Developmental Approach to Complex PTSD: Childhood and Adult Cumulative Trauma as Predictors of Symptom Complexity," *Journal of Traumatic Stress*, 2009.

Duran, Eduardo. *Healing the Soul Wound: Counselling with American Indians and Other Native Peoples*, Teachers College Press, 2006.

Haskell, Lori, and Melanie Randall. "Disrupted Attachments: A Social Context Complex Trauma Framework and the Lives of Aboriginal Peoples in Canada," *Journal of Aboriginal Health*, National Aboriginal Health Organization, November 2009.

Jeffries, Rod. Conference presentation to the Assembly of Manitoba Chiefs, 2007. Available online.

LaBoucane-Benson, Patti. "Moving Beyond Lateral Violence," presentation at the Growing Our Relations: Wahkohtowin conference, North Central Alberta Child and Family Services, 2013.

Maslow, Abraham H. *Toward a Psychology of Being*, Wiley, 1998.

Menzies, Peter. "Intergenerational Trauma from a Mental Health Perspective," *Native Social Work Journal* 7, November 2010.

Miller, John. "Ipperwash and the Media: A Critical Analysis of How the Story Was Covered," Aboriginal Legal Services of Toronto, 2005.

Native Women's Association of Canada. *Aboriginal Lateral Violence: What Is It?*, 2011. Available online.

Nunavut Wellness. "Inuit Men and Empowerment." No date. Available online.

Pard, Allan, John Wolf Child, Clarence Wolf Leg, Blair First Rider, Kathy Brewer, and Trevor R. Peck. "The Blackfoot Medicine Wheel Project," *Back on the Horse: Recent Developments in Archaeological and Palaeontological Research in Alberta*, Occasional Paper No. 36, Archaeological Society of Alberta, 2016.

Partridge, Cheryle. "Residential Schools: The Intergenerational Impacts on Aboriginal Peoples," *Native Social Work Journal* 7, November 2010.

Peck, Richard. Executive summary, Special Prosecutor Decision on Criminal Charges Against Michael Bryant, 2010.

Sinclair, Murray. "The Historical Relationship Between the Canadian Justice System and Aboriginal People," presentation to the Aboriginal Justice Learning Network, Constituency Group Meeting, Aylmer, Quebec, April 16–18, 1997.

Westphal, Maren, Mark Olfson, Margarita Bravova, Marc J. Gameroff, Raz Gross, Priya Wickramaratne, Daniel J. Pilowsky, Richard Neugebauer, Steven Shea, Ráfael Lantigua, Myrna Weissman, and Yuval Neria. "Borderline Personality Disorder, Exposure to Interpersonal Trauma, and Psychiatric Comorbidity in Urban Primary Care Patients," *Psychiatry* 76(4), Winter 2013.

Chapter 5: Invisible Roots

Alexander, Pamela C. *Intergenerational Cycles of Trauma and Violence*, W.W. Norton & Co., 2015.

Everett, Barbara, and Ruth Gallop. *The Link Between Childhood Trauma and Mental Illness: Effective Interventions for Mental Health Professionals*, Sage Publications, 2001.

Figley, Charles R., and Laurel J. Kiser. *Helping Traumatized Families*, Second Edition, Routledge, 2013.

GreyWolf, Iva. "Out of the Darkness," presentation to the American Psychological Association Division 35 Mid-Winter EC Meeting,

Section 6 Alaska Native/American Indian/Indigenous Women, Seattle, Washington, January 2011.

LaBoucane-Benson, Patti, Ginger Gibson, Allen Benson, and Greg Miller. "Are We Seeking Pimatisiwin or Creating Pomewin? Implications for Water Policy," *The International Indigenous Policy Journal* 3(3), 2012.

Chapter 6: Fractured Narratives

Bisbey, Stephen, and Lori Beth Bisbey. *Brief Therapy for Post-Traumatic Stress Disorder: Traumatic Incident Reduction and Related Techniques*, John Wiley & Sons, 1998.

Hylton, John H., with Murray Bird, Nicole Eddy, Heather Sinclair, and Heather Stenerson. "Aboriginal Sexual Offending in Canada," Aboriginal Healing Foundation, 2006.

Ralph, Naomi, Kathy Hamaguchi, and Marie Cox. "Transgenerational Trauma, Suicide, and Healing from Sexual Abuse in the Kimberley Region, Australia," *Pimatisiwin: A Journal of Aboriginal and Indigenous Community Health* 4(2), Winter 2006.

Richter-Levin, Gal, and Irit Akirav. "Amygdala-Hippocampus Dynamic Interaction in Relation to Memory," *Molecular Neurobiology* 22, 2000.

Schauer, Maggie, Frank Neuner, and Thomas Elbert. *Narrative Exposure Therapy: A Short-Term Intervention for Traumatic Stress Disorders After War, Terror, or Torture*, Hogrefe & Huber, 2005.

Van der Kolk, Bessel A., James W. Hopper, and Janet E. Osterman. "Exploring the Nature of Traumatic Memory: Combining Clinical Knowledge with Laboratory Methods," *Trauma and Cognitive Science*, 2001.

Venable Raine, Nancy. *After Silence: Rape and My Journey Back*, Crown Publishers, 1998.

Chapter 7: What the Body Remembers

Allen, Billie, and Janet Smylie. "First Peoples, Second-Class Treatment: The Role of Racism in the Health and Well-Being of Indigenous Peoples in Canada," The Wellesley Institute, 2015.

Arkle, Madeline, Max Deschner, Ryan Giroux, Reed Morrison, Danielle Nelson, Amanda Sauvé, and Kelita Singh. "Indigenous Peoples and Health in Canadian Medical Education," Canadian Federation of Medical Students (CFMS) position paper, 2015.

Atleo, E. Richard (Umeek). *Principles of Tsawalk: An Indigenous Approach to Global Crisis*, University of British Columbia Press, 2011.

Belcourt, Billy-Ray. "Meditations on Reserve Life, Biosociality, and the Taste of Non-Sovereignty," *Settler Colonial Studies*, January 2017.

Belcourt, Billy-Ray. "Settler Structures of Bad Feeling," *Canadian Art*, January 2018.

Bourassa, Carrie, Kim McKay-McNabb, and Mary Hampton. "Racism, Sexism, and Colonialism: The Impact on the Health of Aboriginal Women in Canada," *Canadian Woman Studies* 24(1), 2004.

First Nations Information Governance Centre. First Nations Regional Health Survey 2008/10: National Report on Adults, Youth, and Children Living in First Nations Communities, 2012.

Hill, Louis Paul. "Understanding Indigenous Canadian Traditional Health and Healing," theses and dissertations, Wilfred Laurier University, 2008.

Hoffman, Ross. "Perspectives on Health within the Teachings of a Gifted Cree Elder," *Pimatisiwin: A Journal of Aboriginal and Indigenous Community Health* 8(1), 2010.

Kaler, Shamdeep Norry, Kelli Ralph-Campbell, Sheri Pohar, Malcolm King, Rose Laboucan, and Ellen L. Toth. "High Rates of Metabolic Syndrome in a First Nations Community in Western Canada: Prevalence and Determinants in Adults and Children," *International Journal of Circumpolar Health* 65(5), 2006.

Kaptchuk, Ted J. *The Web That Has No Weaver: Understanding Chinese Medicine*, McGraw-Hill, 2000.

Katz, Esther. "Recovering After Childbirth in the Mixtec Highlands," *Médicaments et Aliments: L'Approche Ethnopharmacologique*, March 1993.

Kirmayer, Laurence J., Christopher Fletcher, Ellen Corin, and Lucy Boothroyd. "Inuit Concepts of Mental Health and Illness: An Ethnographic Study," Culture and Mental Health Research Unit, Institute of Community and Family Psychiatry, Jewish General Hospital & Division of Social and Transcultural Psychiatry, Department of Psychiatry, McGill University, 1994.

Kurtz, Donna L. M., Jessie C. Nyberg, Susan Van Den Tillaart, Buffy Mills, and The Okanagan Urban Aboriginal Health Research Collective. "Silencing of Voice: An Act of Structural Violence — Urban Aboriginal Women Speak Out About Their Experiences with Health Care," *Journal of Aboriginal Health*, National Aboriginal Health Organization, January 2008.

Long, David Alan, and Terry Fox. "Circles of Healing: Illness, Healing, and Health Among Aboriginal People in Canada," *Visions of the Heart: Canadian Aboriginal Issues*, Harcourt Brace & Company, 1996.

Loppie Reading, Charlotte, and Fred Wien. *Health Inequalities and Social Determinants of Aboriginal Peoples' Health*, National Collaborating Centre for Aboriginal Health, 2009.

Maté, Gabor. *When the Body Says No: The Cost of Hidden Stress*, Vintage Canada, 2004.

Mitchell, Terry L., and Dawn T. Maracle. "Healing the Generations: Post-Traumatic Stress and the Health Status of Aboriginal Populations in Canada," *Journal of Aboriginal Health*, National Aboriginal Health Organization, March 2005.

Native Women's Association of Canada. "Aboriginal Women and Traditional Healing: An Issue Paper," 2007. Available online.

Obomsawin, Raymond. "Traditional Medicine for Canada's First Peoples." No date. Available online.

Reading, J. "The Crisis of Chronic Disease Among Aboriginal Peoples: A Challenge for Public Health, Population Health, and Social Policy," University of Victoria Centre for Aboriginal Health Research, 2009.

Regroupement provincial des comités des usagers. "Patient Engagement and Health Literacy: An Indigenous Cultural Context," presentation at the National Symposium on Patient Engagement, October 25, 2011.

Richmond, Chantelle A.M., Nancy A. Ross, and Julie Bernier. "Exploring Indigenous Concepts of Health: The Dimensions of Métis and Inuit Health," Aboriginal Policy Research Consortium International, 2007.

Robben, Antonius C.G.M. "How Traumatized Societies Remember: The Aftermath of Argentina's Dirty War," *Cultural Critique* 59, Winter 2005.

Van der Kolk, Bessel A. *The Body Keeps the Score: Brain, Mind, and Body in the Healing of Trauma*, Penguin, 2014.

Van der Kolk, Bessel A. "The Body Keeps the Score: Memory and the Evolving Psychobiology of Post-Traumatic Stress," *Harvard Review of Psychiatry* 1(5), 1994.

Young, David, Grant Ingram, and Lise Swartz. *Cry of the Eagle: Encounters with a Cree Healer*, University of Toronto Press, 1989.

Chapter 8: Sacred Being

Alberta Health Services. "Honouring Life: Aboriginal Youth and Communities Empowerment Strategy." No date. Available online.

Archibald, Linda, Jonathan Dewar, Carrie Reid, and Vanessa Stevens. "Dancing, Singing, Painting, and Speaking the Healing Story: Healing Through Creative Arts," Aboriginal Healing Foundation, 2012.

Cajete, Gregory. "Rebuilding Sustainable Indigenous Communitites," presentation at the Celebrating Indigenous Knowledges: Peoples, Lands, and Cultures conference, Department of Indigenous Studies, Trent University, 2010.

Cree School Board. "Cree Culture and Values." No date. Available online.

Hauge, Ashild Lappegard. "Identity and Place: A Critical Comparison of Three Identity Theories," *Architectural Science Review*, March 2007.

Kirmayer, Laurence J., Christopher Fletcher, Robert Watt. "Locating the Eco-Centric Self: Inuit Concepts of Mental Health and Illness," ResearchGate, December 2008.

Landa, Michael J. "Easterville: A Case Study in the Relocation of a Manitoba Native Community," thesis submitted to the Faculty of Graduate Studies in partial fulfillment of the requirements for the degree of Master of Arts, Department of Anthropology, University of Manitoba, 1969.

Radu, Ioana, Lawrence M. House, and Eddie Pashagumskum. "Land, Life, and Knowledge in Chisasibi: Intergenerational Healing in the Bush," *Decolonization: Indigeneity, Education, & Society* 3(3), 2014.

Thistle, J. *Indigenous Definition of Homelessness in Canada*, Canadian Observatory on Homelessness Press, 2017.

Waldram, James B. "Relocation and Social Change Among the Swampy Cree and Métis of Easterville, Manitoba," a thesis submitted to the Faculty of Graduate Studies in partial fulfillment of the requirements for the degree of Master of Arts, Department of Anthropology, University of Manitoba, 1980.

Yellow Horse Brave Heart, Maria. "Historical Trauma and Boarding School Trauma," slide presentation from the Takini Network. No date. Available online.

Chapter 9: Recreating the Structures of Belonging

Alfred, Gerald Taiaiake. "Colonialism and State Dependency," *Journal of Aboriginal Health*, National Aboriginal Health Organization, November 2009.

Armstrong, Jeannette. "En'owkin: What It Means to a Sustainable Community," *Ecoliteracy: Mapping the Terrain*, Center for Ecoliteracy, 2000.

Glendinning, Chellis. "Recovery from Western Civilization," *Elmwood Quarterly* 8(1), 1990.

Grand Council of the Cree. "Social Impact on the Cree of the James Bay Project." No date. Available online.

Lloyd, David. "Colonial Trauma / Post-Colonial Recovery?" *Interventions: International Journal of Post-Colonial Studies* 2(2), 2000.

Mann, Michelle. "Capitalism and the Disempowerment of Canadian Aboriginal Peoples," *Journal of Aboriginal Economic Development* 1(2), 2000.

Mignone, Javier, and John O'Neil. "Social Capital as a Health Determinant in First Nations: An Exploratory Study in Three Communities," *Journal of Aboriginal Health*, National Aboriginal Health Organization, March 2005.

Tuck, Eve and K. Wayne Yang, "Decolonization Is Not a Metaphor," *Decolonization: Indigeneity, Education & Society* 1(1), 2012.

Zohar, Danah, and Ian Marshall. *The Quantum Society: Mind, Physics, and a New Social Vision*, William Morrow, 1994.

Chapter 10: Killing the Wittigo

Abadian, Sousan. "Cultural Healing: When Cultural Renewal Is Reparative and When It Is Toxic," presentation at Healing Our Spirits Worldwide conference, August 7, 2006.

Archibald, Linda. "Decolonization and Healing: Indigenous Experiences in the United States, New Zealand, Australia, and Greenland," Aboriginal Healing Foundation, 2006.

Bopp, Michael, and Judie Bopp. "The Esketemc (Alkali Lake) Community Story: A Case Study," Four Worlds Centre for Development Learning, 2011.

Briere, John, and Catherine Scott. *Principles of Trauma Therapy: A Guide to Symptoms, Evaluation, and Treatment*, Sage Publications, 2006.

Buller, Ed. "A Cost-Benefit Analysis of Hollow Water First Nation's Community Holistic Healing Process," Aboriginal Policy Research Consortium International, Paper 134, 2004.

Chansonneuve, Deborah. "Addictive Behaviours Among Aboriginal People in Canada," Aboriginal Healing Foundation, 2007.

Courtois, Christine A. "Complex Trauma, Complex Reactions: Assessment and Treatment," *Psychotherapy: Theory, Research, Practice, Training* 41(4), 2004.

Doxtater, Lauren, Gayle Broad, Jude Ortiz, Mike Storozuk, Paul Dupuis. "Neighbourhood Resource Centre: A Collective Impact Assessment," NORDIK Institute, January 2016.

Duran, Eduardo. *Healing the Soul Wound: Counselling with American Indians and Other Native Peoples*, Teachers College Press, 2006.

Furniss, Elizabeth Mary. "A Sobriety Movement Among the Shuswap Indians of Alkali Lake," a thesis submitted in partial fulfillment of the requirements for the degree of Master of Arts, Faculty of Anthropology and Sociology, University of British Columbia, 1987.

Inuit Tapiriit Kanatami. National Inuit Suicide Prevention Strategy, 2016. Available online.

Jablonka, Eva. "Cultural Epigenetics," *Biosocial Matters: Rethinking Sociology-Biology Relations in the 21st Century*, Maurizio Meloni, Simon Williams, Paul Martin, eds., Wiley Blackwell, 2016.

John, Ed. "Indigenous Resilience, Connectedness, and Reunification — From Root Causes to Root Solutions: A Report on Indigenous

Child Welfare in British Columbia," Ministry of Children and Family Development, 2016.

Kirmayer, Laurence, Cori Simpson, and Margaret Cargo. "Healing Traditions: Culture, Community, and Mental Health Promotion with Canadian Aboriginal Peoples," *Australasian Psychiatry* 11 supplement, 2003.

Kirmayer, Laurence J., Megha Sehdev, Rob Whitley, Stéphane F. Dandeneau, and Colette Isaac. "Community Resilience: Models, Metaphors, and Measures," *Journal of Aboriginal Health*, National Aboriginal Health Organization, 2009.

Kral, Michael J., Lori Idlout, J. Bruce Minore, Ronald J. Dyck, and Laurence J. Kirmayer. "Unikkaartuit: Meanings of Well-Being, Unhappiness, Health, and Community Change Among Inuit in Nunavut, Canada," *American Journal of Community Psychology* 48, March 2011.

Krichauff, Skye. *Memory, Place, and Aboriginal-Settler History: Understanding Australians' Consciousness of the Colonial Past*, Anthem Press, 2017.

McFee, Dale R., and Norman E. Taylor. "The Prince Albert Hub and the Emergence of Collaborative Risk-Driven Community Safety," Canadian Police College Discussion Paper, 2014.

McIvor, Onowa, Art Napoleon, and Kerissa M. Dickie. "Language and Culture as Protective Factors for At-Risk Communities," *Journal of Aboriginal Health*, National Aboriginal Health Organization, November 2009.

Menzies, Peter. "Developing an Aboriginal Healing Model for Intergenerational Trauma," *International Journal of Health Promotion & Education* 46(2), 2008.

Menzies, Peter. "Understanding Aboriginal Intergenerational Trauma from a Social Work Perspective," *The Canadian Journal of Native Studies* 27(2), 2007.

Pearlman, Laurie Anne, and Christine A. Courtois. "Clinical Applications of the Attachment Framework: Relational Treatment of Complex Trauma," *Journal of Traumatic Stress* 18(5), October 2005.

Pinderhughes, Howard, Rachel A. Davis, and Myesha Williams. "Adverse Community Experiences and Resilience: A Framework for Addressing and Preventing Community Trauma," Prevention Institute, 2015.

Quinn, Ashley. "Reflections on Intergenerational Trauma: Healing as a Critical Intervention," *First Peoples Child & Family Review* 3(4), 2007.

Sawatsky, Murray J., Rick Ruddell, and Nicholas A. Jones. "A Quantitative Study of Prince Albert's Crime/Risk Reduction Approach to Community Safety," *Journal of Community Safety and Well-Being*, March 2017.

Todd, Roy. "Between the Land and the City: Aboriginal Agency, Culture, and Governance in Urban Areas," *London Journal of Canadian Studies* 16, 2000/2001.

Tousignant, Michel and Nibisha Sioui. "Resilience and Aboriginal Communities in Crisis: Theory and Interventions," *Journal of Aboriginal Health*, National Aboriginal Health Organization, November 2009.

Trouillot, Michel-Rolph. "Abortive Rituals: Historical Apologies in the Global Era," *Interventions: International Journal of Post-Colonial Studies* 2(2), 2000

Turpel-Lafond, Mary Ellen. "Paige's Story: Abuse, Indifference, and a Young Life Discarded," Office of the BC Representative for Children and Youth, 2015.

Urban Society for Aboriginal Youth, YMCA Calgary, University of Calgary. "Intervention to Address Intergenerational Trauma: Overcoming, Resisting, and Preventing Structural Violence," *Intergenerational Trauma and Aboriginal Youth*, 2012.

Zembylas, Michalinos. "The Politics of Trauma: Empathy, Reconciliation, and Peace Education," *Journal of Peace Education* 4(2), 2007.

INDEX

The use of *fig* following a locator indicates an image.

Aboriginal Approach to Dispute
Resolution process, 310
Aboriginal Corrections Policy
(Public Safety Canada), 289
Aboriginal Healing Foundation
(AHF)
on chronic headaches in
survivors, 187
healing initiatives of, 2–3
on intergenerational trauma,
28–30, 38, 44, 224
on shame, 135
on trauma as a way of life, 97
abuse
ADHD and, 211
CPTSD and, 39, 60
developmental trauma disorder
and, 86
dissociation and, 73, 161
Duplessis orphans and, 63, 65

health effects of, 187–190
in Indigenous communities, 2,
229
intergenerational trauma and,
28–30, 84
normalizing of, 77–78
re-enactment of, 132, 155–156,
166
in residential schools, 2, 10, 47,
157
see also emotional abuse; sexual
abuse; trauma
abuse family trees, 164–165 *fig*
addiction
materialism and, 257
need for control and, 70, 193
role of in community
dysfunction, 296–297
as symptom of trauma, 288–289
see also alcohol addiction

ADHD, 210–211
affect
    need for both positive and
      negative, 135
    nine types of, 134
    Silvan Tomkins on, 133–135
agency
    healing and, 55
    loss of sense of, 48–49, 93, 101,
      146, 193
    medicine circle/wheel and, 52,
      82, 108
    regaining sense of, 53, 165, 301, 307
agribusiness, 243, 247
Ahousaht First Nation, 192–193, 258
alcohol addiction, 53, 163, 195,
    287–288, 296
Alexie, Robert Arthur, 4
Alexis, Cameron, 254
Alfred, Gerald Taiaiake, 243, 247
anger
    control and, 48, 73–74, 92, 153
    episodic outbursts of, 118
    fear and, 117, 148
    projection of, 114, 117, 121
    vs rage, 97
Angry Indian
    Attawapiskat women's press
      conference and, 116
    Darcy Allan Sheppard story
      and, 113–115
    as living in the moment of
      trauma, 117
    reclaiming of term, 96
    sexist framework and, 121
    struggle to establish emotional
      boundaries, 112–113

    use of term, 95–96
    versions of, 96–97, 104
Anishinabek, 25, 42–43, 164, 289, 322
Anthropocene, 263–264
antlers, proper disposal of, 225–226
Arnaquq-Baril, Alethea, 96
art, accessing feeling through, 80
Aseniwuche Winewak, 216
As'in'i'wa'chi Ni'yaw, 216
Assembly of First Nations (AFN)
    as out of touch, 252
    Youth Council, 251–252
Atikamekw, Quebec, 309
Atleo, Shawn, 316
Atleo, Umeek Richard, 192–193
Attawapiskat, Ontario, 37, 115–117,
    313

balance
    Eeyou on, 231
    in families, 142
    as integral to health, 230–231
    lack of and dis-ease, 16, 192–194,
      238
    Nehiyawak on, 107–108, 207
    relationships and, 50–51
band councils
    as colonial system, 41
    market capitalism and, 251–252
    problems with model, 263,
      310–313
banishment, 169–170, 309
basic needs, Maslow's hierarchy of
    needs, 104–105 fig
being cognition, 109
being values, 109
Belcourt, Billy-Ray, 3–4, 189, 257–258

biological processes, intergenerational
    trauma and, 20
blame
    culture of, 102
    as defensive cover, 137–138
    of victims, 50
    in workplace, 119
blood memory, 20–21
Bobbish, Davey, 256
Brave Bull Allard, LaDonna, 249
Bryant, Michael, 113–115

Cajete, Gregory, 239
Calliou, Brian, 310–311
Campiou, Fred, 146–147
Canadian Pacific Railway (CPR), 9
cancer
    in Fort Chipewyan, 258
    polio vaccine experiments and,
        49–50
    rate of in Indigenous peoples,
        188
    traditional food sources and,
        254–255
captivity, 39, 45
Cardinal, Clifford, 41–42, 50
Cardinal, Kiana, 252
Cassandra (teacher), 90–91, 97–100
Celina (TCM practitioner), 143–145,
    161–162, 222–223
ceremonies
    banning of, 28, 41
    healing with, 209, 234, 280–281,
        287
    helping offenders with, 168
    loss of, 23
    natural world and, 239

socialization and, 121
    Walking Out ceremonies, 256
    wealth-sharing ceremonies, 244
chaos junkies, 93
Chenoo story, 266–272, 274–278
child welfare
    as indifferent, 306
    innovative programs in,
        288–289, 308–310
children
    bonding with caregiver, 72
    as caregivers, 74–75
    coping strategies in, 78
    dissociation in, 70, 73–74, 79
    efforts to bring family into
        balance, 142
    experience of trauma, 66–68,
        152–154
    health effects of trauma in,
        187–188
    neglect of, 71, 73–74, 77–78, 288
    securely attached children, 72,
        79
    see also Indigenous children/
        youth
Chisasibi, Quebec, 236–238, 256
Christian church, 7, 29, 50, 225–226,
    243
chronic pain
    abuse and, 189
    suicide and, 42
chronic stress
    diabetes and kidney disease
        and, 201
    racism and, 188
chronic trauma
    incarceration rates and, 54

chronic trauma (*continued*)
  memory disturbance and,
    152–153
  physical manifestations of,
    177–186
  poverty and, 106–107
  within context of control, 43
  see also complex post-traumatic
    stress disorder (CPTSD);
    trauma
Circle of Care program, 309
Clara (patient), 195–198
Clyde River, Nunavut, 319–320
colonization
  Anthropocene and, 263–264
  chronic stress of, 188
  chronic trauma and, 41, 243,
    280
  components of, 243
  CPTSD and, 60
  damage to Indigenous
    communities and, 3, 23–24,
    27
  disharmony caused by, 17
  health effects of, 189, 199, 213
  Indigenous slavery and,
    245–246
  intergenerational trauma and,
    18–19, 164–165, 188
  loss of agency and, 93, 146
  market capitalism and, 255
  processes of, 28, 41, 84, 247
  programs addressing, 236–237
  resource extraction and, 257
  story of the Seven Fires and,
    209
  tools of, 93

  trauma of, 36, 41, 46
Columbus, Christopher, 6
Community Holistic Circle Healing
  (CHCH) program, 288–289
community hubs, 292–294, 298–300
Community Mobilization Prince
  Albert (CMPA), 296
co-morbid diagnoses, 67–68, 195
complex post-traumatic stress
  disorder (CPTSD)
  abuse and, 39, 60
  as being stuck in time, 52
  control and, 35, 39–40, 52, 55, 60
  effect on sense of self, 236
  feeling of separateness due to,
    232
  memory management and, 139
  need for multi-step approach to,
    278–280
  origins of, 39
  overview of, 60–61
  and relationship with control
    figure, 283–284
  stages of healing from, 284–285,
    289
  swinging between extremes
    in, 103
  see also chronic trauma; post-
    traumatic stress disorder
    (PTSD)
connection
  in children, 69–70, 73–74
  to community, 263
  to family, 37, 103, 105, 147
  loss of, 146
  to the natural world, 213, 218,
    224, 227–228, 235–236

connection (*continued*)
  in pre-colonial Indigenous
    societies, 223–224
  see-also disconnection
control
  addiction and, 70, 193
  anger and, 48, 73–74, 92, 153
  captivity and, 45, 54
  colonization and, 38, 84
  CPTSD and, 35, 39–40, 52, 55, 60
  as factor in intergenerational
    trauma, 35
  of Indigenous peoples by
    systems, 40–41, 69, 205,
    258–259, 280, 290
  loss of sense of self and, 43–44,
    46, 49
co-operation
  funeral and, 1–2
  philosophy of, 261
coping strategies
  in children, 78
  creating new, 80
  fixed worldview, 102
  individual differences in, 132–133
  unlearning, 290
Corey O'Soup, 315
corporations, rights of, 262
Couture, Joseph, 311–312, 317–318
cradleboards/moss bags, 120–121
Cree Board of Health, 283
crime severity index, 296
criminal justice system
  author's father's experience of,
    65–66, 301–302
  need for trauma-informed
    approach in, 295–297

overrepresentation of Indigenous
    peoples in, 54, 167–168
  poverty and, 53
  R. v. Gladue and, 54
  see also prisons
cultural genocide, 45–46, 55, 249, 278,
  311

Dakota Access Pipeline, 248–249
Dane-zaa, 216
dangerous offender status, 54–55
Danis (student), 68–79, 74–77, 76 *fig*,
  84–85
Davis Inlet, Labrador, 306–307
death rate, 11
decolonization, 171, 205, 237, 245, 290
deficiency cognition, 109–110, 112
Delgamuukw decision, 252–253
Dene, 258, 295
depression
  diet and, 212
  grief and, 235–236
  intergenerational trauma and,
    29, 44, 48
  materialism and, 257
  root causes of, 3
developmental trauma disorder, 86–87
diabetes, 11, 188, 200–201, 283, 296
disconnection
  Chenoo story and, 277
  colonization and, 51
  as dangerous to collective
    societies, 272–273
  inability to create relationships
    and, 312
  lateral violence and, 100
  see also connection

dis-ease
    holistic medicine and, 191
    imbalance and, 16, 192–194, 238
    in Indigenous communities,
        189–190
    origin of term, 16–17
    as teacher, 214
disempowering narratives, 121–122
dissociation
    in children, 70, 73–74, 79, 86, 161
    in CPTSD, 60
    in PTSD, 35, 57–58
    traumatic memory and, 153–157
dreams
    of bears, 175
    meaning of colours in, 205–206
    of unknown apartments, 176
Duplessis, Maurice, 62–64
Duplessis orphans, 62–64 fig, 66,
    173, 301
Duran, Eduardo, 119

Easterville, Manitoba, 228
Eeyou
    changing from sharing society,
        255–256
    land-based healing program of,
        236–237
    on maintaining balance, 231
    rate of health issues in, 283
ego security, 120
Eighth Fire, 25, 209
elders, 310–312
Elsipogtog, New Brunswick,
    264–265
emotional abuse
    definition of, 71

developmental trauma disorder
    and, 86
    in Indigenous communities, 2
    intergenerational trauma and,
        28, 30
    wittigo (whitikiw) and, 274
    see also abuse
emotional neglect
    definition of, 71
    see also neglect
empathy, 87, 227
English-Wabigoon River, 42–43
en'owkin, 261
enteric nervous system, 189–190
environmental violence, 257
epigenetics, 20, 101, 188, 238
Esk'etemc, British Columbia, 286–288
Eskimo Identification Canada tags,
    44
ethnic cleansing, 9
European Enlightenment,
    worldview of, 22

falsely empowering narratives, 121–122
family systems
    different coping strategies in,
        132–133
    intergenerational trauma and,
        19–20, 141
    need for stories in, 138–139
    sexual abuse in, 141
fear
    anger and, 117, 148
    everyday impacts of trauma
        and, 29–30
    lateral violence and, 94
    of police, 40

fear (*continued*)
  PTSD and, 58
  purpose of, 134
  stress response and, 201
  toward Indigenous peoples, 320
fetal alcohol spectrum disorder
  (FASD), 30, 53, 168
Fifth World, 25
Five Elements Theory, 196–197
flashbacks
  author's experience of, 149–152
  as symptom of PTSD, 57
  traumatic memory and, 152–154
Fondation Thierry LeRoux, 322
food security/insecurity, 254, 260,
  286, 296
Fort Chipewyan, Alberta, 258, 295
foster care
  author's mother's threats of,
    71, 219
  experiences of, 172
  individual stories of, 113, 157, 172,
    307
  overrepresentation of Indigenous
    children in, 83–84
fracking, 264
freeze response, 98–99

Gaikezheyongai, Sally, 209
genocide
  in Canada, 8–10, 18
  cultural genocide, 45–46, 55, 249,
    278, 311
Giiwedin Anang (North Star)
  program, 309–310
Gladue decision, 167–168, 170
  see also R. v. Gladue

globalization, impact on planet of,
  264
Goodfish Lake First Nation, 41–42,
  49–50
Gordon Residential School, 157
Grassy Narrows
  (Asubpeeschoseewagong),
  Ontario, 42–43
Gregoire, Pierre, 172
Grizzly Bear Spirit, 261–262

haka, 220–223
hardship, 146–147
Harper, Elijah, 208–209
Haudenosaunee, 216, 223, 242, 244,
  254, 311
headaches
  author's experience of, 177,
    205–206
  in survivors of residential
    schools, 187
healing
  from CPTSD, stages of, 284–285
  as long-term process, 288–290
  need for culture-based
    programming for, 281–282,
    286
  purging and, 275–276
  role of kindness in, 274–275
  as social process, 52–53, 276
healing circles, 240–243
healing lodges, 321–322
helplessness, 46, 60, 87, 154
Herman, Judith Lewis
  on acute vs chronic trauma, 44–45
  on anger, 48
  CPTSD and, 39

Herman, Judith Lewis (*continued*)
  on extremes in CPTSD, 103
  on self-perception, 232
  on stages of healing from
    CPTSD, 284–285, 289
holistic medicine
  dis-ease and balance and, 193
  Indigenous peoples and,
    191–194, 196–199, 204–205
  recovery from trauma and, 204
  vs Western biomedical system,
    196–198
Hollow Water, Manitoba, 164–165
  fig, 288–289
Holocaust survivors, 19–20, 49
home, Indigenous concept of, 231–232
homelessness, 231–232
hongi, 220–221, 223
hot-cold balance, 207–208
Hudson's Bay Company, 216, 225
human development
  Maslow's model for, 104–105,
    108–109
  see also personality development
hunting
  monetization of, 255
  Young Hunter program,
    226–227

identity, sense of, 168–170
identity narratives, 173–174
Idle No More, 51
Idlout, Lucie, 44
Inca, 25, 244
Indian, settler use of term, 94–96
Indian Act, 41, 263, 278, 312–313
Indian Agents, 9, 247

Indian Residential Schools. *see*
  residential schools
Indian Resource Council, 251
Indigenization, 285
Indigenous 4Rs, 50–51, 85, 282, 292
Indigenous children/youth
  effects of poverty on, 213
  Fondation Thierry LeRoux and,
    322
  health issues in, 209–211
  lack of traditional education for,
    226–227
  programs aimed at, 226–227,
    234–235, 290–292
  rate of ADHD in, 210–211
  rate of foster care placement
    in, 83
  sexual abuse of, 162–165, 287–289
  suicide rate in, 313–314
  trauma-informed care for, 302–304
  Urban Society for Aboriginal
    Youth (USAY) and, 234–235
  Violence on the Land, Violence
    on Our Bodies, toolkit
    for, 257
  see also child welfare; children
Indigenous Clean Energy (ICE), 260
Indigenous communities
  abuse in, 2, 229
  alcohol addiction treatment in,
    286–289
  community hubs for, 292–294,
    298–300
  crime rates in, 54
  crime-risk reduction strategies
    in, 296–299
  cycle of trauma in, 22–23

Indigenous communities (*continued*)
dialysis centres in, 201
displacement of, 228, 246–247
distress felt in, 314–315
dysfunctional relationship with
police, 40
effect of colonization on, 3,
23–24, 27
food sovereignty projects in,
260–261
health care in, 201–202,
204–205
innovative child welfare
programs in, 288–289
issues of leadership in, 316–317
lack of power of, 279–280
land-based healing programs in,
236–238
lateral violence in, 47, 122–123,
229–230
manifestations of unresolved
issues in, 11–12
mental wellness programs in,
313–314
pre-colonization, 109–110, 162,
223–224, 239, 243–244, 282
pre-contact, 16–18
rate of PTSD in, 36
reintegration of offenders in,
66, 169–170
relocation of, 306–307
social inequities in, 286
suicide prevention strategies in,
285–286, 313
Sustainable Development Goals
(SDGs) for, 259–260
traditional ceremonies in, 256

training community counsellors
in, 319–320
use of abuse family trees in,
164–165 *fig*
worsening condition of, 278
Young Hunter program,
226–227
Indigenous cultures, as flexible,
253–254
Indigenous healing practices,
203–204, 234
Indigenous homelessness, 231–232
Indigenous lands
appropriation of, 28, 48, 51, 84,
243–246, 253
economy of Canada and, 246
federal extraction of resources
from, 279–280
see also land
Indigenous peoples
activism of, 247–249, 251,
261–262, 264–265, 317
annihilation of, 245–246
death rate in, 11
economic systems of, 243–245
health problems of, 188, 194–196,
199–200, 209–210
holistic medicine and, 191–194,
196–199, 204–205
incarceration rates of, 54
life expectancy of, 11
marginalization of, 243
as plot devices for settler stories,
94–95
pre-colonization identities of, 55
state surveillance of, 249–251
suicide rate in, 11, 283, 285–287, 307

Indigenous peoples (*continued*)
traditional relationship with
natural world, 230–231
traditional response to trauma,
280–281
trauma-informed care for,
302–304
in urban areas, 280, 296–297
Indigenous programming in
schools, 90–91
Indigenous prophecies, 25, 209
Indigenous science and philosophy
denigration of, 205
food as medicine in, 213
as holistic, 191, 203, 208
importance of life essence in,
199
loss of, 202, 246
role of change in, 12
vs Western biomedical system,
207–208
wisdom in, 26–27
Indigenous slavery, 245–246
Indigenous storytelling, 6, 138–139,
225, 234, 237
see also narratives
Indigenous students
graduation rate of, 283, 299–300
negative emotion in, 68–70
rate of PTSD in, 36–37
teaching, 80–83
Indigenous trade routes, 243–244
Indigenous Treaty Alliance, 251
Indigenous women and girls
abuse of, 39–40, 162–163
attitudes toward, 217
exploitation of, 256–257

National Inquiry into Missing
and Murdered Indigenous
Women and Girls, 115–116,
164
Innu, 207, 225, 243, 306–307
intergenerational trauma
abuse and, 28–30, 84
breaking the cycle of, 282–283, 302
colonization and, 18–19, 164–165,
188
control as factor in, 35
difficulty discussing, 24
emotional abuse and, 28, 30
everyday impacts of, 28–30, 38,
91
first identification of, 18–19
healing from, 26–27
healing lodges and, 321–322
in Holocaust survivors, 19–20
patterns of abuse created by, 84
vs PTSD, 38
transposition of, 21
internalization, 29, 49, 52
internalized racism, 92–93
Inuit
community programs of,
318–320
Eskimo Identification Canada
tags and, 44
on hot-cold balance, 207
loss of connection to natural
world, 227
on maintaining balance, 231
naming systems of, 43–44
subversion of Angry Indian
label by, 96
suicide rates of, 11, 283, 285–286

Inuit Tapiriit Kanatami (ITK), 283, 285–286, 318
Ipperwash Crisis, 95
Irniq, Peter, 43–44
irritable bowel syndrome, 187–188

James Bay and Northern Quebec Agreement, 255–256, 283
Jeffries, Ron, 93
Jumbo Glacier ski resort, 261–262

Kanehsatake (Oka), Quebec, 51, 95, 209, 241
Kanienkehaka, 216, 243
Karetak, Joe, 226–227
Katt, Mae, 36–37
Kellermann, Natan, 19–20
Kestenberg, Judith, 21
Kettle and Stony Point First Nation, 95
kidney disease, 188, 200–201
kindness, healing role of, 274–275
Kinew, Wab, 24–25
Ktunaxa Nation Council, 261–262

LaBoucane-Benson, Patti, 122–123, 146
Laboucan-Massimo, Melina, 250–251
Labrador (Nitassinan), 224, 243
Lac La Ronge First Nation, 313–314
Ladner, Kiera, 310, 312–313
Lafontaine, Alika, 201–202
land
    as commodity, 256
    connection to, 230, 249, 307
    disconnection from, 55
    loss of, 23, 40, 48
    see also Indigenous lands
land-based healing, 234–238, 286
land-based learning, 260
Larocque, Brad, 95
Las Casas, Bartolomé de, 6–7, 10–11, 17
lateral violence
    description of, 92–94
    disconnection and, 100
    effect on cultural identity, 165
    externalization of self-hate and, 119–120
    in Indigenous communities, 47, 122–123
    wittigo (whitikiw) and, 273
    in the workplace, 143
Le Grande Noirceur, 62–64
LeMay, Rose, 27
Lenape, 8
LeRoux, Thierry, 322
life essence, 20, 199
life expectancy, 11
Lipton, Steve, 53
Little Gramma (author's great-grandmother), 125–126, 174–176
loneliness, 140, 187
Low, Barbara, 249

Macdonald, John A., 9
Mackenzie, Alexander, 216
malnutrition, 186–187
Mâmawêyatitân Centre (Regina), 294
Manitoba Keewatinowi Okimakanak, 313
manitow
    connecting to, 222
    description of, 20, 22, 224

manitow (*continued*)
  flow of, 196, 205
  medicine circle / wheel and, 82
  meridians and, 191
  mother and child and, 120
  rebalancing and, 238–239
  see also qi
market capitalism
  campaigns against, 247–251
  colonization and, 243–245
  effects on Indigenous peoples
    of, 258–259
  as negative force, 256
  resistance to, 254
Maslow, Abraham
  developmental model, 104–105
  research with Niitsitapi,
    108–109, 120
  on self-actualization, 106
Maslow's hierarchy of needs, 104–105 *fig*
Maté, Gabor, 93, 193, 213
Maya, 25
McGregor, Glen, 115–116
McKay, Catherine, 320–321
McQuarrie, Dallas and Susan, 264
medicine circle / wheel
  anger and, 80
  connection and, 193
  Niitsitapi and Nehiyawak, 107
  power of volition and, 51
  purpose of, 13
  quadrants of, 13–15 *fig*
  versions of, 12–13
medicine people
  pre-colonization, 202
  in today's Indigenous
    communities, 203–204

memory
  encoding of, 153
  formation of, 153
  management of, 139
  post-catastrophic memory, 23
  retrieval of, 153, 162
mental health
  diet and, 212–213
  Gladue decision and, 168
  lack of services for, 53
  programs addressing, 236–237,
    313–315
  social / environmental
    conditions and, 257–258
mercury poisoning, 42–43
meridians, manitow and, 191
Methot, Suzanne
  ancestry of, 174–176
  childhood of, 31–34, 33 *fig*, 56
  coherent narratives of, 172–173
  coping strategies of, 117–118, 133
  dreams of, 175–176, 205–206
  experience of blaming, 137–138
  experiences in school system,
    88–92, 161, 217–220
  father, 62–66, 80, 131, 301–302
  flashbacks, 149–152
  healing circle and, 240–243
  Maori haka and, 220–223
  mother, 64–65, 71–73, 75, 124–129,
    147–148, 158–160, 304–305
  mother's diary, 125–128, 127 *fig*,
    158–159
  naturopathy and, 184–185,
    205–206
  physical manifestations of
    trauma in, 177–186

Methot, Suzanne (*continued*)
   physical therapy and, 181–183
   re-enactment of childhood
      abuse, 155–156, 166
   sexual abuse of, 151, 155, 162,
      172–173
   sexual identity and, 166
   as "Sexy Suzi," 32–33, 218
   siblings of, 129–132
   talking circles and, 232–234
   traditional Chinese medicine
      (TCM) and, 143–145, 161–162,
      222–223
   work at Indigenous magazine,
      118–119, 121
   see also Little Gramma (author's
      great-grandmother);
      Thelma (author's
      grandmother); Thomas
      (author's grandfather)
Métis, 41, 113–114, 217, 258, 302
microbiome, 212
Mihirangi, 220–223
Mi'kmaq, 193, 264, 290
Monday Night Healing Circle,
   240–243
Mushkegowuk, 37
Mushuau Innu, 306–307
Muskotew Sakahikan Enowuk, 51,
   216, 242

'Namgis First Nation, 262
Napoleon, Val, 16
narratives
   about movement and change,
      5–6, 172
   abuse family trees and, 164–165 *fig*

Chenoo story, 266–272, 274–278
of colonization, 26, 52, 83–84
creating coherent narratives,
   153–154, 157, 160–161,
   164–167
disempowering narratives,
   121–122
falsely empowering narratives,
   121–122
healing stories, 139
identity narratives, 173–174
Indigenous narratives, 83–84,
   171–172, 176
loss of, 23
need for in families, 138–139
from settler perspective, 95–96
of sexual abuse, 172–173
story of the Seven Fires, 209
stuck in old stories, 17, 52, 72, 97,
   101, 192
of terror, anger, grief, and loss,
   5–6, 45–46, 97
   see also Indigenous storytelling
National Collaborating Centre for
   Aboriginal Health, 3
National Inquiry into Missing and
   Murdered Indigenous Women
   and Girls, 115–116, 164
National Israeli Center for
   Psychosocial Support of
   the Holocaust and Second
   Generation, 19
Native Women's Association of
   Canada (NWAC), 92, 203
Native Youth Sexual Health
   Network, 257
Natuashish, Labrador, 306–307

natural world
  developing connection to, 75–76,
    213, 227, 235, 321
  disconnection from, 29, 208,
    224, 228
  fighting for, 247
  lack of rights for, 262
  lessons from, 230–231
  personhood status for, 262
needs
  belonging needs, 112
  esteem needs, 112
neglect
  definition of, 71
  developmental trauma disorder
    and, 86
  effects on children of, 73–74
  normalizing of, 77–78
  suicide crisis and, 288
Nehiyawak
  cultural beliefs of, 50 51
  on dis-ease, 214
  in Fort Chipewyan, 258
  on good health, 199–200
  on hot-cold balance, 207
  polio vaccine experiments on,
    41–42
  wittigo (whitikiw) and, 23
  worldview of, 224–225
Neighbourhood Resource Centre
  (NRC), 298–299
Nelson Jail, 127–128 fig
nervous systems, 189–190
Niitsitapi, 108–109, 120, 199–200 fig
Nisga'a, 51
Nishnawbe Aski Nation, 163
Nishnawbe-Aski Legal Services, 310

Nisichawayasihk First Nation, 308–309
Nitassinan (Labrador), 224, 243
Northern Gateway pipeline, 249
Nunavut Suicide Prevention
  Strategy, 319
Nuu-chah-nulth, 192–193

Oakalla Prison Farm, 65–66, 125, 301
Obed, Natan, 318–319
O'Connor, John, 258
oil and gas industry
  cancer and, 254, 258
  environmental violence caused
    by, 257
  federal government as security
    arm of, 251
Oji-Cree, 208–209
Oka (Kanehsatake), Quebec, 51, 95,
  209, 241
Okpik, Harry, 205
Our Life's Journey, 319–320
Outside Looking In, 291

Pangowish, Rolland, 252
parenting programs, 306
Pashagumkum, Eddie, 236–238
Paul, James Clifford, 170–171
Peace Country, Alberta, 215–216
Penashue, Elizabeth, 225, 243
Pequot Massacre, 8
Percy (student), 210–211
personality development
  chronic trauma and, 104
  effects of trauma on, 92–93
  interruption of, 302
  normal course of, 37
  see also human development

Peskotomuhkati, 125, 175–176, 274
Peter Ballantyne Cree Nation, 313
Petit, Marcel, 172
pêyâhtakêyimowin, 230–231
pipelines
    anti-pipeline movement, 251
    Dakota Access Pipeline, 248–249
    Woodfibre LNG natural gas
        pipeline, 317
Piungituq, Aisa, 319
police. see Community Mobilization
    Prince Albert; Royal Canadian
    Mounted Police (RCMP)
polio vaccine experiments, 41–42,
    49–50
post-traumatic stress disorder (PTSD)
    causes of, 57
    vs intergenerational trauma, 38
    memory management and, 139
    rates of, 36
    residential schools and, 37–38
    symptoms of, 35–36, 57–59
    see also complex post-traumatic
        stress disorder (CPTSD)
poverty
    chronic trauma and, 106–107
    health effects of, 213
Prince Albert, Saskatchewan, 296
prisons
    alternatives to, 167–168, 288–289,
        321–322
    chronic trauma and, 41
    disproportionate numbers of
        Indigenous peoples in, 11
    Oakalla Prison Farm, 65–66, 125,
        301
    rate of PTSD in, 36

    see also criminal justice system
projection of negative emotions
    as coping strategy, 114, 116–117, 301
    onto children, 89, 159–160
    by perpetrators, 101, 167
psychodynamic processes,
    intergenerational trauma and,
    19–20
purging, as part of healing, 275–276

Qat'muk, 261–262
qi, 196–197, 205
    see also manitow
quantum entanglement, 206–207
quantum mechanics, as basis
    of Indigenous science and
    philosophy, 207

R. v. Gladue, 54
    see also Gladue decision
racism
    chronic stress and, 188
    colonization and, 28
    dominant society justifications
        of, 94
    epistemological racism, 205
    as internalized, 92
    as ongoing, 38–39
    in schools, 69
rage vs anger, 97
Ray, Carl, 191–193, 192 fig
reciprocity
    Indigenous philosophy of, 3
    see also Indigenous 4Rs
reconciliation
    beginning of in Canada, 25
    rights of nature and, 262

reconciliation (*continued*)
trauma-informed systems and, 295
reconnection, 147, 284–285
Redfern, Madeleine, 96, 116–117
re-enactment
of abuse, 71–72, 132
author's experience of, 155–156
of childhood roles, 142–143
sexual abuse and, 165
as symptom of PTSD, 57
of traumatic events, 47, 153–154
reintegration, of offenders, 66, 169–170
relationships
fear of, 141–142
Indigenous philosophy of, 3
see also Indigenous 4Rs
reserves, 41, 45, 200–201, 280, 287
residential schools
abuse suffered in, 2, 10, 47, 157
chronic trauma and, 41
CPTSD and, 39
cultural genocide and, 45
history of, 9–10
intergenerational impacts of, 2–3, 28–29, 141
malnutrition in, 186–187
national system of, 9–10
negative health outcomes for students of, 186–187
numbering system in, 44
PTSD and, 36–38
resiliency, 18, 48, 81, 130, 313
respect
Indigenous philosophy of, 3
see also Indigenous 4Rs

responsibility
Indigenous philosophy of, 3
see also Indigenous 4Rs
risky behaviour, 113, 115, 153–154
Rivers, Dustin (Khelsilem), 317
Roland (teacher), 88–90, 97–99, 102–103
Royal Canadian Mounted Police (RCMP)
abuse of Indigenous girls and women by, 39–40
arrests of protesters by, 253
on crime rate in Natuashish, 307
dysfunctional relationship with Indigenous communities, 39–40
as part of resource team, 288
removal of children from their homes by, 10
surveillance of activists by, 249–250

Sagitawa, 215–217
Sagkeeng First Nation, 229, 309
Saik'uz First Nation, 316–317
self
control and sense of, 43–44, 46, 49
CPTSD and sense of, 49
creating own sense of, 82
erasure of sense of, 44–45
impoverished sense of, 103–104, 121, 227–228
positive sense of, 103
structures of, 43
two kinds of, 34–35
self-actualization, 104–105 *fig*, 106–107, 109
self-hatred, 48–49, 119

self-sabotage, 30, 78

Seven Fires story, 209

Seven Sacred Teachings, 109–111 *fig*, 292

sexual abuse
author's experience of, 151, 155, 162, 172–173
author's mother's experience of, 158
of children, 162–165
culture of silence around, 163–164
Gladue decision and, 167–168
Hollow Water, Manitoba, program, 288–289
need to create coherent narrative around, 164–167
rates of in Indigenous women, 162–163
suicide crisis and, 163–164
see also abuse

sexual offenders, reintegration of, 169–170

shaking tent ceremonies, 191, 192 *fig*

shame
author's experience of, 32
effect on parenting, 142–143
vs guilt, 141
intergenerational trauma and, 135–136
toxic shame, 141, 143
Tyrell (author's neighbour) and, 136–137

Sheppard, Darcy Allan, 113–115, 117

Sheshatshiu, Labrador, 172, 243

Siksika First Nation, 108

Simard, Daniel, 63–64

Sinclair, Murray
on cultural genocide, 278
on deaths in residential schools, 10
on effects of raising children in institutions, 100–101
on government policies leading to dysfunction, 17–18
on sense of identity, 168–170

Sixties Scoop, 41, 83, 116

social capital, 255, 263, 265

social isolation, 42, 70, 187, 314

social structures
as broken, 2–3
disruption of, 45
effect of institutions on, 298
reclaiming of, 51

sociocultural processes, intergenerational trauma and, 19–20

solvent abuse, 306–307

Soule, Jay (Chippewar), 96

spirit names, 56, 175

Sqilxw, 261

Squamish First Nation, 251, 317

squaw, use of term, 31–32, 217

St. Jean de Dieu insane asylum, 63

Starblanket, Noel, 252

Stewart, Abe, 226

Stonechild, Dale, 156–157

stories. *see* narratives

STR8 UP program, 322

stress. *see* chronic stress; complex post-traumatic stress disorder (CPTSD); post-traumatic stress disorder (PTSD)

suffering
  ancestral suffering, 21–22, 46
  human vs political, 265
suicide
  epidemic of, 313–314
  grief and shame and, 235–236
  rate of in Indigenous peoples,
    11, 283, 285 286, 307
  sexual abuse and, 163–164
Sûreté du Québec, abuse of
  Indigenous girls and women
  by, 40
Sustainable Development Goals
  (SDGs), 259–260
sweat lodge, 45, 168, 207, 280, 287
Sylvio, Albert, 63–64
symptomology, 190–191, 204–205

Taino, 6–7
talking circles, 232–234
Tetlit Gwich'in, 4
Thelma (author's grandmother)
  ancestry of, 174–176
  marriage and background of,
    124–127
  refusal to help her daughter, 130
  trauma experienced by, 159–160
Thistle, Jesse, 231–232
Thomas (author's grandfather),
  124–127
Thomas-Müller, Clayton, 249
Thrasher, Michael
  on conditions for creating
    change, 52
  on the medicine circle/wheel,
    12–13, 16, 80
tipi, 107–108

Tittel, Wolfgang, 206–207
Tomkins, Silvan Solomon, 133–135
Traditional Chinese Medicine
  (TCM), 143–145, 161–162, 196–197,
    222–223
transposition, 21
trauma
  holistic medicine and, 193–194
  narratives of, 121–122, 154
  perpetrators of, 49, 61, 123,
    163–164, 166–167, 309
  stress responses to, 99–100
  see also chronic trauma;
    intergenerational trauma
Trauma-Informed Care for Children
  and Families Act (U.S.), 302–303
trauma-informed systems, 302–304
Tremblay, Ron, 249
trickster stories, 162
Tr'ondëk Hwëch'in First Nation, 260
Truth and Reconciliation
  Commission (TRC)
  on diet in residential schools,
    186–187
  on need for culture-based
    programming, 306
  on residential schools, 9–10
tsawalk, 192–193
Tsilhqot'in decision, 253
tuberculosis (TB), 10–11
Turpel-Lafond, Mary Ellen, 305–306
Tyrell (author's neighbour), 136–137,
  140
Tzotzil Maya, 207–208

United Nations Declaration on the
  Rights of Indigenous Peoples, 250

Urban Aboriginal Peoples Study,
11, 280
Urban Society for Aboriginal Youth
(USAY), 234–235

Van de Vorst family, 320–321
van der Kolk, Bessel
CPTSD and, 39
on creation of chaos, 93
on developmental trauma
disorder, 86–87
on securely attached children,
72
on trauma early in life, 66–68
Van Dusen, Julie, 115–116
violence. *see* lateral violence
Violence on the Land, Violence on
Our Bodies, 257

Walker, David Edward, 211
Walking Out ceremonies, 256
warrior societies, 51
Wemigwans, Mary, 44, 52
Western biomedical system
as dehumanizing, 194–196
vs holistic medicine, 196–198
vs Indigenous science and
philosophy, 207–208

lack of knowledge about
dreams in, 206
limitations of, 189–191
Wet'suwet'en, 251–253
Whitestar, Evan, 291–292
Willier, Russell, 246
wittigo (wihtikiw)
Chenoo story, 266–272, 274–278
killing of, 274, 315, 320, 322
as mental illness, 272
as possession, 23
as symbol in modern Indigenous
societies, 273–274
wittigo psychosis, 272
Women in Indigenous Leadership,
317
women's circles, 51
Woodfibre LNG natural gas
pipeline, 317

Yaakswiis Warriors, 253
Yellow Horse Brave Heart, Maria
on ancestral suffering, 21–22
on disenfranchised grief,
235–236
on PTSD in Indigenous
communities, 36
Young Hunter program, 226–227

SUZANNE METHOT is a Nehiyaw writer, editor, educator, and community worker born in Vancouver, British Columbia, and raised in Peace River, Alberta. Her work has been published in anthologies including *Steal My Rage* and *Let the Drums Be Your Heart*. She has worked in the non-profit sector, in the classroom, and in advocacy and direct-service positions in Indigenous community–based agencies. She is co-author of the textbook *Aboriginal Beliefs, Values, and Aspirations*, and she currently lives in Toronto, Ontario.

At ECW Press, we want you to enjoy this book in whatever format you like, whenever you like. Leave your print book at home and take the eBook to go! Purchase the print edition and receive the eBook free. Just send an email to ebook@ecwpress.com and include:

- the book title
- the name of the store where you purchased it
- your receipt number
- your preference of file type: PDF or ePub?

A real person will respond to your email with your eBook attached. And thanks for supporting an independently owned Canadian publisher with your purchase!